THE ORIGINS AND EVOLUTION OF
THE MOSES NATIVITY STORY

STUDIES
IN THE HISTORY OF RELIGIONS

(*NUMEN* BOOKSERIES)

EDITED BY

H.G. KIPPENBERG • E.T. LAWSON

VOLUME LVIII

Moses nativity scenes from the fresco at Dura-Europos

THE ORIGINS AND EVOLUTION OF THE MOSES NATIVITY STORY

BY

JONATHAN COHEN

E.J. BRILL
LEIDEN • NEW YORK • KÖLN
1993

The paper in this book meets the guidelines for permanence and durability of the Committee on Production Guidelines for Book Longevity of the Council on Library Resources.

BS
580
.M6
C64
1993

ISSN 0169-8834
ISBN 90 04 09652 3

© *Copyright 1993 by E.J. Brill, Leiden, The Netherlands*

All rights reserved. No part of this publication may be reproduced, translated, stored in a retrieval system, or transmitted in any form or by any means, electronic, mechanical, photocopying, recording or otherwise, without prior written permission of the publisher.

Authorization to photocopy items for internal or personal use is granted by E.J. Brill provided that the appropriate fees are paid directly to Copyright Clearance Center, 27 Congress Street, SALEM MA 01970, USA. Fees are subject to change.

PRINTED IN THE NETHERLANDS

CONTENTS

Introduction 1

Chapter I. The Moses Nativity Story in the Bible 5

Chapter II. The Moses Nativity Story in Post-biblical Sources . . 29
    The Book of Jubilees (46–47) 29
    Ezekiel the Tragedian 32
    Biblical Antiquities (Chapter 9) 37
    Philo 40
    Flavius Josephus 46
    Stephen's Oration 59
    The Fresco at Dura-Europos 62

Chapter III. The Midrash 67
    Differentiation of the Story 67
    Reasons for the Exile and the Decrees 71
    Redemption 76
    The Length of the Enslavement 78
    Dealing Wisely 84
    Lest they Multiply and the Enslavement 87
    Lest They Multiply and Murder of the Sons 91
    The Hebrew Midwives 92
    The Annunciation 95
    Abraham 105
    Mistakes of the Magicians 106
    The Fate of the Masses 108
    Anonymity of the Parents 115
    The Second Marriage 117
    The Three Months of Concealment 121
    Restoration of the River 121
    One of the Hebrews' Children 124
    Pharaoh's daughter 126
    Typological Motifs 127
    The Tale of the Crown 129
    Concluding Remarks 131

Chapter IV. The Asatir	137
Chapter V. Notes on Rashi's Commentary	143
Chapter VI. Christian Sources	157
The Gospel according to Matthew	157
The Protevangelium of James	171
Appendix A. The Tidings to the Shepherds (Luke 2:6–20)	177
Appendix B. Notes on Ibn Ezra's Short and Long Commentaries	181
Appendix C. The Asatir, Chapters 8 and 9	187
Appendix D. List of Abbreviations	189
Bibliography	191
Index	197

ACKNOWLEDGMENTS

The distinguished scholars from whose books I derived greater understanding have been mentioned in explicit references throughout this volume. To the list of scholars to whom I am indebted one must add my first teacher, my father David Cohen. His oral teachings provided the setting from which I developed the ideas contained in this book.

The book, including the primary sources appearing in it, was translated by Rachel Rowen. In translating the primary sources we availed ourselves of existing translations, as far as possible, but re-examined and compared all the texts, adapting them as necessary. Rachel Rowen also typeset the book, using $\mathcal{A}_{\mathcal{M}}\mathcal{S}$-T$_{\!E\!}$X and making various modifications in order to incorporate the Hebrew and Greek passages. She also prepared the files needed to process the index.

INTRODUCTION

It is widely recognized that the order in which motifs appear in a story does not necessarily reflect the chronology of the motifs' origins; a motif appearing in the beginning of a work may very well have been incorporated at a later date, sometimes even after the work was completed. This is true both of written works produced by a single author, as well as of oral traditions developed by many contributors over a period of generations. The relation between the account of a hero's birth and the story of his life as a grown man illustrates this disconnection. Although the obvious place for a nativity story is at the beginning of the narrative, nevertheless in the vast majority of works one can show that the account of the hero's birth was incorporated in the last stages of the story's formulation. Such late incorporation is a logical consequence of the process of its literary creation. The singularity of the adult hero is the core around which the literary work takes shape, the focal point which paves the way and generates the desire to express this singularity from the outset.[1] The story of the birth of Moses provides a clear illustration of the inverse relationship between the late origin of the motif and its incorporation at the beginning of the narrative. Although the Moses nativity story is incorporated into the first two chapters of Exodus, it is actually far less ancient than the rest of the text into which it is set. The evidence for the late date of addition of the birth story has been discussed at length and will be presented further on.

If we analyze nativity stories we see that the constants are not confined to the creative process; rather, they extend further, also subsuming elements of form, fixed models around which these stories take shape. Heroes differ greatly from one another in terms of their life, their character, their era; but the descriptions of their birth are amazingly uniform. These two observations seem to be related. The fixed element in the creative process gives rise to a set model; but the similarity between prototypes is at times so great that this explanation becomes inadequate and must be supplemented by assuming migration and reciprocal

---

[1] Cf. H. Gressmann's brief summary, *Das Weihnachtsevangelium auf Ursprung und Geschichte untersucht*, pp. 1–6. Also compare Ginzberg's comments on the legend of Rashi's birth (על הלכה ואגדה, pp. 239–240).

influence of prototypes. The ever resurgent desire to complete the saga of the hero's life with an account of his beginnings follows, as it were, the literary genre designed from the outset to serve this role.

This study deals with philological and literary questions, in an attempt to trace the sinuous course of the creation of literary forms, showing how, from obscure beginnings, story patterns are shaped by instilling in them singular content, how they meld, interact and go their separate ways, in a never-ending process. Such a study is not built on historical investigation, rather it can provide the historian with insights, especially in terms of the extreme caution required in drawing inferences from traditions whose content and form are in large measure subservient to literary and theological configurations.[2] This study seeks not only to discover the various traditions, distinct from each other at the outset, but also to understand the way in which each one emerged and developed. In this respect, it has a close affinity to Gunkel's school of form criticism. However, unlike this school, it does not rest on *a priori* literary foundations, such as holding that the primal structure comprises a whole, free of internal contradictions, and that the composite structure is always later than the "pure" one. The development of the traditions, as revealed in this study, indicates that tension between various elements of the literary form sometimes is present from the earliest point at which we can trace those traditions; close analysis of the evolution of a tradition sometimes shows that the later story actually serves to reconcile tension between original elements.[3]

We shall endeavor to describe the development of the tradition in its entirety. Gunkel's followers generally confined their analysis of the history of a form to Scriptural material (but see Gressmann's notes on the Moses story, in Chapter 2). Aggadic scholars, such as Bacher, Ginzberg, Heinemann, Lieberman, and others, for various reasons refused to admit Bible criticism into their study of Aggadah.[4] Analysis of post-biblical traditions, however, shows that although fixing the formulation of a story in Scriptures marks an important milestone in the development of the pattern, it does not put an end to the pattern's development. Elements that were in conflict with one another in the biblical story continue their

---

[2] See the enlightening remarks of Raglan (*The Hero*) on this question. Despite opposing trends in Bible study, his remarks have not lost their pungency.

[3] Also see Y. Kaufmann, תולדות האמונה הישראלית (henceforth cited as *Toledot*), Vol. 2, Bk. 2, p. 654, note 18, and the literature cited there.

[4] This lack is particularly notable in Ginzberg's monumental work, *Legends of the Jews*. For example, Ginzberg does not draw a connection between the legends of the birth of Moses and the particular features of the biblical story. For this reason the interpretive aspects of the *midrash* are not sufficiently stressed in his work. Cf. the chapters which follow on the evolution of the story in later sources.

course, even after the biblical formulation is set, and trends that originate in Scripture reach their culmination in later literary works. Of course the literary crystalization of the story mould in Scriptures, setting the limits within which the motifs develop, has a decisive impact on this conflict. These limits, as we shall see, are quite broad. Tracing the evolution of a motif, aside from being of intrinsic interest, can also help us understand the dynamics of the creation of the ancient story. Needless to say, drawing inferences about the origins of a motif on the basis of its evolution in a literary corpus which dates largely to a later period must be done with the utmost caution and reserve. The assumptions set forth here bear a close affinity to Loewenstamm's approach in *The Evoluton of the Exodus Tradition* and in many of his articles.[5]

---

[5] "The Death of Moses," "The Making and Destruction of the Golden Calf," "Die Geburtsgeschichte Moses" and others. Unlike Loewenstamm, I believe greater weight should be given to the possibility that the complexity of the biblical text in its final form, as we have it today, is what shapes the evolution of the tradition. Often this possibility should be prefered over the assumption, naturally more attractive to the commentator, that the evolution of a tradition reflects the continuation of conflicting traditions that predates the formulation of the biblical text. Thus, even Loewenstamm's fundamental assumption in his pioneering article, "The Death of Moses," must be subjected to close scrutiny. Indeed, one must weigh seriously the possibility that the various approaches to the death of Moses are a reaction to the finished text in Deuteronomy, and not, as he assumes, the remains of pre-Deuteronomic traditions. Cf. also Zunz, p. 125 in the German edition, p. 58 ff. in the Hebrew edition. It would not be out of place to quote Gressmann's words of caution: *Es ist nach wie vor sehr unwahrscheinlich, dass das Rabbinische Schrifttum wirklich "alte Traditionen" bewahrt haben sollte, die über das Exil hinaus reichen* (ZAW n. F. III, 1926, p. 307). Cf. note 3, p. 155, in "Voraussetzungen der Midraschexegese." Indeed, Gressmann's very own comments on the Moses nativity story are conclusive testimony to the fact that one cannot establish *a priori* principles, rather one must consider each case in its own right. Also, cf. the principles set forth in Seeligmann's article, "Voraussetzungen der Midraschexegese."

CHAPTER ONE

THE MOSES NATIVITY STORY IN THE BIBLE

The incorporation of the legend of the birth of Moses into the tradition of the exile in Egypt is characteristic of the way in which a nativity story is worked into traditions that were unrelated at the outset. The evidence for this has been set forth clearly by Gressmann,[1] and therefore I shall only review the main points in brief.

(1) The murder and annihilation motif disappears completely after Exodus 2:10; i.e., after it has served its purpose of introducing the birth of the savior. The motif also detracts from the crescendo in the theme of increasing enslavement in Chapter 5, verse 21.[2] Nor is there any subsequent mention of other motifs associated with the nativity: the miraculous way in which Moses was rescued, and in particular his adoption: **and he became her son** (Ex. 2:10), and his growing up in the Pharaoh's palace. In all the encounters between Moses and Pharaoh there is not even the slightest allusion to this background.[3]

---

[1] For a detailed discussion, see his book, *Mose und seine Zeit*, pp. 1–16; a review of the opinion of other scholars, including the author, may be found in Childs, *Exodus*. Ibn Ezra's commentary (cf. Appendix) provides some bold critical insights.

[2] On the difficulty posed by the disappearance of the murder decree, see Nachmanides (1:10): "It seems to have been quite short-lived, for in the time of Aaron there was no such decree, and when Moses was born it seems to have been abrogated. Perhaps Pharaoh's daughter, in her compassion for Moses, asked her father not to enforce the decree; or when it became known that the decree had come from the King, he abrogated it. [According to Nachmanides, the king ordered his entire people to cast the sons into the Nile, and did not directly command his ministers in order to leave himself the option of denying having issued the edict, if necessary.] Or perhaps it was issued in accordance with the prediction of the astrologers, as the Sages said (*Sotah* 12b). For it was all a scheme against them, that the dastardly act not be found out." Nachmanides continues, "And this is the meaning of the people saying to Moses, ye have made our savor to be abhorred in the eyes of Pharaoh ... to put a sword in their hand to slay us (Ex. 5:21); i.e., hating us even more, they will invent a pretext to say that we are insurgent, and now they will kill us openly by the sword, and no longer by devious means." Nachmanides' comments here show that he is aware that the story of increasing enslavement loses its climactic force if we assume that the slaughter of the sons was an ongoing practice.

[3] Cf. Josephus, who tries to set this "oversight" right (*Antiquities* 2.281–282).

(2) In terms of its literary genre, the nativity story is distinct from the tradition of the enslavement to which it was appended; one being an historical fragment, the other a legendary tale.

(3) Without exception, all other Scriptural accounts of the exile in Egypt dwell solely on the theme of enslavement and do not recall the motifs of annihilation or of Moses' miraculous nativity. Thus it is clear that the ancient traditions were not familiar with the nativity legend. Discerning this is of the utmost importance, since it releases us from evaluating the various methods of assigning sources to documents, advanced by different Bible scholars. Moreover, the evidence for the late date of the nativity story's incorporation removes the underpinnings for source differentiation according to the classical documentary view. What is surprising is that many scholars (including Gressmann!) did not sense this.[4]

Many parallel texts from the folk literature of other peoples reveal that the story of the birth of Moses took shape within an existing pattern. Having noticed this, E. Meyer has said that the Moses nativity story should be viewed as belonging to the category of migratory legends.[5] Gressmann developed this point further, comparing our story primarily to the legend of the birth of Sargon.[6]

> Sargon the mighty king of Agade, am I.
> My mother was *enītum*,[7] my father I knew not.

---

[4] In terms of the late incorporation of the story, it is surprising that many scholars, including Gressmann himself, give so much weight to the absence of an Egyptian parallel to the story. Indeed, there is no close Egyptian parallel; but, in our humble opinion, this could be purely incidental. Moreover, there is a later semi-Egyptian source that has a legend about a savior, albeit typologically closer to the legend of Abraham being born in a cave (see p. 106 below). In *Contra Apionem* (1.292) Josephus cites the account given by Chaeremon, the first century B.C.E. Greco-Egyptian scholar, of the birth of Ramesses: τὸν δὲ Ἀμένωφιν ... εἰς Αἰθιοπίαν φυγεῖν καταλιπόντα τὴν γυναῖκα ἔγκυον, ἣν κρυβομένην ἔν τισι σπηλαίοις τεκεῖν παῖδα ὄνομα Ῥαμέσσην, ὃν ἀνδρωθέντα ἐκδιῶξαι τοὺς Ἰουδαίους εἰς τὴν Συρίαν. "Amenophis ... fled to Ethiopia, leaving his wife pregnant. Concealing herself in some caverns she gave birth to a son named Ramesses, who, on reaching manhood, drove the Jews into Syria." Also cf. Loewenstamm (entry on Moses, *Encyclopedia Biblica*, Vol. 5, pp. 485–486), who accepts the account of Moses' Egyptian upbringing as historical fact, even though he agrees with Gressmann's identification of the story's archetype. One must also reject his suggestion that this Egyptian background accounts for the constant tension between Moses and his people, for Scripture never alludes to this tension being associated with his Egyptian education. Loewenstamm seems to have forgotten having noted (after Gressmann) that there is not the slightest trace of the Moses nativity story in any other biblical source.

[5] *Die Israeliten und ihre Nachbarstämme*, pp. 46–48.

[6] Translation from E. A. Speiser, ANET (3rd. edition), p. 119.

[7] Thus in Akkadian. Cf. ANET (2nd. edition). For an explanation of the word,

The brother(s) of my father loved the hills.
My city is Azupiranu, which is situated on the banks of the Euphrates.
My *enītum* mother conceived me, in secret she bore me.
She set me in a basket of rushes, with bitumen she sealed my lid.
She cast me into the river which rose not (over) me.
The river bore me up and carried me to Akki, the drawer of water.
Akki, the drawer of water, lifted me out as he dipped his e[w]er.
Akki, the drawer of water, [took me] as his son (and) reared me.
Akki, the drawer of water, appointed me as his gardener.
While I was a gardener, Ishtar granted me (her) love.
And for four and [. . .] years I exercised kingship.

The common motifs are immediately apparent: the secretive, unobserved birth; the *enītum* mother, putting her son in an ark; explicit reference to the mother sealing the ark with pitch; and the infant who is drawn out of the water by a stranger. This is a very common pattern in folk literature;[8] we may presume that it was not invented by Sargon, but actually predated him.[9] As Loewenstamm has shown,[10] two motifs attest dependence of the biblical story on the pattern which appears in the Sargon legend. The first is the motif of the ark. In the Babylonian story

---

see below.

[8] Cf. Gressmann, *op. cit.* The literature on this subject is quite extensive. See the bibliographical references in Gaster, *Myth, Legend, and Custom*, p. 380, note 1. Cf. especially D. B. Redford, "The Literary Motif of the Exposed Child"; G. Binder, *Die Aussetzung der Königskinder Kyros und Romulus*; M 371 in Thompson's *Motif Index of Folk-Literature*.

[9] The abandoned child motif itself is extremely widespread. Therefore it belongs to the classification of the migratory legend. This, however, hardly suffices to account for the frequency of the pattern. Cf. Binder's overview. For the more general motif of water carrying the object to its destination, cf. Günter, *Die Christliche Legende des Abendlandes*, p. 73ff. One cannot rule out the possibility that the pattern emerged independently in a number of places, and that what we have here is a preset mold. It seems methodologically undesirable, however, to deal with this question here; therefore we shall only present examples whose literary interdependence is possible, and indeed probable. For an illustration of the archetypal approach, see Otto Rank's imaginative work, *The Myth of the Birth of the Hero*. Although such endeavors as his should not be ruled out on principle, nevertheless it should be noted that the big shortcoming of Rank and his ilk (such as Campbell) is that their form analysis is not accompanied by philological analysis. For example, see Rank's reconstruction of the Moses nativity story according to the mold which he determined for it (*op. cit.*, pp. 82–83). This shortcoming was inherited by psychoanalytic scholars from their great teacher, Freud. See Freud's classic work, *Der Mann Moses und die monotheistische Religion*. We must also note that our study uses such terms as pattern, form and type in a fundamentally different way. They do not refer to a symbolic or allegorical form, and they do not lead to another reality. They specify only a literary pattern, aspiring to express a theological idea through means commonly used in literary works.

[10] S. E. Loewenstamm, "Die Geburtsgeschichte Moses."

the careful construction and sealing of the ark stem from the setting, for the mother places the ark in the river, presumably even upstream where the current is strong, and the river carries off the ark to the distance. In the biblical story, however, the mother places her child in the reeds on the shore of the Nile (Exodus 2:3), not in a place where the strong current of the river will wash him away. His sister even positions herself some distance off, to find out what fate will befall him. The detailed account of the ark's construction, found in verse 3, is not justified by its context in the narrative. This indicates that the origins of the motif are not in the biblical story itself, rather in some archetype to which the biblical story is heir. Placing the ark in the reeds on the shore of the Nile also is somewhat inconsonant with the etymological conclusion of the story: **Because I drew him out of the water.**

The second motif is the absence of a father. In both narratives, the father plays no part in the ark's construction. In the Sargon narrative, the father does not appear at all; in the biblical narrative, he disappears immediately after the introduction. Modern scholarship, which has concerned itself greatly with the absence of the father in the Sargon narrative, does not seem to be aware of a parallel problem in Exodus. Loewenstamm mentions Abarbanel as one exegete who discusses the problem and attempts to resolve it in his own way.[11] In the Sargon legend this exclusive role of the mother is understandable and necessarily stems from the fact that the father was unknown: "My father I knew not." But in the Exodus story, where the mother's role is given even greater emphasis—the story adds that it was she who hid the child—the absence of the father is reason for wonderment. Examining this motif produces evidence that, as in the first motif, the biblical story form developed from a form patterned after the Babylonian narrative.[12]

Why the father's absence and what purpose it plays are questions in their own right. Reviewing the occurrences of this pattern,[13] we see that in the vast majority of cases the father or mother is a god. Of the thirteen instances cited by Redford as parallels of the Sargon nativity story, ten clearly associate the hero with a divine father or mother. An explicit divine element is lacking only in three instances:

---

[11] In his commentary on Chapter 2 of Exodus, Abarbanel says: "Note that Scriptures attribute all these deeds to the mother of Moses, and make no mention of his father; perhaps because he had already died, or was not present, or had despaired of the situation and did not want to go to pains, saying, 'let me not see the death of the child,' etc.; and the latter is correct."

[12] It is true that the second argument, the absence of the father, does not hold as well as the first, placing the ark in the river; for in many stories of abandoned heroes the mother plays the principal role, often because it is the father who is the newborn child's primary foe.

[13] Cf. Redford, *op. cit.*

the births of Zal and Darab in Persian mythology, and the birth of Ptolemy Soter. According to the legend of Ptolemy's birth, an eagle hovered over him and fed him. The eagle is the bird of Zeus; thus it seems the legend would like to intimate that Zeus' attitude towards Ptolemy is one of father to son (cf. Binder, p. 72). The Persian variants lack reference to a divinity, but one should note the close affinity between the nativity legend of Zal and myth. As the legend has it, he was fed by a divine bird on a mountaintop above the clouds (*ibid.*, p. 179). Lambert's interpretation of the Akkadian word *enītum*, a puzzle to scholars for many years,[14] also points in this direction. As Lambert has shown, this word refers to the status of a priestess bound to chastity; and if, nevertheless, such a priestess does bear child, and perhaps even in the temple, such a birth would attest that the deity is husband and father.[15] To these considerations one must add the general fact that in the pagan world attributing divine progenitorship to the hero is a dominant theme, occurring in dozens of variations. For a Babylonian example, see the Code of Hammurabi, Col. II, A:13-14.[16]

Perhaps in the Sargon legend the mother's bearing in secret and sending off her child can be accounted for as an attempt on the part of the priestess to conceal her contact with the god or to ward off her being accused of breaking her vow of chastity. Be that as it may, the general assumption that the need to cover up an illicit birth explains the motif of the father's absence does not seem to hold for several reasons:

(1) The recurrence of the pattern over many generations and across various cultures indicates that it is an archetype mythological pattern, and not an actual explanation of fact.
(2) It does not explain why it is precisely the important figures who are born under such circumstances.

---

[14] W. G. Lambert and A. R. Millard, *Atraḫasis*. Cf. *ibid.*, p. 102; notes on p. 165. Also see note 1, p. 13. Cf. C. Cohen, "The Legend of Sargon and the Birth of Moses," pp. 46-51. Speiser accepts this interpretation in his translation in the 3rd edition of ANET, and renders it there as *high priestess*.

[15] Cf. Gressmann, *Mose*, p. 10, note 4; he considers this possibility but is reluctant to accept it; however he has a different translation of *enītum*. The motif of a priestess bearing child notwithstanding her duty to be chaste occurs in the nativity stories of Telephos (for the many versions which exists, see Binder, p. 130), and of Romulus and Remus; cf. Roscher, *Lexicon* IV, p. 174ff. Clearly one must be extremely cautious in comparing distant sources; nor should such comparisons be granted undue importance. Yet the fact that these distant sources all juxtapose a priestess bearing child with the divine origins of the newborn at least indicates the reasonability of such a motif. In the *Protevangelium of James*, Mary appears as a priestess.

[16] Cf. also Kaufmann, *Toledot*, Vol. 1, Bk. 2, pp. 337-343, and Loewenstamm, "Beloved is Man that he was created in the Image."

(3) This assumption has an internal contradiction. Even its proponents recognize that the story serves to cover up the fact of an extra-marital birth by doing away with the father. Therefore, even if we were to accept the possibility, which I see as altogether unnecessary, that the pattern sometimes serves to cover up an illicit birth, this in itself attests that the pattern wishes to say just the opposite—that not knowing the identity of the father does not indicate the worthlessness of the son, but rather attests his elevated status, and the supreme expression of this elevated status is having the deity as father.

(4) Going one step further, it seems more reasonable to suppose that accounts of illicit births are the product of the pattern than to suppose that the pattern resulted from the fact of an illicit birth. This can be seen in the evolution of traditions in the history of Christianity. The story of the virgin gave rise among the opponents of Christianity to the tradition that Jesus was born as a bastard, most likely a later tradition than that of the virgin mother, since there is no hint of such accusations having been made against Jesus, his mother, or his disciples in the New Testament itself or in coeval Jewish sources (cf. Strack und Billerbeck, Vol. 1, pp. 36–43). Also such testimony in Christian sources appears entirely in sources that are already familiar with the virgin birth (cf. Brown, *The Birth of the Messiah*, pp. 535–537).[17]

Unlike the story of the birth of Moses, the murder motif does not appear in the Sargon nativity story. There is no need to assume, as Gressmann does, that this motif should be added. Our method does not require it in order to account for the mother's deeds; parallels of this pattern indicate that the pattern of the foundling often appears separately, even going back to very ancient examples. In other words, both literary analysis as well as literary findings indicate that here we are dealing with two essentially distinct patterns.[18]

The murder motif in the biblical story raises many difficulties.[19] Why

---

[17] The attempt to infer a slanderous tradition from Jesus being called the son of Mary, in Mark 6:3, is quite tenuous. Jesus is also compared there to his brothers, and surely with no intention of implying that they, too, were bastards. Furthermore, we must note that the text is of dubious accuracy. The ancient Papyrus 45 apparently reads "son of the carpenter," in parallel to Matthew and as in Luke and John. Cf. Nestle-Aland, *Greek English New Testament*. Thus, this may reflect the same trend of refraining from calling Joseph the father of Jesus, which we discussed in our studies of birth traditions (J. Cohen, pp. 228, 182).

[18] Cf. Redford, *op. cit.* Redford collected abandoned hero legends that did not include attempted murder, and included them in the first group, in which he also placed the Sargon nativity legend. *Ibid.*, pp. 211–214.

[19] Once more, after Gressmann.

is it directed only at newborns? Why only the sons? The explanation given in the story—lest the people become numerous—does not provide an answer to these questions, and it also conflicts with the historical motif of enslavement, since a slave-owner's supreme interest is to increase the number of his slaves. Moreover, the measures the king takes to reduce their numbers are not effective and would better have been directed at the females. It should also be noted that everywhere the theme of slavery appears (even in Exodus), with the sole exception of Exodus, Ch. 1, it is not coupled with a desire to reduce the number. The association of annihilation with slavery also leaves something to be desired literarily. We have already mentioned above that the story of increasing enslavement in Chapter 5 loses all its climactic force if one supposes that it was preceded by murder of the sons. Analysis of the structure of the nativity story also reveals a certain lack of clarity. The Pharaoh's designs of murder are directed at the entire people, whereas in the biblical narrative they introduce the birth of the lone child, the sole subject of interest of the legend; and from the moment he comes on the scene, the entire motif of annihilation or fear lest the people multiply disappears. On the contrary, as the story continues, the desire that the people remain in Egypt comes to dominate. As Gressmann puts it: "There is a conflict between the exposition of the story and the point it seeks to prove." Moreover, we never hear whether the plot to murder the sons took place, whether indeed the Israelite sons were cast into the Nile. Similarly, unlike the motif of slavery (Ex. 2:23), the sons being thrown into the river elicits no reaction on the part of the people.[20] These difficulties, coupled with close analysis of parallels in the literature of other peoples, especially the parallel in the New Testament, Matthew 2, and the version of the story which appears in *Antiquities*, led Gressmann to conjecture that also the Moses nativity story originally began with the motif of foreknowledge, which, as formulated in our story, heralded the birth of the savior who, according to the natural structure of the pattern, was destined to bring destruction to Pharaoh and his people. Thus Pharaoh does not fear the entire people, but only the birth of a certain male; and it is this birth which he tries to prevent, and fails dismally. Not only is the child saved; but the daughter of the would-be murderer is the one who brings him up. One should add to Gressmann's remarks that accepting his conjecture brings out even more strikingly the independence of the birth story, considering that glossing over the

---

[20] In the first instance, as well, the narrator did not describe the reaction of the people to the murder decree, or to its annulment, parallel to his description of the impact of the enslavement (Ex. 1:11–14). But the absence of such a reaction is consonant with the conspiratorial nature of the murder decree at the hands of the midwives.

Pharaoh's death (Ex. 2:23) hardly suits the substance of the foretold events. Indeed, compare *Tanḥuma Buber* (חזריע 10), page 125 below, where the structure is "corrected."

At this point our reconstruction of the story departs from Gressmann's. We believe that one can still detect two patterns in the narrative.

The first pattern, that of the ark, paralleled in the Sargon nativity legend, is comprised of the following basic elements: a priestess bound to chastity, bearing child in secret, placing the child in an ark, the child being drawn out of the water, and his growing up as a foundling. **The second pattern**, that of the murder, paralleled in the New Testament and in many other stories, is comprised of the following basic elements: foreknowledge, an attempt at murder, the failure of this attempt, and the motif of a foundling.[21] Moses, as an illustrious figure, attracted these patterns of nativity stories. And, in addition to the usual factors that lead to a hero being associated with a certain story pattern, an etymological element (Ex. 2:10) also came into play. Thus both these patterns became incorporated into the tradition of the Israelites' enslavement and increase in numbers. In its present form, the Moses nativity story is a blend of these three elements. We cannot describe precisely how these traditions came to be melded together, since what we see is primarily the final outcome. Yet we may surmise that the motivation for the attempts at murder was taken from the tradition of the Israelites becoming more numerous; that the attempts at murder came from the second pattern; and that the first pattern, the ark pattern, borrowed its motivation for the mother's actions from the second pattern, that of the murder. Pharaoh's edict that every newborn son be thrown into the Nile came to replace the original reason for the motif, found in the

---

[21] This pattern is also very widespread. Redford places the stories belonging to this pattern in the second group (pp. 215–217), and lists 13 parallels (*op. cit.*). A surprising number of them come from Hellenistic sources, although some are about non-Greek heroes, such as Cyrus and Gilgamesh. This pattern was also known to Persian legends, (*ibid.*). To his examples one should add the incorporation of the pattern into a myth in the cosmology of Orpheus: οὓς καὶ δήσας κατεταρτάρωσεν, ἐκπεσεῖσθαι αὐτὸν ὑπὸ τῶν παίδων τῆς ἀρχῆς μαθών. "He [Uranus] bound them [his sons] and cast them into Tartaros, because he had found out that his sons would seize power from him" (Diels, 1B 13). Redford's observation that there is no ancient Egyptian source among the various examples of the abandoned hero pattern is important to our study of the history of the biblical story. This observation is especially striking in the *Westcar Papyrus*, which recounts how the king in power received tidings of the birth of the founder of a new dynasty; yet the text does not mention any measures taken by the king in connection with this annunciation in order to prevent the birth. Note, however, the close affinity between this story and the obvious motif (*ibid.*). Also cf. Brunner-Traut, "Die Geburtsgeschichte der Evangelien im Lichte ägyptologischer Forschungen," pp. 101–102, and note 4, above.

Babylonian pattern—the priestess, bound to chastity, bearing child—a motif which was not understood and could not continue to exist in the biblical narrative. Perhaps the lack of understanding of the mother's actions served as another factor pressing for incorporation of the murder theme in order to provide a motive. With the utmost caution, we add the conjecture that the origins that shaped the account of the attempt at murder precisely by throwing the sons in the Nile, the account of the child born in secret and placed in an ark, and the account of the child drawn out of the water all stem from the first pattern, that of the ark. But Moses being raised by the daughter of the one who issued the decree stems from the second pattern, that of the murder, by the symmetric argument that the murder is prevented by the daughter of its instigator and the infant is raised in the palace of the would-be murderer.

The tri-part relationship between the three principal components of the story—the midwives, the ark, and the birth of Moses—clearly shows that the two birth patterns were originally independent. According to the narrative in its present state, the birth of Moses is related only to the second decree, that of throwing the sons into the Nile (Ex. 1:22), and to the subsequent story of the ark, in which Moses is saved due to having been concealed: **she hid him three months** (Ex. 2:2), and due to the ark: **she took for him an ark of bulrushes** (Ex. 2:3). But the narrative draws no connection between his being saved and the actions of the midwives. In other words, the story of the midwives plays no role in introducing the saga of the savior. This is most remarkable. The story of the midwives would have no grounds for existence without the birth of the savior, at which the story is directed and which gives the story its *raison d'être*. Yet the narrative does not join the story of the midwives with the story of the birth. The very statement of the problem hints at a possible solution. The instruction to the midwives is an original element of the murder pattern. This pattern was intended from the outset to introduce the birth of the savior, and as such was drawn towards the figure of Moses. In this original pattern the savior's deliverance was due to the midwives' refusal to carry out the king's edict; but in the struggle between the various traditions regarding the birth, the ark motif gained the upper hand and set a distance between the murder motif (at the hands of the midwives) and the savior himself. Perhaps this conflict of traditions, which separated the murder motif from the savior, also led to the disappearance of the annunciation of the savior's birth, which in the original pattern served as the sole reason for the murder motif at the hands of the midwives. We cannot rule out the possibility that the impact of the murder motif worked its way into Jewish tradition gradually. First came a decree against the sons, without any reason for the decree; and only in subsequent stages of evolution did the tradition fill in the details of the pattern. In other words, one should view Scriptures as reflecting an early stage in terms of the evolution of tradition in Jewish sources. (Cf. below, in the chapters on *Asatir* and Rashi's commentary and their relationship to the tradition in the New Testament.) Yet the very edict against the sons cannot be severed from the ruler's fear of a lone savior; otherwise we have no explanation why the decree should have been directed only at the sons. Therefore we must say that if the Aggadah truly reflects a later stage of development, in this instance it is closer to the source from which Scriptures derived the decree to murder the male infants.

The drawback of mixing traditions is that it sometimes leads to tension between various motifs and to a lack of structural clarity, but as we shall see below, it is precisely this tension that serves as the point of departure for the rich development of motifs.

Delimiting the literary unit. It is no simple task to determine the exact bounds of the literary unit. Actually, determining where the unit ends is not so difficult. Verse 10 is clearly the end of one unit, and verse 11 the transition to the next. A similar concluding verse may be seen in the narrative of the birth of Samson, Judges 13:24–25. The principal difficulties are encountered in finding where the unit begins. This is understandable; for, according the Gressmann's conjecture, in our story this part was damaged and has reached us without the motif presaging things to come, which he surmises appeared at the beginning of the narrative. In the introduction to the narrative, verses 11–14 form a unit in two respects. First, in terms of their literary genre they comprise an historical fragment. Second, they include only the ancient motifs of enslavement and proliferation.[22] Therefore it is reasonable to view this passage, even as presently formulated, as predating the birth legend. This can also be seen from the way this passage relates to the story of the midwives which follows. The final version of the story views the instruction to the midwives as stemming from the failure of enslavement. According to this structure, verse 12: **But the more they afflicted them, the more they multiplied and grew. And they were grieved because of the children of Israel** ought to have come at the end of the unit, after verse 14, in order to sum up the failure and explain the Pharaoh's next action. The fact that the verse is in the middle of the unit attests the independence of the unit. On the other hand, verses 8–10 contain a number of mixed motifs. Alongside the ancient motif of natural increase, we have the motif of getting the better of the Israelites by dealing wisely with them, a motif which finds direct

---

[22] Cf. Deuteronomy 26:5–8, where the proliferation of the Israelites is not accompanied by any fears on the part of the king. Also cf. Psalms 105:24.

expression in verse 15, and not in verse 11.[23] Therefore one should view these verses as combining the birth legend with the motif of slavery and natural increase. It is hard to view these verses as having a separate and distinct literary existence; in any event, we must relinquish any attempt at isolating specific words or phrases. In summary, the limits of the birth story are from Exodus 1:15 to 2:10; verses 11–14 do not belong to it at all; and verses 8–10 are the result of melding the birth tradition with the slavery and proliferation tradition, after the opening of the birth story had disappeared.[24]

Analysis of parallels to the Moses nativity story led us to conclude above that this story should be viewed as the result of blending three basic elements: the tradition of enslavement, joined with two archetypes of birth stories—the murder pattern and the ark pattern. By the point at which the story has developed in Scriptures we can no longer reconstruct the complex process of interlacing one tradition with another. Moreover, one may cast doubt on the very notion of such interlacing being early or late, for it seems that the various component elements influenced one another from the outset. Nevertheless, we can describe the result of these various elements coming together.

The impact of ancient traditions on the nativity legend. We begin with the impact of ancient elements of the story—exile and a foreign land, enslavement and proliferation—on the nativity legend. To this influence one should attribute the Egyptian setting of the story. The king is the Pharaoh, the princess is the Pharaoh's daughter, and the river is the Nile. Also the motivation for the murder decree in the story—fear of the people becoming numerous—was drawn from ancient traditions and pushed aside the original reason for the decree—fear of a lone savior. It is hard to know why the motif of foreknowledge of the birth of a savior disappeared from the story, but this probably happened when the various elements of the story were interwoven. It stands to reason that this change was abetted by a process of nationalization of the story which occurred as the various elements were joined together, and that this resulted from the influence of the ancient tradition on the birth patterns; for the decisive difference between these patterns and the more ancient story units is that the birth patterns deal with

---

[23] Meyer's perceptive insight, *op. cit.*, p. 41. One cannot rule out the possibility that the motif of dealing wisely actually grew out of the difficulty in understanding the enslavement as a direct means of annihilating the people. If so, the motif of dealing wisely should also be viewed as an element that came into being as a result of the tradition of enslavement being combined with the nativity story.

[24] Again there is no need here to discuss the various traditions that are embedded in the enslavement story, since the nativity legend was incorporated into the enslavement tradition at a late date, after the various traditions regarding the enslavement came into existence and blended with one another.

a single individual, whereas the ancient traditions describe the entire nation.[25] Compare Genesis 15:13-14, Deuteronomy 26:5-9, and other sources. True, a legend should not be challenged by posing questions of reality, but with hindsight it seems that joining a legend about an individual with a tradition concerning a nation created the question that ancient commentators have struggled with since the time of Ibn Ezra: How could two midwives have assisted the births of a nation of six hundred thousand?[26]

The impact of the tradition of enslavement, in which the hero is the entire nation, is more evident in the story of the midwives (the murder pattern) than in the ark pattern. In the story of the midwives the decree is directed against the masses, and in parallel the salvation becomes a deliverance of the masses. However, in the story of the ark, which, as we recall (cf. p. 13 ff., above), retained the connection with the birth of a lone savior, the rescue of the single hero is mentioned but the fate of the masses is forgotten; we do not know what befell the rest of the newborn sons, whether they were drowned in the Nile or were saved. As a result, the narrative assumes the following structure: the first murder decree, directed against the masses (1:16); rescue of the masses (1:17); a second murder decree against the masses (1:22), rescue of an individual (2:1-10). Note that this structure is deficient in that it lacks symmetry; compare later sources, cited below, that try to amend the structure.

One can also attribute the appearance of the father from the House of Levi in the narrative's introduction to the influence of the general setting within which the nativity stories were embedded; although, as we have seen, this influence was limited to the beginning of the narrative.

The influence of the nativity legend on the ancient traditions. The parallel change that took place in the ancient traditions regarding the exile as they were melded with the birth motifs is no less far-reaching. The impact of the decrees to murder the sons worked its way into the tradition of the enslavement. Only in Exodus 1 (and nowhere else) is the enslavment described as a means for annihilating the people. Perhaps this change in the enslavement motif has to do

---

[25] Perhaps verse 12 is the first link in the chain of viewing the enslavement of the Israelites as directed against their proliferation, even though this was not the intent of the original verse, as attested by the sources cited above. Cf. note 22 above.

[26] Later midrashic commentaries show to what extent the Aggadah is oblivious of this very real question. *Midrash Sekel Tob* on Exodus 1:15 comments: "to the Hebrew midwives—It is written with incomplete orthography (למילדה העבריח), to indicate that there were only two." Hadar Zekenim commentary by the Tosafists says: "A ו is missing in למילדות, to the midwives, to teach us that there was only one midwife, namely Yocheved; Miriam, however was a young girl and not a midwife, but she was panting (פועה) for child, and therefore our Sages said Puah was Miriam" (*Torah Shelemah*, Vol. 8 (שמות), p. 37, n. 156*).

with the loss of the original reason for the murder decrees—fear of the individual savior. However, in addition to this striking difference, which Gressmann explains correctly, mention must be made of one other, albeit less prominent, difference which is of great significance to the later evolution of the story. In the present structure of the story, the motif of enslavement is subordinate to the birth traditions. Here the enslavement appears as the first design in a climactic tri-part series, building up to the appearance of the savior. This subordination radically changed the motif of enslavement. While in Genesis 15:13, the enslavement is portrayed as a protracted affair: **and shall serve them; and they shall afflict them four hundred years** (cf. also Numbers 20:15); in Exodus 1, because it is subservient to the history of one individual and is placed parallel to the decrees against the sons, the motif appears as a shallow episode, devoid of historic depth.[27][28] This contrasts with the motif of the miraculous increase in numbers which appears before the ascent of the new king (v. 7). Unlike the enslavement, there is an inherent contradiction between the nature of the people's proliferation and its being included during the reign of a single king.

Reciprocal impact of the birth motifs on one another. We have already suggested that the birth legend encapsulates two fundamentally distinct patterns and have tried to trace the origins of each original component. It should be added that in the unification of the two patterns it is evident that pride of place went to the ark pattern as opposed to the murder pattern, since the motif of being rescued by means of the ark appears in direct connection with the birth of the savior, whereas rescue by means of the midwives becomes only a matter

---

[27] An element of tension is also created by the enslavement persisting after the birth of the savior, unlike the decree against the sons, which disappears once it has fulfilled its role (according to Gressmann, *op. cit.*). Loewenstamm, "Die Geburtsgeschichte Moses," also presents the solutions offered by the Midrash, which we shall discuss later.

[28] Aside from the compression of historical time, one also encounters its protraction. Take the instructive example of Zimri, who reigned all of seven days, and nevertheless the author of the Book of Kings sums up his life and accounts for his death with the standard formula: **for his sins which he sinned in doing evil in the sight of the Lord, in walking in the way of Jeroboam, and in his sin which he did, to make Israel sin** (I Kings 16:19). This sort of tension between the description of national history vs. personal biography is typical of biblical historiography and has far-reaching implications. For example, the conquest of the land is described as taking place entirely under Joshua; the struggle between Israel and Judea is couched in terms of a struggle between **"the man of Israel"** and **"the man of Judah"** (cf. II Samuel 19:42-44), etc. Perhaps the fact that the Pentateuch concludes with the death of Moses and not with the conquest of the land should be attributed, among other reasons, to this approach to biography. This, however, is a matter for much more extensive discussion.

of momentary deliverance. To further illustrate the complexity of reciprocal influence, we must add that the first deliverance motif could assume such a form because, under the influence of the ancient sources, the murder decree was directed against the entire people, not against a single son; for, it stands to reason that in the original pattern the midwives' refusal to fulfill the king's orders sufficed to save the one infant. Also the weakening of the ark motif, which we dwelled on following Loewenstamm, became possible due to the interweaving of the patterns, because the motif of the danger threatening the infant in the ark can be eliminated without detriment to the motif of danger in the story as a whole, where the murder design lends it sufficient expression.

The results of combining the three components.[29] We noted above, after presenting Gressmann's analysis of the tensions created by joining the birth legend with the enslavement story, that this only reveals one aspect of the narrative, because its complex structure and wealth of motifs stem largely from this special process of combining materials. The present story has three edicts—enslavement, murder of the males by the midwives, and throwing the sons into the Nile—which appear in a triple, climactic structure, each successive edict harsher than the previous one.[30] There is development even from the first murder decree to the second one: the first was done in secret, by stratagem; the second in the open, without pretense; and the fact of there being a second attempt was the result of the failure of the first.[31] Analysis of the story shows that each of these three decrees stems from a different origin, and the dialectic between the murder decrees is the result of combining two separate patterns. The outcome is a complex narrative, with a triple and a double structure, quite far removed from the simple and clear patterns in the literary parallels. Although this structure reveals elements of tension between its basic components, which differ in origin, nevertheless, as surprising as this may seem, the interweaving of the

---

[29] We have already discussed some of the elements of tension generated in the narrative as a result of combining the nativity story with the account of the enslavement (cf. p. 10–12).

[30] It should be noted, however, that this structure is not completely smooth, for there is a larger distance between the second decree (murder at the hands of the midwives) and the first (enslavement), than between the second decree and the third (casting the sons into the Nile). Moreover, the second decree was an utter failure, whereas the first was implemented although it did not achieve its objective. The Septuagint's three-fold repetition ἴσχυον σφόδρα in verses 7, 12, and 20 underscores the connection between proliferation, enslavement, and midwives.

[31] Cf. Gressmann, *Mose*, p. 2, where he notes correctly that the structure here, as well, is lacking; for the first decree, that of enslavement, is carried out openly. These shortcomings are further evidence that originally the nativity legend and the tradition of enslavement were not connected.

basic components in the narrative also produces the opposite effect—a deeper bond between the parts.

The Sargon nativity story has none of the symmetry found in our story, where the person who draws the infant out of the water and rescues him—a figure appearing at the end of the story—is none other than the princess who, by her actions, undoes the murderous designs of her father—the figure who opened the story. It seems that the motif of the foundling was thus changed. In Sargon, the person who abandoned the child had more lofty status than the person who found him; in Scriptures it is the other way around. Likewise, the parallel murder patterns do not have the symmetry found in our story between the method of murder—throwing into the Nile—and the method of rescue—an ark in the Nile.

Even the seam between the deliverance brought about by the midwives (the murder pattern) and the deliverance by means of the ark (the ark pattern) was artfully done. In our story it is an Egyptian princess, daughter of a foreign king, who draws the child out of the water. Here we see an interweaving of elements taken from the murder pattern and the ark pattern. Thus the first deliverance parallels the second, for it is likely that the midwives assisting the Hebrews were Egyptian women. To the evidence for this brought by Shadal (Samuel David Luzzatto) and Ehrlich, we add a decisive factor which emerges from our analysis.[32] In

---

[32] We quote Shadal: "The Alexandrian translator [i.e., the Septuagint], Jerome [i.e., the Vulgate], Josephus, and Abarbanel all believe that midwives were Egyptian; and thus it seems, for how could he have commanded Israelite women to destroy all the male newborns of their people and have believed that they would not reveal the plot? But Le Clerc has argued that if the midwives were not Hebrews the text should have said לעבריות, and Rosenmüler added the gloss that it should have said את העבריות; but this argument does not hold, for it is true that the text could have said למילדות את העבריות, but one could equally well have left out the particle את, as in האדם האכל הבסר (Jeremiah 31:29). Moreover, the argument based on the verse that the midwives feared God is no argument, since the text does not say *YHWH*, but rather *Elohim*; and anyone who believes in a deity, be it a false god or the true God, would fear taking the life of an innocent babe, regardless of what people they belonged to. For example, we read of Amalek, that he **smote the hindmost of thee, even all that were feeble behind thee, when thou wast faint and weary; and he feared not God** (Deuteronomy 25:18). My dear disciple Jacob Pardo, of blessed memory, adds that if the midwives belonged to another people, it would be correct to say that they spared the sons out of fear of God, and not out of love; but had they been Hebrews, there would have been no need to mention fear of God, because every person loves his own people." One should add to Shadal's commentary the instructive example from Genesis 42:18, where Joseph, disguised as an Egyptian, says: **for I fear God.** Cf. also Gen. 20:11 and Job 1:1. In general, Wisdom literature, which is known not to have any Israelite nationalistic elements, often uses the phrase "fear of God." Ehrlich comments on verse 22: "From the fact that the verse says **all his people** we may infer that the midwives were Egyptian, as I said; for the words **all his people** would not have been used here if the midwives

the typical murder pattern the king entrusts the infant to a close confidant, and, as in our story, commands him to kill the child clandestinely and guilefully, so that no one know. It should be noted that the motif of deliverance at the hands of a gentile woman occurs frequently in Scriptures; thus the midwives and Pharaoh's daughter should be added to the list of Rahab and Yael (and perhaps also the harlot of Gaza?).

Juxtaposed to the second deliverance is the scene between Pharaoh's daughter and Moses' sister. As Loewenstamm showed in his above-mentioned article ("Die Geburtsgeschichte Moses"), this juxtaposition reflects one of the unique features of the biblical story: a bias towards curtailing the motif of the abandoned child,[33] which is a fundamental el-

---

had not also belonged to his people." Shadal's remarks can be supplemented by the sources cited in Ginzberg, Vol. 5 (Moses), note 17, p. 393. (See p. 93 below; The Midrash, note 65.) Also cf. *Torah Shelemah*, Vol. 8, p. 38, n. 166; and *ibid.*, Kasher's note. It is possible that the *Asatir* also holds that Shiphrah and Puah were Egyptian. See note 4 in our chapter, The Asatir, below. Also compare Shadal's arguments to the remarks of Rabbenu Ephraim: "It has been asked why Pharaoh ordered to have the sons killed by the midwives, and did not have them killed by the Egyptians who were his servants." But the reason which he gives is different.

[33] This bias exists in other narratives, as well. For example, see the birth of Samuel, which uses the motif of the robe (I Samuel 2:19; as it has been noted, the robe figures prominently in the Book of Samuel, cf. 15:27-28 and 28:14); see also our chapter on Matthew, p. 167. One can connect this literary bias with parallels from the socio-religious-judicial realm, which among the Jews placed an obligation on parents to raise their children, as opposed to the practice of murder or ἔκθεσις found among other nations. The different Jewish practice occasioned comment, dating back to Hecataeus of Abdera, who remarked τεχνοτροφεῖν τε ἠνάγκαζε, i.e., "He (scil. Moses) required to rear their children" (cf. Stern, Vol. 1, p. 33, note 8). Also Tacitus (*Historiae* V.5) wrote that in the Jews' opinion *necare quemquam ex agnatis nefas*, i.e., "they (scil. the Jews) regard as a crime to kill any late-born child" (cf. Stern, Vol. 2, p. 41, note 5:3. Stern also cites the remarks of Josephus in *Contra Apionem*, 2.202: τέκνα τρέφειν ἅπαντα προσέταξεν, καὶ γυναιξὶν ἀπεῖπε μήτ' ἀμβλοῦν τὸ σπαρὲν μήτε διαφθείρειν, ἀλλ' ἢν φανείη τεχνοκτόνος ἂν εἴη, ψυχὴν ἀφανίζουσα καὶ τὸ γένος ἐλαττοῦσα., i.e., "The Law orders all the offspring to be brought up, and forbids women either to cause abortion or to make away with the fetus; a woman convicted of this is regarded as an infanticide, because she destroys a soul and diminishes the race." Compare these remarks of Josephus to the horrifying example cited in Deissmann, *Licht vom Osten*, p. 134, quoting the letter of the poor day-laborer Hilarion to his beloved wife Alis, who apparently had informed him that she was with child. After asking her to care for the son which they already have, he adds instructions concerning the child to be born: ἐὰν ἦν ἄρσενον ἄφες, ἐὰν ἦν θήλεα ἔκβαλε, i.e., if it is a son, let him live, and if it is a daughter, abandon her. He concludes with a touching avowal of his love: πῶς δύναμαί σε ἐπιλαθεῖν· ἐρωτῶ σε οὖν ἵνα μὴ ἀγωνιάσῃς; "How could I ever forget you. I beg of you, do not worry." Also note how the Midrash feels compelled to apologize for Abraham abandoning Terah before the latter had died (*Genesis Rabbah*, לך לך XXXIX, p. 369; *Torah Shelemah*, Vol. 2, p. 525, n. 114; and Rashi on Genesis 11:32). Also see Pharaoh's Daughter, p. 126 ff.

ement in the Babylonian pattern. This bias is most poignantly expressed by the mother becoming the child's nurse. The transition to this new motif is elegant and natural, and only minute analysis can reveal its complexity in terms of the evolution of its component parts. Pharaoh's daughter concludes: **This is one of the Hebrews' children** (v. 6), because the motif of murder directed at an individual (which comes from the second pattern) in our story has been nationalized due to the influence of the ancient tradition. Moses' sister[34] immediately comes forward

---

[34] It seems reasonable that the sister was brought into the story to strengthen the motif of the mother's love and to counteract the motif of abandonment, which the narrative seeks to minimize. It is hard say for certain whether she entered the story secondarily, or whether from the outset the censorious attitude towards child abandonment created both the mother, who placed the ark on the bank of the river, and the sister, as well. The motif of abandonment, stemming from the Babylonian archetype, is curtailed in our story by means of the mother and sister, thus creating the imbalance between taking such extreme care in the ark's construction and then placing it in the reeds, which, following Loewenstamm, we noted above. One senses in the very appearance of the sister that she is by nature foreign to the archetype. This is made all the more evident by the fact that her presence introduces a heroine whom the narrative cannot assimilate. Her appearance in verse 4 comes as a surprise. We have been told nothing of her existence, nor is there room in the narrative, in which the conception of Moses follows fast upon the mother being taken to wife, to tell of her birth; for the archetype requires that the motif opposing the birth be directed at the savior. Loewenstamm notes that mentioning the sister before her actual appearance would have given her too much weight in the story and thus would have hurt the flow of the narrative. (Compare this to Nachmanides' explanation in note 38, below.) While we do not deny the validity of Loewenstamm's remark, we have a different explanation. Contrary to prevalent opinion, we believe that the contradiction created by the appearance of the sister cannot be attributed to a melding of various sources. Although our explanation is close to that of documentary theory, we believe the contradiction here is not the result of a hybrid of independent stories, but rather of the particular development of the story within the context of the archetype yet shaped by the biblical bias censuring abandonment, a bias which is foreign to the basic archetype and contradicts its fundamental elements.

As for the contradiction itself, proximity of elements whose co-existence is discordant is one of the touchstones of biblical thought. Here we shall only give a brief and allusive sketch, since exhaustive treatment of the topic goes beyond the scope of the present work. In the extreme, one finds a statement and its opposite, one after the other; for example, I Samuel 15:29: **And also the Strength of Israel will not lie nor repent; for he is not a man, that he should repent,** which comes only a few verses before the conclusion of the chapter: **and the Lord repented that he had made Saul king over Israel** (15:35); or Numbers 22:20, where the Lord says to Balaam, **rise up, and go with them,** followed by verse 22, and **God's anger was kindled because he went.**

In less extreme cases one finds contradictory points of view in the same narrative unit. A good example is the relationship between the power of the deity and the magical power of the blessing and the curse in the story of Balaam. The only power acknowledged by the story is that of God, and everything happens by His word; yet the course of the narrative, in which the deity intervenes to prevent Balaam's curse, shows that the narrator acknowledges the power of the curse and believes in the power of the blessing. A similar motif may be seen in the story of Samson and his hair. Samson's prayer, Judges 16:28, is preceded by the brief statement, **Howbeit the hair of his head began to grow again after he was shaven** (16:22). There are many instances, akin to the above, where the entire story is based on a point of view whose complete acceptance contradicts the author's viewpoint. To mention only one, we have the trial to which God puts his chosen one, in which there is an implicit assumption that the deity does not know the future: **for now I know that thou fearest God** (Genesis 22:12); yet such an explicit statement surely would have come as a surprise to the author and his circle.

In some of the passages mentioned the problem is somewhat alleviated by separating the verses and ascribing them to different sources; but this does not provide a complete solution, since it only answers the problem how the motifs were created, but not of how they were blended; in other words, the problem is shifted from the author to the redactor. Furthermore, source differentiation certainly does not solve the problem posed by the last two examples—the attitude towards blessing and curse and the question of trials in general. Moreover, tension between opposing outlooks can sometimes be found in a single verse; as in I Kings 18:37: **Hear me, O Lord, hear me, that this people may know that thou art the Lord God, and that thou hast turned their heart back again.** (Shadal struggled in vain with this verse in the introduction to his commentary on the Book of Isaiah.) We must admit that this is simply a different mode of thought, a non-critical way of thinking which has no self-awareness. For the purposes of our discussion, one particular feature of such thought is of decisive importance: its insensitivity to the notion of contradiction. This insensitivity finds double expression. The mode of thought is poor at discerning contradiction; and when it becomes dimly aware of a contradiction, it does not regard it as problematically as we do. Surely these two basic facts are connected. If one does not sense that the coexistence of A contradicting B poses an insoluble problem, one can hardly do well at identifying such contradictions. Cf. also Albright's remark, cited in H. L. Ginsberg, *The Legend of King Keret*, p. 33, that the Ugaritic poet is not bound by the law that the whole cannot be more than the sum of its parts. Compare Judges 8:30 and 9:5. The appearance of the sister in our narrative should also been seen in this context.

Careful consideration of this feature leads to far-reaching conclusions regarding differentiation of sources or traditions. It is not the very existence of a contradiction or of tension between elements that attests the separate existence of the sources, but rather the question whether it is literarily or theologically reasonable to suppose that such elements would emerge in the same tradition. The lack of consistency in the redaction of the biblical text also pertains here. Cf. the material cited by Seeligmann in "מחקרים בתולדות נוסחה המקרא," note 20, and in his book, *The Septuagint Version of Isaiah*, p. 64.

This characteristic of biblical thought continues into Jewish writings up to Rashi's time; yet, alongside it, sometimes we see talented casuistry, identifying contradictions and resolving them. It is instructive, for example, that Rashi makes no comment on verses 29 and 35 of I Samuel 15, or other places. In those places where he does see fit to comment, he clearly does not find the weight of the problem overbearing. It is interesting that in *Tractatus Theologico-Politicus*, at the end of Chapter 10, Spinoza cites a critical remark of Rashi on I Chronicles 8:1,29, saying: "Nam R. Selomo ob., manifestissimas contradictiones, quas in relatis genealogiis observavit coactus est in haec verba erumpere"; this interpretation, however, apparently does not belong to

with the offer: **Shall I go and call to thee a nurse of the Hebrew women, that she may nurse the child for thee?** (v. 7). This offer appears completely natural, for it stems from the same narrative reality that underlies the conclusion drawn by the Pharaoh's daughter, a reality in which many Hebrew women were left with no son to nurse.[35] Thus the transition from the Pharaoh's daughter to the child's mother is built entirely on the way in which the tradition of national exile and the individual nativity story are interwoven. As such, it attests that one should view the curtailed motif of abandonment as belonging to the Scriptural stage in the development of the tradition.

There is also an element of inherent dissolution of tension in the pronouncement by the Pharaoh's daughter, **This is one of the Hebrews' children.** This dissolution of tension stems from the essential nature of the foundling motif, insofar as this motif serves to point out the elevated origins of the hero while at the same time concealing those origins. In the Babylonian parallel this tension is not dissolved.[36] Nevertheless, this dissolution of tension immediately gives rise to another element of tension, since the Pharaoh's daughter is going against her father's command. In the complete version of the narrative, which included tidings of the birth of a savior who would be the king's nemesis, the knowledge which the princess has, albeit partial, poses an even more serious problem, since the pattern requires that the identity of the child being reared in the house of his would-be murderers not be known to those who found him. Perhaps we may go one step further and suggest that the episode which begins with the words **This is one of the Hebrews' children,** (which already bears a biblical mark insofar as it is based on the idea of murder of the masses and reflects a tendency to curtail the motif of abandonment) emerged in the narrative only after the introduction, which from the outset maintained that the edict was directed against a single individual destined to harm the king, had been lost. In any event this tension, like the tension created by the appearance of Moses' sister, attests how basically foreign the connection with the mother is to the pattern that requires the severance of the child from his mother; for it is clear that when Pharaoh's daughter says **This is one of the Hebrews' children,** her words are intended to explain why the story

---

Rashi, and Spinoza's remark serves as further proof that Rashi was not the author of this commentary. But this is a complex issue, beyond the scope of the present discussion.

[35] Cf. Nachmanides (Ex. 2:6): "For she said it was to save him, or not to see the child die, that they put him there; and why would an Egyptian do so?" This explanation is first found in Philo, *Life of Moses* 1.15. See below.

[36] In the parallel stories there are many solutions to this tension: dressing the hero in expensive clothing, placing valuable objects at his side, a letter, etc.

has her turn to the Hebrew women for a nurse; namely, to restore the mother of Moses to her son.

The two-fold trend of revealing and concealing emerges in the wording of the introduction to the narrative, as well. There Levi and daughter of Levi are disclosed, but the names of the parents, Amram and Yocheved, are kept under cover.[37] This reluctance of the pattern to reveal the names of the parents is most impressive, considering how far the pattern has been influenced by historicization. Apparently this should be attributed not only to the heritage of the pattern, but also to the general biblical tendency to minimize the importance of the hero's lineage in order to stress his singularity, stemming from his individuality. The deity shows his grace to a nobody, a son of the common people, and elevates him over the entire nation.[38] Hence biblical anonymity requires not only that the parents go unnamed, but also that they be unimportant; in contrast, the Sargon nativity legend has only the first of these elements. This dualism in the statement of the introduction also sheds light on a grammatical problem grappled with by many commentators: the presence of the particle את preceding an indefinite object.[39] Ehrlich's commentary on the fountain of water in the wilderness (Gen. 16:7) is apt here: "**The fountain of water** is mentioned using the definite article, yet we do not yet know what fountain it is; similarly, we have **And he lighted upon the place** (Gen. 28:11) as well as **And he sat down by the well** (Ex. 2:15); for this is the practice of Scriptures in referring to things and places that are important due to the events being recounted. For the narrator knows his story, and sees it all before him, from beginning to end; and when he comes to tell of the main event or place, his faculty of imagination has the upper hand and he cannot help but speak of it as if the story had reached its conclusion, as he beholds it before his eyes. Also see my commentary on *Now the asses were lost* (I Sam. 9:3)."[40] The author also withholds the sister's name. But later

---

[37] Cf. Cassuto's commentary on Exodus, p. 8 (p. 17 in the English translation). Nor is the sister's name mentioned.

[38] The ultimate expression of this tendency is the besmirching of the chosen one's origins, as in the Sages' legends about Terah. This motif is especially developed in Christianity, but its development there goes beyond the scope of this work. Nachmanides gives an interesting explanation (2:1): "The text does not mention the name of the man, or the name of his wife, because that would have necessitated specifying their ancestry, mentioning who their fathers and fathers' fathers were, back to Levi; but here the text wished to be brief and get directly to the birth of the savior."

[39] Loewenstamm, "Die Geburtsgeschichte Moses," and Gesenius, p. 364, ¶ 117d.

[40] Cf. Gesenius, p. 407f, par. 126.4(q–t), also cf. Avineri היכל רש״י Vol. 3, p. 87, par. 317, named after its end. Besides the examples cited there, one can add Ibn Ezra's *Short Commentary on Exodus*, p. 193, note 1, as well as the comments of Sh. Abramson in R. Jonah ibn Janah's ספר הרקמה, p. 734. J. Blau's remarks in his

sources, which we shall cite further on, do not maintain this element of anonymity.

The complexity and charm of the Moses nativity story[41] can be explained, to the extent rationally possible, as the product of the primordial richness of the story's sources combined with the Bible's narrative talent. This two-fold setting is also related to the most striking singular feature of the story: the almost complete absence of any direct presence of, or reference to, the deity (except for v. 20), as a result of which the religious message is born by the events themselves and their interrelationships. Looking at the fundamental elements in the narrative, we see that the story essentially preserves the features of its components. The Babylonian nativity legend transpires between the motif of Ishtar's love, which appears at the end, and the motif of the priestess bearing child by the deity, which provides, in our opinion, the setting and foundation for the story. The miraculous course of events attests these two basic elements. No god or goddess enters the wondrous story itself, from the *enītum* bearing child in secret until the appearance of Akki, the drawer of water. Only after the miracle has been completed do we have the line, "Ishtar granted me her love."

The main thrust of the murder motif in parallels from the literature of other peoples is the omnipotence of fate and of the predestined event, discovered by a dreamer or diviner whose very ability to presage the future underscores his powerlessness to change it. Not only man, but also the gods, are subject to this supreme law. The gods certainly are not in command, and the deliverance of the child who is born is certainly not attributed to them.

The story of the midwives (the murder motif) is situated at the beginning of the process of moving away from the original pattern. Two stages in this process can be discerned in the story. The first is a modest shift occurring at the core of the pattern. The deliverance of the newborn sons is explained by the comment that the midwives feared God. But this does not yet indicate clear divine intervention in the story; rather, as parallel texts indicate, this expression, especially when used with respect to non-Jews, signifies a general fear of transgression, shared by all. The expression is especially common in Wisdom literature.[42]

The end of the story removes the pattern even further from its origins. God repays the midwives for their righteousness (verses 20–21). Note the structure of verse 21. The end of the verse, **that he made them**

---

article "החל בהוראת התחיל בדבר והמשיך בו," p. 53, about stretching verbs also pertain to this matter.

[41] See Loewenstamm's remarks, *op. cit.*
[42] Cf. note 32, above.

houses, juxtaposed to **And it came to pass, because the midwives feared God** transforms the general, distant deity of "the fear of God" to an historical, revealed deity. We must, however, be more precise and note that this element is marginal to the pattern. The main thrust of the story of the deliverance of the male sons is only indirectly connected with God.

The description of the enslavement of the children of Israel in Egypt diverges from the usual historiographic setting found in Scriptures. It is not attributed to any sin, nor is it explained as a punishment; and there is certainly no element of repentance. These characteristic features of the Egyptian exile are retained in most biblical references to the exile. Specifically, note Genesis 15:13. The very predestination of the hardships of exile tends to undermine attempts at providing a moralistic explanation of events. Perhaps what we have here is a vestige of a pre-biblical approach in which there is a predestined, fixed chronology.[43] Most likely the explanation given in verse 16, that **the iniquity of the Amorites is not yet full**, which accounts for the event in terms of a moral cause, namely the sin of the Amorites, represents the first step towards imposing the usual biblical pattern. Later, in the chapter on the *Midrash*, we shall describe the subsequent stages of this development.

Whatever the reasons may be for this exceptional treatment of the bondage in Egypt, it is accompanied by severance of the deity from what transpires, with the vantage point of the text being that the deity only becomes the God of the nation from the moment of awakening to the exodus. Indeed, note the particular way the text is phrased: **and the children of Israel sighed by reason of the bondage, and they cried, and their cry came up unto God by reason of the bondage** (Ex. 2:23), careful not to say that the children of Israel cried out to God.[44] Compare Ezekiel 20:5, **and made myself known unto them in the land of Egypt**.

To these singular points we must also add the lack of desire for re-

---

[43] Cf. Kaufmann, *Toledot*, Vol. 1, Bk. 2, pp.449–450.

[44] Barukh ha-Levi Epstein, the gifted commentator and author of תורה תמימה, noted this in his book, תוספת ברכה: "There is no mention in this section that they cried out to God (i.e., prayed), but only that **their cry came up unto God**, and here the verse ends by noting that it was by reason of the bondage. Thus, the text does not necessarily mean that they prayed, but that they cried because their bondage was so hard." Cf. also Loewenstamm, *The Evolution of the Exodus Tradition*, pp. 6–9 in the Hebrew, pp. 23–30 in the English translation. We must add the general observation that prayer is extremely rare in ancient biblical prose. Therefore this should be seen as one of the indicators that the text belongs to an ancient level. Indeed, the places where ancient texts do mention prayer require very close examination; but further discussion of this subject must be left for another occasion.

demption on the part of the Israelites, which is also connected with the tenuousness of the connection between God and events during the exile. They sigh by reason of the bondage, but no request for redemption accompanies this sigh, for such a request would have required addressing God directly. Thus the unique line, found in the traditions that the narrative combined as it evolved, is continued by not having a direct presence of the deity in the nativity legend and by refraining from mentioning God.

The nativity legend, as most scholars agree, was incorporated into the story of the exodus at a fairly late stage, but its integration into the existing story line was quite successful. It now serves as the transition to direct divine intervention. In the story of enslavement God is completely disassociated, in the nativity legend His hand guides the course of events, and at the burning bush He reveals Himself to His chosen prophet and delivers His people.

One crucial reservation must be added to the conclusions of this chapter. The origins of the nativity story are shrouded in the past, and therefore any attempt to reconstruct the course of the story's development from its origins to its present biblical form can be nothing more than conjecture. Yet the speculative nature of such a discussion should not make the conclusions that we shall draw further on any the less reasonable. The origins of the nativity pattern are concealed not only from us; they were also concealed from those who shaped the pattern later in its development. Whether or not our conjecture on the origins of the story is correct, it is almost certain that the creator (or creators) of the story in Matthew was influenced by the story of the birth of Moses but was no longer aware of its origins; this is all the more true of the authors of the Midrash. Thus, even if our explanation of the two-fold structure of the Moses nativity story is not correct, this two-fold structure exists all the same, irrespective of its origins, and as such has had an impact on the molding of later stories in Jewish and Christian literature.

CHAPTER TWO

THE MOSES NATIVITY STORY IN POST-BIBLICAL SOURCES

THE BOOK OF JUBILEES (46–47)

Integrating the life of the individual into the history of the generality is the principal distinctive feature of the biblical tradition in its present form. As we have seen, this fundamental differentiation of sources can be detected even in the current structure of the story, which places the enslavement as the first link in an ascending three-part chain. The double foundation—the enslavement tradition vs. the nativity legend— shows through the triple structure. Moreover, as we tried to show in the previous chapter, the structure of the nativity legend itself, uniting two originally independent patterns, is far from simple. The double foundation of the biblical story (the enslavement and the nativity legend) and the double structure of the nativity legend itself are what shaped the version found in the Book of Jubilees; not, of course, because its author was familiar with the original differentiation of the elements of the biblical story, but because the differentiated biblical elements left their mark even after being woven into the biblical narrative.

A parallel can be found for most of the details in the story in the Book of Jubilees either in the Bible itself or in the Aggadah, except for the surprising statement that Amram remained in Canaan after Joseph's death[1]: *And Amram, your father, was left with them* (46:10). This verse comes before the description of the enslavement (verses 12–15). Amram's return to Egypt—"*your father came from the land of Canaan*" (47:1)—is noted after this description, and thus is interposed between the account of the enslavement and the decree to slaughter the sons, which follows immediately (47:2). This structure severs the enslavement from the murder decree and weakens the connection between them, even though in Jubilees, as well, the king of the enslavement is also the king who issues the decree against the sons. The enslavement and the murder decree appear as two separate elements, not as a series of decrees in which each successive decree stems from the failure of the previous one. As in

---

[1] Quotes from the Book of Jubilees are taken from O. S. Wintermute's translation in *The Old Testament Pseudepigrapha*, ed. James H. Charlesworth.

Scriptures, the decrees are not associated with transgression, and God plays no manifest role in the story.

The nativity story in the Book of Jubilees has none of the duality of pattern which in the Bible led to the problematic structure divorcing the story of the midwives from any connection with the nativity of Moses. Like most of the later sources (listed below, in the section on Josephus), the author gave up the superfluous story of the midwives and thus created a lucid structure in which the failure of the kings' decree leads to the rescue of Moses, the hero of the story from the outset. In describing the king's decree—"*that they should throw all of their male children who were born into the river*" (47:2)—the author does not repeat the king's apprehension of the Israelites' proliferation, an apprehension which, as in the biblical story, he uses to explain the enslavement (46:13). By not explaining the decree to throw the sons into the Nile in terms of fear of the Israelite multitude, and by limiting the time of the decree to "*seven months, until the day when you were born*" (47:3), the decree is automatically seen as directed primarily against the birth of Moses, even though, in contrast to Josephus and the Midrash, the Book of Jubilees does not mention the annunciation of the savior's birth.[2] On the formu-

---

[2] According to the Book of Jubilees, the edict remained in force for seven months. Kasher notes quite rightly (*Torah Shelemah*, Vol. 8, p. 46, n. 202 of his commentary) that there is no need for Ginzberg's correction (Vol. 5, p. 399, n. 56) suggesting that the text should accord with *Sotah* 12b, namely, it should read עד יום השלסה "*until the day you were cast [into the Nile],*" instead of עד יום הולדתך "*until the day you were born.*" As Kasher notes, the tradition that the edict was in effect only until the day of Moses' birth is also found in *Pirke R. Eliezer*, Ch. 48 (cited below, p. 82), where we read that Pharaoh abrogated the degree after the magicians had informed him that "*Lo, he has been born but is hidden from our sight.*" The fact that verse 47:3—"*And they continued throwing [them into the river] seven months, until the day when you were born*"—comes before the child is hidden also weakens Ginzberg's argument. It could well be that the tradition in the Book of Jubilees maintains that the decree was in force from the day Moses was conceived until the day he was born. [In *Sirāj al-'uqūl* (cited in *Torah Shelemah*, Vol. 8, p. 36, n. 155) we read: "*At the very hour that the mother of Moses conceived, Pharaoh dreamed ... and told Egypt's magicians forthwith. The magicians were alarmed and investigated with their astrology. Then they said: this son is already in his mother's womb, ... *" (On the ancient material embedded in this midrash, cf. Lieberman, מדרשי תימן, pp. 18 ff.)] In further support of this possibility, it should be added that, in contrast to Scriptures, the Book of Jubilees first mentions the begetting and only after that the decree which continued until the birth. There is no escaping the far-reaching inference from the structure of the Book of Jubilees and the midrashic parallels that the annunciation of the birth of a savior also underlies the account in the Book of Jubilees. The edict was issued when his mother conceived and abrogated when she gave birth. The tradition that Moses was born in the seventh month is widespread (cf. Ginzberg, Vol. 5, p. 397, n. 44; and below, p. 108; *Torah Shelemah*, Vol. 8, p. 56, n. 13 of the commentary). The predilection of the Book of Jubilees towards the number seven is also striking. Note, for example, the way the chapter begins: "*And on the seventh week of the*

lation of the edict—*"issued an order concerning them that they should throw all of their male children ... into the river"*—compare Ezekiel the Tragedian and Acts of the Apostles 7:19. According to this version it is the Israelites themselves, not the Egyptians, who throw the children into the Nile. (See the section on Ezekiel the Tragedian, below.) Unlike Scriptures, the Book of Jubilees states explicitly that the edict was actually carried out: *And they continued throwing [them into the river] seven months* (47:3). Of course elucidating the birth story comes at the expense of the logic of the narrative as a whole. The reason given for the enslavement, whose contribution to keeping down the Israelites' numbers is hard to understand, is precisely the fear lest the people become numerous. No such difficulty exists in Scriptures, where the first decree against the sons appears immediately after the enslavement, and where the brief (perhaps editorial?) remark, "and the people multiplied, and waxed very mighty" (Ex. 1:20), is incorporated between the first murder decree and the second.

Opposition to abandoning the son is well-developed in the Book of Jubilees. The detail that Moses stayed in the ark seven days is added to the account of the ark being placed on the banks of the Nile: *and she placed you in it seven days. And your mother came in the night and suckled you and [in] the day Miriam, your sister, guarded you from the birds* (47:4). The *Asatir*, as well, recounts that Pharaoh's daughter found Moses on the seventh day. According to the Book of Jubilees, Moses was twenty-one years old when he was brought into the royal court (9). It stands to reason that opposition to child abandonment was a factor in protracting the length of time he spent with his father.[3]

---

seventh year in this forty-seventh jubilee." This approach, however, does not justify Moses having been concealed for three months, since it presents the edict as having been abrogated upon the birth. This difficulty is resolved elegantly in the midrashic accounts that associate abrogation of the edict with Moses being cast into the Nile—which took place after the period of concealment (cf. p. 107, below). Perhaps these midrashic versions should indeed be viewed as a later stage in the evolution of the motif.

[3] We concur with the version accepted by Wintermute, which reads: "*And after you completed three weeks (of years) they brought you into the royal court.*" This reading seems logical since, according to the chronology in Jubilees, Moses was born "*in the fourth week, in the sixth year, in this forty-eighth jubilee*" (47.1), i.e., in the year 2386; he fled to Midian "*on the sixth year of the third week of the forty-ninth jubilee*" (48.1), i.e., in 2428; and he spent "*three weeks of years*" (47.10), i.e., twenty-one years, in Pharaoh's house. Unless we take it that he was brought to Pharaoh's house at the age of twenty-one, we cannot account for the interval of forty-two years from his birth until his departure from Pharaoh's house. Therefore it is our humble opinion that one cannot accept the views of Ginzberg (Vol. 5, p. 406, n. 76) and Kasher (*Torah Shelemah*, Vol. 8, p. 72, n. 81), who hold that Moses was twenty-one years old at the time of his flight to Midian. Perhaps the present

The Book of Jubilees does not mention the marriage of Moses' parents at all, and therefore Miriam's appearance on the scene does not raise any problems. The chronological setting proposed by the Book of Jubilees can also accommodate Aaron without difficulty.

The biblical figure of the mother as wet-nurse is joined in the Book of Jubilees by the father (47:9). This accords with the general trend of later sources to give the father greater weight. Recall that the father also appeared in the beginning of the story, although the Jubilees version preserves the more eminent position of the mother in the story of the ark itself.

Ezekiel the Tragedian

Ezekiel the Tragedian gives an account of the birth of Moses in his drama, Ἐξαγωγή, which has come down to us in fragments cited by Clement of Alexandria[4] and by Eusebius.[5]

Two preliminary remarks are in order before we compare Ezekiel the Tragedian's version of the story to that of Scriptures. Firstly, in evaluating the differences in Ezekiel's version one must take into account the fact that the birth of Moses is described through Moses' own monologue. One must expect the dynamics of a theatrical production to entail certain changes. Thus not every change that we encounter can necessarily be attributed to tensions stemming from the original text or to attempts at interpreting the text. Secondly, Ezekiel's version does not reveal any midrashic influence. The few parallels which do exist to various midrashim may reasonably be attributed to a common response to the text and not to direct literary dependence.

Following the biblical source, Ezekiel refrains from mentioning God. None of the major events mentioned—neither the descent to Egypt, nor the hardships of exile, nor the miraculous deliverance of Moses—are explicitly associated with God. The suffering of the Jews is not a punishment; rather, as in the Bible, it stems solely from the king's villainy.

---

contaminated version of Jubilees was supported by the Aggadah's propensity for a prochronistic representation of the hero's attainment of perfect wisdom. It is well known that theme of the hero miraculously reaching maturity is a favorite motif in legends. Cf. Luke 2:41–52 and Ginzberg, Vol. 5, p. 401, n. 64. (Two errors occur in the references given by Ginzberg. Instead of Luke 3:52, the reference should be Luke 2:52; and instead of Acts of the Apostles 8:20, the reference should be Acts 7:20.)

[4] *Stromateis*, Book I, 23.155f.

[5] *Praeparatio Evangelica*, Book IX, 28:1–3. Our English citations are taken from R. G. Robertson's translation in *The Old Testament Pseudepigrapha*, ed. James H. Charlesworth (pp. 803–819), save for a few instances in which we have diverged from Robertson's rendition in order to bring out a specific point.

Ezekiel's dependence on the description of the enslavement in Exodus is clearly seen in the fact that he, too, confines the length of the enslavement to the reign of a single Pharaoh, and the Pharaoh who enslaves the Israelites is the one who issues the decree against the sons. In Ezekiel, however, the loss of depth is less keenly felt than in Exodus, since his account continues the suffering in a direct line until the Tragedian himself: *"suffering, oppressed, ill-treated even to this very day by ruling powers and by wicked men."* Viewing the exile, in which he himself was suffering, as stemming solely from the king's wickedness appropriately reflected the attitude of Alexandrian Jewry and of Jews in the Diaspora in general.[6]

The lower bounds of the hardships of the exile also run deeper in Ezekiel's version. His description does not include the death of Joseph and the change in the Egyptians' treatment of the Israelites; rather, one has the impression that the Israelites' suffering is from the outset part and parcel of their descent to Egypt.[7] Only excerpts of Ezekiel's account are extant, yet it seems that his account also had an element of tension between the continuation of the enslavement and the disappearance of the murder decree.

The role of the enslavement as a means of annihilating the Israelites is obscured in Ezekiel. The king's fear—*"seeing how our race increased in swarms"*—is indeed described; but there is no explicit mention of the purpose of the enslavement being to reduce their numbers. On the other hand, Ezekiel retains the motif of scheming against the Israelites—*"Pharaoh ... devised against us this grand scheme"*—and, as in the Bible, in his text, too, one senses the difficulty that this motif finds no direct expression in the continuation of the story. The absence of such direct expression is even more keenly felt in Ezekiel's work since he, too, omits the story of the midwives, as do the Book of Jubilees, other Hellenistic sources (Josephus and Philo) and some of the Sages' homiletical commentaries.[8]

It stands to reason that a brief, dramatic production would seek to shorten the introduction and hasten to the main point—the birth of the hero—and therefore would skip the story of the midwives, which, as we recall, is not connected with the birth of Moses and is not crucial to understanding the development of events up to his birth. Perhaps the Hellenistic sources also had difficulty with the story's lack of realism, i.e., with how only two midwives could possibly have assisted all the births of an entire nation; although, thus far, the earliest mention we

---

[6] See the examples in Seeligmann, *The Septuagint*, pp. 111ff.

[7] Compare I Samuel 12:8: **When Jacob was come into Egypt, then your fathers cried unto the Lord.** Also see *Genesis Rabbah* XCVI.1 (p. 1192).

[8] See sections on the same, p. 96 below.

have found of this question dates to Ibn Ezra.

Ezekiel does not mention annunciation of the birth; therefore his version, as well, offers no explanation why the king's edict should have been directed precisely at the sons. As far as we can tell from the way the edict is formulated—ἔπειτα κηρύσσει μὲν Ἑβραίων γένει τἀρσενικὰ ῥίπτειν ποταμὸν ἐς βαθύρροον ("*He ordered next the Hebrew race to cast their infant boys into the river deep*")—the Hebrews were ordered to throw their sons into the river themselves. This tradition is also found in the Book of Jubilees 47:2 (cf. p. 31 above) and Acts of the Apostles 7:19 (cf. p. 60 below); also see our chapter, The Asatir (note 1), and Robertson's translation of Ezekiel.[9] As in the biblical original, here too, Ezekiel proceeds directly from the king's decree—"*to cast their infant boys into the river deep*"—to the birth of Moses, and does not state explicitly whether the king's decree was actually carried out. This detail remains unclear; although, again as in the original, one has the general impression that it was indeed carried out.

Ezekiel's version also makes no mention of the marriage of Moses' parents. Perhaps this is due to the dramatic structure which calls for brevity. Be that as it may, omitting the marriage removes the difficulty of Moses already having an older sister Miriam (and a brother Aaron). In addition, by omitting the marriage, the figure of the father disappears from the story entirely, leaving only the mother and the sister to play a role. This is in sharp contrast to all the other Hellenistic sources and the dominant trend in the legends of the Sages.

The account of concealing the child is reported in Ezekiel's version without any changes; but in the next stage of the story, the description of the mother placing her son by the river, Ezekiel's version has no ark. As Loewenstamm notes, the absence of the ark is the logical conclusion of placing the child on the bank of the Nile. The baby, placed by the side of the river, no longer needs an ark. We must add that although removing the ark obviates the tension inherent in lavishing detail on the construction of an object which basically plays no role in the story, the absence of the ark actually brings to the fore the inappropriateness of Pharaoh's daughter's etymological remark—**Because I drew him out of the water**—to the story. Ezekiel was apparently aware of this tension, for his version introduces the shore in addition to the river: ὄνομα δὲ Μωσῆν ὠνόμαζε, τοῦ χάριν ὑγρᾶς ἀνεῖλε ποταμίας ἀπ' ἠόνος "*And she, the princess, named me Moses, since she took me from the river's soggy shore.*"

An interesting detail is added to the description of the mother's actions: κόσμον ἀμφιθεῖσά μοι "*and adorned me with fair array.*" Dressing

---

[9] J. H. Charlesworth (ed.), *The Old Testament Pseudepigrapha*, p.808, note g.

the abandoned child in a special garb is a common motif in legends of foundlings in the literature of many peoples.[10] Aside from bringing out the mother's concern, this motif also intimates the elevated status of the foundling. We know of no parallels to this motif in other Moses nativity stories.

In Ezekiel's version the theme of the child's abandonment is clearly diminished. Unlike the Bible, where the sister watches from afar (Ex. 2:4), Ezekiel reduces the distance between the infant and his sister and calls her by name: "*and Miriam, my sister, watched close by.*" In his version Pharaoh's daughter herself lifts the infant, whereas in the Bible we read that she **sent her maid to fetch it** (Ex. 2:5). This turns the handmaids who accompany Pharaoh's daughter into a mere ornament devoid of any role. Ezekiel also reduces the length of time the child is away from his mother by adding various expressions of dispatch to the hero's actions. The princess, "*straightaway seeing me, she took me up*"; Miriam went "*running to the princess*," who in turn "*pressed her on*"; and even the mother "*with haste did come herself.*" In the Bible, first Pharaoh's daughter says, **Take this child away, and nurse it for me, and I will give thee thy wages**, and only afterwards is the child handed over: **And the woman took the child, and nursed it**; but in Ezekiel the transferal of the child is hastened and precedes the negotiations: Moses' mother "*with haste did come herself, and took me in her arms. The sovereign's daughter then said, 'Woman, nurse this child and I will render you a wage.'*" As further evidence of reducing the theme of abandonment, we see that Ezekiel hastens to give Moses to his mother but, in contrast, tarries to give him to Pharaoh's daughter. Ezekiel has Moses returned to Pharaoh's daughter later, only after "*seeing that my infancy had passed.*"[11] Moreover, he tells us in detail what Moses' mother did when her son was in her charge: "*she did declare to me pertaining to my father's race and gifts of God.*" This addition also reduces the distance between Moses, growing up in the king's court, and his family and his people.[12]

---

[10] For example, the legend of the birth of Cyrus. See Herodotus, Book I, 111.

[11] Cf. the parallel motif in I Samuel 1:22: **But Hannah went not up; for she said unto her husband: 'I will not go up until the child be weaned, and then I will bring him, ... and there abide for ever.'** Also see The Book of Jubilees, p. 31, above.

[12] A similar motif is found in the Book of Jubilees 47:9, only there the person giving the instruction is Amram. Perhaps in this manner the text seeks to resolve the question of how Moses came to know that the Jews were his brethren. Compare Abarbanel's commentary on Exodus 2:11: "For Moses had always cleaved to Yocheved who had raised him and to her sons, and after growing up he knew the truth of the matter from them, that he was one of the Hebrews' children even though Pharaoh's daughter had brought him up as a son; therefore he used to go out unto

Thus Ezekiel's story is structured in such a way that an entire episode separates the account of the princess taking Moses from the riverside and the account of Moses residing with Pharaoh's daughter: *"Throughout my boyhood years the princess did, for princely rearing and instruction apt, provide all things. ... "* Therefore Ezekiel has the etymological explanation—*"And she, the princess, named me 'Moses,' since she took me from the river's soggy shore"*—precede handing over the child; whereas the Bible has the child named immediately after he is handed over, since the child's time spent with his mother is described in brief and there is no risk of missing the connection between the deed and the name.

Between the time Moses spent with his mother and the time he spent with Pharaoh's daughter, the following remark is interposed: τούτοις μεθ' ἕτερα ἐπιλέγει καὶ περὶ τούτων ὁ 'Εζεκιῆλος ἐν τῇ τραγῳδίᾳ, τὸν Μωυσῆν παρεισάγων λέγοντα *"After other matters, Ezekiel adds further information in his tragedy, introducing Moses, who says."* Whether this remark was made by Eusebius or by Alexander Polyhistor is a question in its own right. Possibly a passage is missing here; but there is no way of knowing what it might have contained.

Also Philo and Josephus mention that Moses was educated as a prince.[13] Ezekiel's remark, ὡς ἀπὸ σπλάγχνων ἐὼν *"as though I had come out of her womb,"* is apparently directed at the tradition appearing in Philo, according to which Pharaoh's daughter pretended that Moses was her son (cf. note 23 in the section on Philo, below). It is a bit far-fetched for Ezekiel to interweave this tradition in his version after having stressed the time Moses spent with his mother. Artapanus (Eusebius, *op. cit.*, IX, 27.3) possibly hints at this tradition by his use of the term ὑποβαλέσθαι. Cf. Liddell and Scott, *Greek-English Lexicon*; also see Herodotus, Book V, 41, where we read of a barren woman who finally conceives but is suspected of putting on pretenses and desiring to adopt a foundling and present him as her son (βουλομένην ὑποβαλέσθαι). Also, see note 62 in Ginzberg,[14] and note p in Robertson's translation.[15]

---

his brethren, the Hebrews."

[13] Cf. Ginzberg, Vol. 5, p. 402, n. 67.

[14] *Op. cit.*, Vol. 5, p. 401. Ginzberg's reference to Hebrews 12:23 should read Hebrews 11:24

[15] Charlesworth, *op. cit.*, p. 809. Ezekiel explains the fact that Moses went out to his brethren as follows: πρὸς ἔργα γὰρ θυμός μ' ἄνωγε καὶ τέχνασμα βασιλέως *"impelled to deeds by my own heart and by the king's device"* or perhaps *"impelled by my heart to acts and deeds befitting a king."* It is hard to say whether τέχνασμα should be understood as part of the subject or as the object. In other words, does Ezekiel attribute Moses' act to a joint initiative of Moses and Pharaoh, or to a decision of Moses alone? Compare this explanation to its formulation in Acts of the Apostles 7:23: ἀνέβη ἐπὶ τὴν καρδίαν αὐτοῦ ἐπισκέψασθαι τοὺς ἀδελφοὺς

BIBLICAL ANTIQUITIES (CHAPTER 9)

Biblical Antiquities[16] is distinguished primarily by the primacy of the more recent component, the legend of the individual, over the more ancient component, the national tradition about the enslavement. A leaning in this direction is also evident in other sources that abbreviate the description of the enslavement (such as Ezekiel the Tragedian) or that transfer the enslavement motif to the end of the story (such as Philo); but in Biblical Antiquities this trend stands out most clearly. Hardly anything remains here of the enslavement motif. It is mentioned out of context in verse 11 (which is lacking in *Sefer Yeraḥmiel* and perhaps is an interpolation) and a brief glimpse of it can be seen in the words the author puts in the mouth of Amram: *"from the time when we became slaves in Egypt, there are 130 years"* (9:3). This statement is itself of interest insofar as it retains the length of the enslavement, in contrast to the episodic nature of the murder decree that prepares the way for the birth of Moses.[17] Also note verse 1: *"And whoever is born from them will be a slave and will serve us"* (cf. p. 92, below). It is interesting to compare Biblical Antiquities with the *Passover Haggadah*, in which it is the individual's story that is completely pushed aside. It may well be that this is related to the strangely perplexing virtual absence of the figure of Moses in the *Passover Haggadah*.

The version in Biblical Antiquities is completely subservient to recounting the birth of Moses. Thus, in addition to the enslavement, also the story of the midwives is pushed aside. We have already noted the surprising fact that in the Exodus version of the narrative the story of the midwives is not connected with the birth of Moses and does not in any way affect his fate. The biblical "let us deal wisely" is rendered in Biblical Antiquities (9:1) as: *Venite consilium habeamus*—"*Come, let us*

αὐτοῦ; and cf. Robertson, note r (Charlesworth, *op. cit.*, p. 810). Nor is it clear what ἔργα means. Robertson takes it to be connected to Moses, i.e., that his heart impelled him to action; but it can also be construed as describing the hard labor of the Israelites (cf. *Tanḥuma Buber* (ויאי), p. 32, note 151; and The Midrash, note 6, below).

[16] English quotes from Biblical Antiquities (*Liber Antiquitatum Biblicarum*), a work ascribed to Philo, are taken from D.J. Harrington's translation in *The Old Testament Pseudepigrapha*, ed. by James H. Charlesworth, pp. 297–377. The Latin edition we have used is that of G. Kisch. The author of Biblical Antiquities draws the material incorporated in his work from midrashic literature. This needs no proof, and will not be mentioned repeatedly. Some of the elements common to *Biblical Antiquities* and midrashic literature will be discussed in the chapters on *Midrash*, where we shall note the motifs that have parallels in Biblical Antiquities.

[17] To understand how the length of the enslavement was set at 130 years, see The Midrash, note 159, below. According to Biblical Antiquities it follows that the length of the enslavement matched the length of the exile.

make a plan."[18] Therefore the story of the midwives, which was needed to support the devious plans alluded to by the words "let us deal wisely," is not missed here.

In Biblical Antiquities, as in Exodus, the murder decree is based on the king's fear of the people who were becoming ever more numerous (9:1). In Biblical Antiquities, as in Philo, only the first part of Exodus 1:10 is present, and the incomprehensible ונלחם בנו ועלה מן הארץ "**and fight against us, and leave the land**" is omitted. Of course omitting the enslavement motif eases the transition from the fear of proliferation to the measures employed against this by the king. Biblical Antiquities explains, although somewhat constrainedly, why the decree was issued only against the male children (9:1). We say constrainedly because the explanation (the desire to take the women and enslave those who would be born of them) is not consonant with the desire to wipe out the people. The secondary nature of this explanation is evident in the fact that it is not given as the explanation of the Pharaoh's decree itself, but as a sort of further clarification.

Unlike the biblical source, Biblical Antiquities mentions God explicitly: "*And the strategy that Amram thought out was pleasing before God*" (9:7). The heroes of the story, Amram and the elders, mention God repeatedly. Nevertheless, the impact of the original is still evident in the fact that the murder decree is not perceived as divine retribution. Amram's remark, "*For God will not abide in his anger*" (9:4), is completely unfounded in the story, and must be viewed as simply conforming to a common manner of speech.

Biblical Antiquities should certainly be viewed as closer in terms of literary genre to the stories in Philo and Josephus than to the rather free stringing together of legends such as one finds in Tractate Sotah; nevertheless, we must admit that the unifying structure that strings together the separate sources is not very tight and that the cohesiveness of the story in Biblical Antiquities does not match that in Philo and Josephus. The independent and distinct origins of the sources in Biblical Antiquities is easily discerned; it seems that the author(s) did not try overly hard to give the work a unified appearance, nor did they care, like Philo or Josephus, whether the flow of the narrative stood to reason.

The loose structure of the story in Biblical Antiquities is particularly evident in the way it handles the two-fold account of taking a wife. To begin with, it should be noted that in terms of the history of the motif the primary reason for its creation was the existence of Miriam watching to see what would befall the child (cf. p. 117 ff.); yet it is precisely this touching scene that is dropped from the account in Biblical

---

[18] Cf. Targum Yerushalmi, Neophyti Targum, and Rashi.

Antiquities. Yet it is clear to the author of Biblical Antiquities that Miriam and Aaron came before Moses: "*And this man had one son and one daughter; their names were Aaron and Miriam*" (9:9). In his version, Miriam prophesies her brother's birth[19] (9:10). But the relationship between the midrashic version, according to which Amram is married (cf. verse 4: "*Now therefore I will not abide by what you decree, but I will go in and take my wife ...*") and the fragments from the biblical version (cf. verse 9: "*And Amram of the tribe of Levi went out and took a wife from his own tribe*") is not at all clear.

Another trend which reaches its fullest development in Biblical Antiquities is the emphasis given the figure of the father. In this respect Biblical Antiquities is even more extreme than Josephus. Amram displaces Yocheved throughout most of the story. Moses' birth is portrayed as the reward for his righteousness (v. 7). The only facets of the story that remain under Yocheved's purview are concealing the child, building the ark, and placing it at the mouth of the river. But these aspects, which comprise the bulk of the biblical story, have been greatly condensed (v. 12). (Moreover, note how Amram is imperceptibly brought into the picture in verse 14: "*And when they had cast him forth.*") Therefore, it should come as little wonder that the figures of Miriam watching from afar and the mother nursing her child have disappeared from the story.

The biblical verse, **and laid it in the flags by the river's brink**, is rendered in Latin as *os fluminis* (v. 12), the meaning of which demands attention.[20] This is certainly not the rendition given in the Septuagint or the Vulgate. Be that as it may, Miriam pronounces prophetically: "*Behold he who will be born from you will be cast forth into the water; for through him the water will be dried up*" (9:10); and verse 14 says of Moses' parents that "*they had cast him forth (proicerent eum).*"[21] The son's abandonment is accompanied by the elders' reproach to Amram: "*Are not these our words that we spoke, 'It is better for us to die without having sons than that the fruit of our womb be cast into the waters'?*" This picture discloses that the fate of the many is secondary and interests

---

[19] Cf. Ginzberg, Vol. 5, p. 396, n. 40; and below, The Midrash, p. 119.

[20] One cannot rule out the possibility that the reference here is to the actual water of the river. Compare *Aeneis* 1.245: *fontem superare Timavi. Unde per ora novem*, as cited in the dictionary of Lewis and Short, 1282(D). Also cf. Tacitus, *Historiae* V.7: *Belus amnis Iudaeo mari inlabitur, circa cuius os lectae arenae admixto nitro in vitrum excocuntur.*

[21] A. Zeron, *The System of Pseudo-Philo* (Hebrew), p. 36, assumes that *os fluminis* is the bank of the Nile, and views the tension between placing vs. casting as proof of the secondary nature of the verse. But one should take into account the fact that this tension already existed in the biblical source and in the evolution of the story over many generations.

neither the biblical story nor the author of this legend. The author of the legend has forgotten that the elders needed no such proof, for the king's decree applied equally to their own sons, who had already been thrown into the Nile.

Philo

In *The Life of Moses* Philo[22] prefaces his account with the statement that what he has to tell about Moses he has learned "*both from the sacred books, the wonderful monuments of his wisdom which he has left behind him, and from some of the elders of the nation; for I always interwove what I was told with what I read*" (1.4). In addition to these two sources, we must add a third—Philo himself. Close analysis of the story reveals the great weight of these three sources in shaping Philo's version, and shows that he often preferred the oral tradition and his own personal inclinations to the original biblical version.

It is hard to know what precisely was included in the account of the elders, from whom Philo learned his story. However, there certainly are many points of contact between Philo and the aggadic and midrashic traditions, as well as Hellenistic sources.[23] Philo generally retains the

---

[22] Quotes from Philo are taken from the Loeb Classical Library edition.

[23] Moses' parents are described as "*the best of their contemporaries*" (1.7) (cf. The Midrash, p. 116, below.) In the Hellenistic sources, this detail may be found in Josephus (2.210). It is worth noting that Philo does not give their names; perhaps this may be construed as reflecting biblical influence (see above, p. 24). Moses is the seventh generation after Abraham (1.7). Note the midrash: כל השביעי חביבין באבות השביעי חביב, אברהם יצחק יעקב לוי קהת עמרם משה ... (*Pesikta de R. Kahana* 23:10, Mandelbaum edition, p. 344. See the textual variants listed there, and also cf. Ginzberg, Vol. 5, p. 395, n. 31). Moses' good looks are important in Philo's account. This probably shows Hellenistic influences at work. Compare the description given in Josephus (*Ant.*, 2.231–232), which also mentions Moses' good looks and size as a reason for the princess's fondness of him. (*ibid.*, 224). Also compare the legend of Cyrus in Herodotus, Book I, 112, which recounts how the shepherd's wife was moved by the beauty and size of the infant Cyrus. Perhaps this reflects the influence of the Septuagint, rendering ἀστεῖον, which apparently also reflects the understanding of the good as the beautiful and certainly refers to the body. See Judges 3:17; Judith 11:23; Susanna 1:7; and compare Hebrews 11:23; Acts of the Apostles 7:20; the Vulgate likewise render this as *elegantem*. The legends of the Midrash also speak of Moses' beauty. See p. 129 below; and also note the remark by Pompeius Trogus: *etiam formae pulchritudo commendabat* in Stern, Vol. 1, p. 335, and *ibid.*, p. 340, note 2:11. The reason Philo gives for ceasing the concealment is that in a monarchy there is commonly always someone who will rush to bring the ruler the latest rumor (1.10). A similar explanation is given in the Book of Jubilees (47:3): "*and they reported concerning her.*" On Pharaoh's daughter's pretenses that Moses is her son, see Ezekiel the Tragedian, p. 36 above. Moses grows up miraculously. On the parallels in the midrashic sources, see p. 129 ff. In the Hellenistic sources this motif also occurs in Josephus (*Ant.*, 2.230–231; see Ginzberg, Vol. 5, p. 401, n. 64). According

original biblical feature of not mentioning the deity as the cause of the people's hardship. He, too, ascribes the exile and its horrors to natural causes. Famine was the cause of the children of Israel's descent to Egypt, and their proliferation and the king's wickedness were the cause of the murder decrees and the enslavement. The fact that the exile is not ascribed to the people's sins is certainly convenient for Philo's apologetics (as it was for Josephus; see p. 53, below). The influence of the biblical source is also apparent in Philo's description of the deliverance. Although, unlike the Bible, Philo does not refrain from ascribing the wonderful confluence of events to God, nevertheless he makes few references to God; when he does mention God he takes care to present what he says as his personal opinion: ἅ μοι δοκεῖ (*in my opinion*) (1.12)—or to include the deity's intervention as a suggested explanation of events (1.17, 19).

Philo not only enlarges on the original biblical text, but also arranges his story according to a structure which does not appear in the Bible and most likely did not appear in his Hellenistic or Jewish sources. Philo inverts the biblical order, transferring the enslavement, which in the Bible appears before the murder decrees, to the end of the narrative, after the nativity story has been completed. Philo's version thus has no causal connection between the enslavement and the nativity story. By detaching the enslavement from the murder decree, Philo avoids the constrained biblical explanation of the enslavement—**lest they multiply**—and only brings in this explanation prior to the king's murder decree. The people are enslaved due to the king's cruelty, which Philo contrasts

---

to Philo, the princess is moved to pity by the baby's cries: "*and seeing him weeping took pity on him*" (1.15). This association also occurs in the Midrash; cf. *Exodus Rabbah* I.24: בא גבריאל והכה למשה כדי שיבכה ותתמלא עליו רחמים כיון שראתה אותו בוכה חמלה עליו. "*Gabriel came and struck Moses so that he would cry and she would be filled with pity for him; when she saw him crying, she had mercy on him*" (*Torah Shelemah*, Vol. 8, p. 65, n. 49; p. 66, n. 54). The portrayal of the princess as barren and longing for a child appears in Artapanus (Eusebius, *Praeparatio Evangelica*, Book IX, 27.3) and Josephus (*Ant.*, 2.232). Using barrenness as an explanation of the desire to adopt a child follows logically from the plot, and can be found as far back as the ancient Indian tale of abandonment, Mahabharata, recounted in detail in Gaster, *Myth*, p. 226; and the story of the abandonment of Hur's son (Redford, *op. cit.*, p. 11). Parallel to this explanation is the motif of the death of the adopting woman's son, as found in the Cyrus nativity story in Herodotus, Book I, 112. Philo's etymology of the name Moses is apparently taken from Hellenistic sources: "*Since he had been taken up from the water, the princess gave him a name derived (ἐτύμως) from this and called him Moses, for (μῶυ) is the Egyptian word for water*" (17). A similar explanation is given by Josephus in *Antiquities* (2.228) and *Contra Apionem* (1.286); cf. Ginzberg, Vol. 5, p. 401, n. 59. (For our purposes, the much discussed question of whether Philo drew on the midrashic parallels directly or whether via intermediate Hellenistic sources is not crucial.)

with the hospitality and protection due the ἱκέτης, the refugee seeking asylum, which the king ought to have granted the Jews (1.35–36) (cf. 3 Maccabees 6:3 ἐν ξένῃ γῇ ξένον ἀδίκως ἀπολλύμενον).

Like Ezekiel the Tragedian, Philo does not mention Joseph's good services to Egypt, even though this would have served his purposes, justifying the demand for equal rights and pointing out the injustice of the king's actions. Also the idea of dealing wisely, whose connection with the enslavement is perplexing, disappears in Philo's version. Another advantage of introducing the enslavement motif later is that the resultant structure reduces the tension stemming from the murder decree having disappeared while the enslavement remained. Presumably this structure was the fruit of Philo's own ideas on the matter, and is the outcome of grappling with the difficulties of the biblical source discussed above. One should note, however, the similarity between Philo's version and *Pirke R. Eliezer* Ch. 48 (see p. 82, below).

Although Philo separates the enslavement from the murder decree, he still has the same king enact the enslavement as the murder decree. Close attention should be paid to the language Philo uses to describe the atrocities of the enslavement: "*This was shown by the way in which they died one after the other, as though they were the victims of a pestilence, to be flung unburied outside the borders by their masters*" (1.39). This description appears to have been influenced by the account of the enslavement in the Bible and its proximity there to the murder decrees. Below (p. 89), we discuss a similar juxtaposition in the Midrash. Perhaps the emphasis which is laid on the hardships of the bondage should be viewed as compensating for its loss of chronological depth. Curtailing the length of the bondage necessarily follows from its having been placed after the birth story.

Thus, in Philo the birth of Moses is recounted only in conjunction with the murder plot, which belongs with it naturally. Moreover, Philo does one better and gives the nativity story a more lucid structure. The circumstances that brought Moses to the king's palace are described in Philo thus: "*As the nation of the newcomers was constantly growing more numerous, the king of the country, fearing that the settlers thus increasing, might shew their superiority by contesting the chief power with the original inhabitants, contrived* (ἐμηχανᾶτο) *a most iniquitous scheme to deprive them of their strength. He gave orders to rear the female infants, since her natural weakness makes a woman inactive in war, but to put the males to death, to prevent their number increasing throughout the cities; for a flourishing male population is a coign of vantage to an aggressor which cannot easily be taken or destroyed*" (1.8–9). Comparing Philo's structure with the original, we see that Philo did away with the structure of the murder decrees in the Bible, and thus a large part of the difficulties that this structure created were dissolved. Philo's version is similar to that of Josephus, but is more far-reaching in several ways: it does not leave the slightest inkling of the double structure of the biblical narrative; it replaces the two distinct murder edicts of the Bible with a single, general order. Thus not only the midwives drop out of the story, but also the order to throw every newborn into the Nile.

The way Philo explains the king's edict merits special attention. As in the Bible (Ex. 1:9–10), Philo explains that the king of Egypt feared lest the people become numerous; but instead of continuing with the enigmatic biblical conclusion of the verse, **and fight against us, and leave the land**, Philo presents his own interpretation: *"fearing that the settlers thus increasing, might shew their superiority by contesting the chief power with the original inhabitants."* Philo does not mention the astrologers' prediction, which we find in Josephus;[24] thus he explains the fact that the king's edict was directed only at the males on the grounds that the women were weak and hence unsuited for war. Postponing the account of the enslavement does away with the tension between enslaving the people yet killing their offspring (cf. p. 10).

The motif of the king's devious scheming should be viewed as inherited from the biblical structure. The idea of dealing wisely, already problematic in the biblical narrative (see above, p. 14), is not associated with the enslavement, which Philo has placed later, nor with the story of the midwives, with which Philo has done away, but rather with the distinction made between the males and females in the murder edict.[25] In contrast to his detailed description of the enslavement, Philo does not describe the actual implementation of the murder decree.

Philo's drastic editing of the narrative indeed removes many of the difficulties inherent in the triple and double structure of the biblical version, but it has its price in terms of literary quality. Not much of the beauty of the original story remains in Philo's version; but esthetics were probably not his primary concern.

---

[24] Although the magicians' forewarning does not appear in Philo in the same magical-legendary form as it assumes in Josephus and aggadic sources, nevertheless at the end of the nativity story Philo describes the king's advisors cautioning him about the young man and mentioning the danger that the latter might seize power, and has them add: *"He is highly ambitious. He is always busy with some further project (προσπεριεργάζεται). He is eager to get the kingship before the time comes"* (1.46). It is hard to say whether the operative factor here was the impact of the legend which Philo was familiar with but did not wish to incorporate in his account due to the legend's unrealistic nature; or whether, as is more likely, it was the force of the pattern that partially restored the motif to its proper place. The idea of a foundling growing up in the king's house and adopted by his only daughter intrinsically leans toward the motif.

[25] Compare Acts of the Apostles 7:19, p. 60 below.

Like the Septuagint and Josephus (*Ant.*, 2.220–221), Philo includes the father as well as the mother in the act of deliverance (cf. also Hebrews 11:23). Philo's story should be viewed as a link in the chain shifting greater weight to the figure of the father (see the discussion of Josephus, p. 48).

Philo retains the biblical formulation of the abandonment being on the river's edge but, as Loewenstamm has noted, does away with the superfluous ark. Another difference from the biblical version is that Philo's version lacks the contrasting parallelism between the edict to cast the sons into the river and the deliverance on the banks of the river; for, as we recall, the king's edict is phrased in a general way. The other biblical elements whose function is to minimize the theme of abandonment— the sister and the mother as wet-nurse—are retained in Philo. The sister's appearance does not pose any problems in Philo's version because he has already mentioned Moses' parents as being married, before the king's edict. In spite of the elements attenuating the abandonment, Philo obviously has difficulty with it. His account of the abandonment is accompanied by a sentimental description of Moses' parents, the purpose of which is to stress their grief and their lack of any other option. Stressing the obvious creates a clear tone of apologetic self-justification (Philo, *Moses*, 1.10–11).[26]

Like Ezekiel the Tragedian, Philo juxtaposes the naming of Moses to his rescue. Also in his version the etymological explanation, *"since he had been taken up from the water"* (1.17), does not suit the story.

Moses' childhood in the king's palace, a subject that is glossed over in the Bible with the aid of the stock phrase **Moses was grown up**, is described by Philo at great length. From the literary structure of his version, it seems that this aspect was of primary importance to him. Philo precedes the account of Moses' deliverance with the remark: *"He was brought up as a prince, a promotion due to the following cause"* (1.8); and he repeats this idea at the end of the story, after the mother hands Moses over to Pharaoh's daughter: *"So now he received as his right the nurture and service due to a prince"* (1.20). Moses' deliverance is not an end in itself, as in the biblical narrative, but is directed at

---

[26] Compare the apologetic tone of line 33: *"And he would have continued to do so [to requite his adopted parents with gratitude] throughout had he not found the king adopting in the country a new and highly impious course of action,"* a line which serves to protect Moses against allegations of ingratitude. Also, consider further on, where a description of Moses retiring to Midian (1.47) replaces the biblical story of Moses fleeing to Midian (but, as far as we can tell, this shows the influence of the Septuagint). The story of the two Hebrews fighting is not mentioned at all. (Josephus, too, does away with this story.) See Rashi's commentary on Ex. 2:14; compare also Targum Onkelos, Gen. 27:43, and note 26 in Chapter 6, below. Wavering over the justness of abandoning Moses will play an important part in medieval commentaries.

the savior being raised and educated in the style of Hellenistic royalty. Indeed, note the anachronism of Moses being trained in Greek wisdom. Compare this to Acts of the Apostles 7:22, "So Moses was trained in all the wisdom of the Egyptians."[27]

Evolution of the version.

Philo's version had a decisive impact on the writings of several of the Church Fathers. The evolution of his version in these writings is of some interest. Philo is the principal source for the account by Clement of Alexandria.[28] As many scholars have noted, Clement's version may be viewed as a precis of Philo's (although other influences have been noted; cf. the index in Ginzberg). But a certain slight change, which happens to be important to our discussion, has not received any attention. Clement indeed describes the king's edict and the child's abandonment according to the Philonic pattern, but he restores the ark to the story. In his version, *"But at last, dreading lest they should be destroyed along with the child, they made a basket of the papyrus that grew there, put the child in it, and laid it on the banks of the marshy river.* (δείσαντες δὲ ὕστερον μὴ συναπόλωνται τῷ παιδί, ἐκ βίβλου τῆς ἐπιχωρίου σκεῦός[29] τι ποιησάμενοι τὸν παῖδα ἐνθέμενοι ἐκτιθέασι παρὰ τὰς ὄχθας τοῦ ποταμοῦ ἑλώδους ὄντος.)" We note Clement's precision in likening the river to a swamp (showing the influence of the Septuagint). Was this in order to do his duty to the river as well as the river bank? In this connection one should note the rather off-hand manner in which the ark's preparation is described in his account. Apparently, from the fact that he has the ark placed on the river bank and not in the river, we may infer that the ark motif was restored under the influence of the biblical story and not after Josephus.

Gregory of Nyssa goes one step further in his *Life of Moses* (pp. 7–8). His version is very close to Clement's and includes the specific detail that Pharaoh's daughter heard a child crying and thus discovered Moses.[30] This detail, which also appears in Clement, is absent from Philo's version.[31] Gregory further embellishes Clement's description of the ark by

---

[27] Cf. Ginzberg, Vol. 5, p. 402, n. 67.

[28] *Stromateis* Bk. I, 23.151–153.

[29] The GCS edition reads οχεῦός, apparently interchanging o for σ. We have followed the reading in the Migne edition (Vol. 8, p. 897).

[30] The child's cries attracting the rescuer (a bird) is a motif found in the description of the birth of Aichmagoras in Pausanias, Περιήγησις Τῆς Ἑλλάδος, Book VIII, 12.2–3, cited in Binder, p. 129.

[31] We must revise our former opinion and point out that Gregory did not necessarily receive this detail directly from Clement; we have subsequently discovered that the motif of a child crying appears in a similar form not only in the Book of Jubilees but also in Origen, *Ex Homilia* II.3–4: *Descendit autem filia Pharaonis, ut lavaretur*

adding details about the ark's construction, and he changes the location of the ark from the river bank to the river itself, where it was situated in the original ark motif: *"Thus, when the threat of the tyrant prevailed, he was not simply thrown into the current of the Nile but was placed in a basket daubed along its joints with slime and pitch, and so was given to the current."* Gregory does not mention the sister watching from afar, probably because of the difficulty in maintaining this motif when the ark was being carried away by the river. Josephus solved this problem by having the sister walk along the river's edge (cf. p. 51.). Perhaps because his account diverges from the biblical story and from the accounts of Philo and Clement, Gregory claims that his version is based on faithfully transmitted first-hand observation of the event. According to his version, Pharaoh's daughter does not need to send anyone to swim into the river (as in *Antiquities*), because the ark is carried downstream and then washed into the reeds. The princess then notices the ark because of the child's crying. Gregory retains the motif of the mother as wet-nurse even though in his version he cannot explain her entry into the story through the sister's offer. In his version Moses is put off by the unfamiliar wet-nurse, *"He was nursed at his mother's breast through the contrivance of one of his close relatives"* (a vestige of the sister). This explanation does not appear in Clement or Philo, but does occur in Josephus and the Midrash.[32]

We can now look back from the place the ark comes to rest in Gregory's version and survey its stops along the way. In the Akkadian story the mother casts the ark into the river herself, after having prepared it for her son with great care. In the Bible the care in constructing the ark is retained, but the mother places the ark in the reeds at the river's edge. In Philo the ark, having become purely ornamental, is removed from the story. The young child is abandoned by both his parents, without an ark, on the edge of the Nile. Clement still has the child abandoned on the river's edge, but restores the ark to the story, although in his version it is made only of reeds. Gregory adds the biblical-Akkadian emphasis on the details of the ark's construction, and the mother and father together place the ark into the river's current, again as in the original pattern.[33]

Flavius Josephus

We begin with a review of certain details in Josephus' version of the

---

in flumine, et audivit plorantem infantem et misit "inquit" et assumpsit eum, etc.

[32] Cf. Rappaport, p. 27, note 118, and p. 114, note 132; and Ginzberg, Vol. 5, p. 399, n. 51.

[33] The ark is restored to the river itself in the Arabic legend, as well. Cf. Grünbaum, *Neue Beiträge*, p. 152ff.

story,³⁴ which have already been studied by various scholars. As in our discussion of the biblical narrative, mention must be made first and foremost of Gressmann's pioneering work. Gressmann confines his comparison to the motif of foreknowledge, which is found in Josephus as well as the Midrash³⁵ and the Jesus nativity story in Matthew, and uses these sources to attempt to reconstruct the original Moses nativity story. (For a review of his analysis, see the beginning of Chapter 1, above.) Perhaps the annunciation of the birth in Josephus, which is put in such words as not to include any direct threat to the king, was influenced by the desire to make the foretelling of the birth of Moses fit in with the details of the biblical story, according to which the king dies of natural causes. (Josephus mentions the death of the Pharaoh in 2.277.) It should be added to the above discussion that although in Josephus the king's murder designs are directed against a specific individual, nevertheless the entire people suffer because the identity of that individual is not known.

In terms of the history of the motif, it is hard to say whether not knowing the identity of the specific individual was a primary motif in the legend of the individual. If so, this is of great significance, since it facilitated combining the legend of the individual with the legend of the nation. The specific individual is unknown, and therefore the generality suffer in order to strike at the individual, as in the New Testament.³⁶ On the other hand, not knowing the child's identity may have been a secondary motif, formed precisely in order to combine the individual's story with that of the masses.

Note with what precision Josephus states the edict to throw newborns into the Nile, explicitly restricting it to Israelite males: " ... *ordered that every male child* born to the Israelites *should be destroyed by being cast into the river*" (206), even though he had already mentioned "*that there would be born to the Israelites ... one ...* " (205). Compare this with the Septuagint's rendition: τεχθῇ τοῖς Ἑβραίοις "*born to the Hebrews*"; or Targum Onkelos and Targum Yerushalmi: ברא דיתליד ליהודאי

---

³⁴ Greek citations from Josephus have been rendered according to the Loeb Classical Library edition, and English citations according to Thackeray's translation there. Sometimes we shall cite references in S. Rappaport, *Agada und Exegese bei Flavius Josephus*, separately or in addition to the usual citations given by Ginzberg and *Torah Shelemah*. For the sources Josephus may have used, aside from Jewish Hellenistic traditions, see also *Antiquities*, 8.159, ἐγὼ δὲ καὶ ἐν τοῖς ἐπιχωρίοις ἡμῶν βιβλίοις εὗρον "*And I myself have discovered in the books of our own country*", and Zunz's note (p. 127, n. b in the German edition; p. 296, n. 5 in the Hebrew edition). We do not concur with Schalit's remarks (in his Hebrew translation of Josephus, Vol. 2, p. 132, n. 227) on the passage from Josephus cited here.

³⁵ Cf. Rappaport, p. 25; *ibid.*, p. 113, n. 126.

³⁶ See the chapter on Matthew; cf. also *The Asatir*, p. 136, on the tension created by knowing the identity of the individual.

"*sons born to the Jews*"; the Neophyti Targum; the Samaritan Targum: לעבראי "*to the Hebrews*"; and Biblical Antiquities, *filium qui natus fuerit Ebreis*. It is hard to say whether these are polemical additions put into the translations in reaction to the Midrashic remark: "*He issued the decree even against his own people*"[37]; or whether, conversely, the Midrash was shaped from the outset by its familiarity with and comparison of two ancient versions of the text. One must consider whether the comment by Josephus, καὶ γονεῖς ὄντες αὐτοὶ πρὸς τὴν ἀπώλειαν ὑπούργουν τῶν γεννωμένων ("*not only were they to be bereft of their children, not only must the parents themselves be accessories to the destruction of their offspring*") (208), alludes to the tradition that the children of Israel were ordered to cast their sons into the river themselves. (See p. 34 above.)

Although Josephus largely retains the original character of the prediction revealed by the astrologers, "*persons with considerable skill in accurately predicting the future*" (205), he does not attribute the deliverance of the infant to the actual force of the edict, as in the mythological source, but rather to "*the will of God*" which "*no man can defeat*" (209). Thus he tones down precisely the element that the Midrash preserves—the automatic nature of the fulfillment of the dream or omen.

Loewenstamm's comparison is based on a different foundation. Unlike Gressmann, contrary to his usual approach Loewenstamm does not believe that the biblical story can be reconstructed from the account given by Josephus. His basic assumptions, as well as his bias, are different. Loewenstamm seeks to show how the various motifs continue to develop even after being set in the biblical story; especially the "unnatural" motifs, i.e., those that do not belong to the original pattern and whose incorporation in the biblical narrative created tension between the basic elements of the story.[38] According to Loewenstamm, these differences in the story as recounted by Josephus indicate that his version is later than the biblical narrative, and that therefore his version may be used only indirectly to help analyze the biblical story. In other words, the presence of a given motif in Josephus cannot in and of itself be used to infer the existence of that element in the pre-biblical version; but sometimes the very way in which the motif is developed provides indirect evidence of a difficulty inherent in the motif's presence in the biblical narrative, and at times one may infer from this that the motif was not original to the biblical story.

A striking difference between the Josephus version and the biblical story, of great significance to the method of analysis proposed here, is the place held in the story by the father. In the Bible the father appears

---

[37] *Sotah* 12a; see below, p. 99 ff., and cf. the parallels cited in *Torah Shelemah*, Vol. 8, p. 46, nn. 202, 203, 205.

[38] Cf. pp. 7–8 above, on the role of the ark and the place of the father.

only in the introductory verse: **And there went a man of the house of Levi, and took to wife a daughter of Levi.** In Josephus the father becomes a major figure, whereas his wife, Yocheved, becomes a marginal character. This change naturally brings with it the end of the father's anonymity. The man of the house of Levi becomes Amram, and in parallel the daughter of Levi becomes Yocheved, and the sister, Miriam. Thus, Josephus completes the process whose beginnings we saw in the relationship of the biblical story to its Babylonian antecedents.[39]

From the endpoint of this process we can look back and summarize its waystations. In the Babylonian story the *enītum* appears by herself, and the father—a god, according to our analysis—does not appear at all (see Chapter 1, pp. 8–10). In the adaptation of the pattern to the Israelite faith the absence of the father plays no role, and the vacuum left by his absence from the story is gradually filled in. In the Bible the figure of the father only enters as far as the introductory verse, but his absence is felt in the remainder of the story. The Septuagint has the father join the mother in enacting the first part of the story: ἰδόντες δὲ αὐτὸ ἀστεῖον, ἐσκέπασαν αὐτὸ μῆνας τρεῖς. Ἐπεὶ δὲ οὐκ ἠδύναντο αὐτὸ ἔτι κρύπτειν, ἔλαβεν αὐτῷ ἡ μήτηρ αὐτοῦ θῖβιν "and having seen that he was fair, **they** hid him three months; and when **they** could no longer hide him, **his mother** took for him an ark ... " Cf. also Hebrews 11:23: **By faith Moses, when he was born, was hid three months of his parents** πατέρων), **because they saw he was a proper child; and they were not afraid of the king's commandment**; and Acts of the Apostles 7:20, which mentions that Moses was **nourished up in his father's house three months**; but the main role in the story—placing the child in the ark—is still reserved for the mother alone. In Philo the father joins the mother as an equal partner. The figure of the father also becomes more dominant in the Midrash. The midrashic shift

---

[39] According to Josephus, Amram was "a *Hebrew of noble birth*" (210). Compare: "*A certain Manoch among the most notable of the Danites and without question the first in his native place*" (*Ant.*, 5.276). There, too, Josephus' version gives the father a greater role. Josephus, the aristocrat, makes it a regular practice to stress the hero's elevated status. Saul's father, Kish, is "*a man of good birth*" (*Ant.*, 6.45). With respect to Saul, Josephus' description goes well with the bias of the biblical text; yet Josephus does not hesitate to controvert the biblical bias when it is different from his own. In the Bible (Judges 6:15) Gideon says, "behold, my family is poor in Manasseh"; but in Josephus (*Ant.*, 5.213) we read that he was "*one of the foremost among the tribe of Manasseh*" (see Thackeray's note on this line). In the Bible (Judges 11:1) Jepthah is the son of a harlot, but in Josephus (*Ant.*, 5.257–260) he is "*a mighty man by reason of the valor of his forefathers*" and his mother "*had been brought to them [the brothers] by their father through his amorous desire.*" What we have pointed out weakens Ginzberg's conjecture (cf. Vol. 6 (Judges), p. 202, n. 106) that Josephus read זרה, foreign, instead of זונה, harlot; and supports his second conjecture, that attributes the change to Josephus' apologetic motives.

of emphasis seems to parallel the stage of the story's development found in Biblical Antiquities, except that the episodic nature of the legends of the Sages, which do not repeat the biblical story from beginning to end, makes this shift in emphasis less pronounced than it is in Josephus, where the father holds full sway.

According to an approach which we advanced elsewhere,[40] we maintain that there is a double parallelism between the Moses nativity story and stories of a barren woman who bears a child. The first parallel is in the present structure of the story, which follows a common underlying pattern according to which the story opens with a motif which runs contrary to the birth—in which respect the motif is equally well served by a murder decree or by barrenness. The second parallel is in the development of the stories from their mythological origins, in which the hero derives his special qualities from his divine progenitorship, to their biblical form, in which the divine father is supplanted by a human father. The birth of Samson (Judges 13) provides a prime example of such a development in stories of barrenness. Although theologically this story is completely severed from its mythological origins, literarily certain elements remain that reflect its original form, attesting that the husband is incidental to the story and is actually unnecessary. The process by which the father works his way into the Moses nativity story, to the point of his complete dominance in Josephus' version, should be compared to the development of the barren woman motif, so that these two parallel developments can shed light on one another. If we compare the Moses and Samson stories, we see that at the biblical stage of the tradition's development the father figure holds a more central place in the Samson story than in the Moses story, where, as we recall, his role is confined to the introduction. But the redoubled importance of Moses did not allow the biblical story to remain frozen in its biblical form; therefore the intrusion of the father into the story continued until its final and most extreme point, as reflected in the version of Josephus. At this final stage the figure of the father fills the entire story, and the mother, deprived of any independent role, is tolerated only as a passive partner of the father.

Above (p. 8) we mentioned Loewenstamm's comment on Abarbanel's unique contribution in the history of biblical exegesis as the first commentator to dwell explicitly on the problem of the father disappearing from the Moses nativity story. It is instructive that Abarbanel also sensed the parallel problem in Judges, as is evident from his question there: "Why did the angel of God appear to the woman and not to Manoah?"

---

[40] J. Cohen, *Masorot*

In contrast to the biblical story, in Josephus (221) the mother does not place the ark on the banks of the Nile; rather, the father, with the mother at his side, launches the ark containing the infant into the Nile, and the river "*received its charge and bore it on.*" The river, which is erased from the biblical story, returns here. (The midrashic parallels will be presented below, p. 122 ff.) This change in Josephus' version of the story requires him to have the sister moving along the riverbank: "... *while Mariam(e), the sister of the child, at her mother's bidding, kept pace with it along the bank to see whither the basket would go*"; whereas in the Bible she remains stationary: **And his sister stood afar off** (Ex. 2:4), since, as we recall, in the biblical narrative the ark does not float down the river. Moreover, Josephus must also have the princess send swimmers to bring her the ark (224).[41] It should be stressed that this difference in the version of Josephus is the opposite of the previous difference. Although the father's place in Josephus is just the opposite of his place in the biblical narrative, the very fact that the father is made the principal hero actually continues a trend already heralded in the Bible. In contrast, giving the river an active role runs contrary to the direction of the biblical story, which does away with the river in order to counter the motif of abandonment. The structure in Josephus attests that restoration of the river to the story was not due to a desire to emphasize the motif of abandonment and severance. Quite the contrary, Josephus maintains the figure of the sister notwithstanding the difficulty which this creates for his version of the story; also, the episode of the wet-nurse is recounted at length.[42] The river's restoration to the story must be attributed to purely literary concerns. The biblical severance between the ark and the river is unnatural; it runs counter to the basic elements of the story. Therefore, as the story developed, this severance was removed. Restoring the river attests the vitality of the pattern, aspiring as it were to return to its natural form.[43]

---

[41] Cf. Loewenstamm, "Die Geburtsgeschichte Moses," p. 199.

In Josephus the Pharaoh's daughter was playing on the banks of the Nile (224), whereas in the bible, her presence is explained by saying: **And the daughter of Pharaoh came down to wash herself at the river** (Exodus 2:5). Compare this to the princess Nausicaa who, playing with her maidens on the riverbank, in the course of her game found Odysseus, who had come up from the sea (*The Odyssey*, 6:100ff.).

[42] Josephus, *Antiquities*, 2.225–227; Rappaport, p. 27, and p. 114, note 132.

[43] We would like to mention two examples, albeit from quite different eras, that run parallel to the change in the role of the river which we have noted in Josephus. The first comes from the realm of art: artists dating as far back as the painter of the frescoes in the synagogue at Dura-Europos (see section on Dura-Europos, below) generally portray the ark in the river itself; and surely we cannot suspect that most of them were familiar with the versions in Josephus or the Midrash. As an

In summary, the return of the river to the Midrash, in Josephus, in paintings, and even in innocent children's songs shows how foreign it is to the original pattern to have the ark motif severed from the river. Indirectly, this development attests the originality of the Babylonian pattern and the dependence of the biblical story on the Babylonian one.

Josephus' version not only differs from the biblical story in terms of many of its details, some of which we have discussed following Gressmann and Loewenstamm and some of which we shall discuss further on, but it also differs essentially in terms of its literary genre. The biblical narrative is clearly legend and, as such, should not be challenged on the grounds of being unrealistic. Josephus, on the other hand, wishes his work to meet the standards of contemporary Hellenistic histories (cf. Schalit's introduction). The difference in genre leads Josephus to enlarge upon the subject. As against the 32-verse treatment of the story in the Bible, Josephus gives an extensive account, spanning several pages and as closely tailored to the taste of his contemporary Hellenistic readers as possible. Many aspects of his version may be attributed to this difference in literary genre.

A) Josephus casts aside the elliptic character of the biblical story.[44] The Bible simply states: **she hid him three months** (Ex. 2:2), without explaining why it was only for this length of time;[45] whereas Josephus

---

interesting anecdote, we note that in a modern painting taken from the *Passover Haggadah*, the artist's solution to the problem of the tension between the ark being swept along by the river while the sister stands on the river's edge was to paint a rope, one end of which was tied to the ark and the other end held in the sister's hand. The second example, from modern times, is supplied by a children's folk song, whose words, "A little ark floats quietly down the Nile," naïvely seek to describe the biblical story. Also see Kasher (*Torah Shelemah*, Vol. 8, p. 60, n. 30) who comments on the Midrash: "*Why did she cast him into the river? So that the astrologers might think that he had already been cast into the water, and would not search for him*" (*Exodus Rabbah* I.21), making the naïve remark: "The *midrash* seeks to answer the question which has perplexed exegetes, namely how Yocheved could have done such a thing as to endanger her child with her own hands by putting him into the river." For him, as well as for some of the exegetes he cites, the river itself has taken the place of the riverbank. In contrast, compare the remark by the author of *Midrash ha-Ḥefez*, ונעלחה פי אל ברדי עלי שאטי אלניל לא פי אלניל מתל קנה וסוף קמלו "*She placed him in the reeds on the bank of the Nile, not in the Nile; as in* 'The reeds and flags shall wither' *(Is. 19:6)*."

[44] See Kaufmann's perceptive remarks on pp. 74–77 of his commentary on the Book of Joshua.

[45] The question why the Bible does not give a reason for Moses no longer being sequestered is one of those questions which we have no right to ask when dealing with the genre of legend. On the actual concealment of the child, see Loewenstamm's simple and persuasive argument ("Die Geburtsgeschichte Moses," p. 208) in which he perceives the concealment as an element which draws out the story. However, Loewenstamm is unnecessarily hard put when it comes to explaining the end of the

cites Amram's fear as the reason the child was not hidden longer—"*and then Amaram, fearing that he would be detected and, incurring the king's wrath, would perish himself along with the young child*"—and is careful to present this reason to Amram's credit by immediately adding: "*and thus bring God's promise to nought*" (219) (cf. Philo, *Moses*, 1.10).

In the Bible the sister's appearance is unexplained; in Josephus she appears "*at her mother's bidding*" (221), perhaps to pay credit to the mother lest she be accused of abandoning her child. In the Bible we read: **And she had compassion on him**; whereas in Josephus we read: "*she, at sight of the little child, was enchanted at its size and beauty*" (224). Compare this to Philo (*Moses*, 1.15). The Midrash, too, makes an effort to account for these elements which are not explained in the Bible. (See the next chapter.)

B) The biblical legend does not mention the deity, and it is only the miraculous confluence of events that attests His hidden hand. Josephus, who gives a running personal commentary, repeatedly states the legend's inexplicit conclusion. The first illustration of this is his comment: "*but no man can defeat the will of God, whatever countless devices he may contrive to that end*" (209). Similar remarks are found in line 222, and especially in line 225: "*for such was the tender care which God showed for Moses, that the very persons who by reason of his birth had decreed the destruction of all children of Hebrew parentage were made to condescend to nourish and tend him.*" Likewise, Josephus does not maintain the severance of the deity from His people; rather, he has Amram actually praying to God (211).

Nevertheless, Josephus is faithful to the biblical account in that he does not view the hardships of the exile as divine retribution for transgression. Amram prays to God: "*beseeching Him to take some pity at length on men who had in no wise transgressed in their worship of Him.*" The absence of any element of transgression in the Bible probably suited the apologetics of Josephus, as it did other Hellenistic sources.

C) Whether deliberately or unconsciously, Josephus' way of presentation, which seeks logical order, leads him to eliminate dualities, contradictions and other difficulties that obscure the narrative. Despite the more extensive nature of the story in Josephus, the marriage of Moses' parents is not mentioned. Josephus chooses to begin his story with the wife being with child (210), apparently in order to overcome the problem

---

concealment after three months. His answer that explaining this would have slowed down the story beyond reasonable limits and in so doing would have given undue weight to a secondary motif is essentially correct, but is not at all to the point. The three months had to come to an end in order to make way for the principal motif, that of the ark. It is the ultimate purpose that determines the cause; the legend, in its teleological approach, sees no need to account for the motif.

of the sister. (The Midrash also grapples with this problem. See p. 117, below, for greater elaboration on its solutions.) Nor does Josephus forget Aaron; but he goes to pains to make him a younger brother, to be born later: "*he shall have a brother*" (216) (but, compare this with line 319, which follows much later).

Josephus senses a problem in reconciling the edict to enslave the people with the desire to reduce their numbers, and therefore he does his utmost to obfuscate the motif. To begin with, Josephus does not mention the children of Israel proliferating and does not attribute the change in the Egyptians' attitude towards the Israelites to the latter's great numbers; rather, he attributes it to the Egyptians' envy of the Israelites' prosperity (201) and to their fear of the Israelites' consequent growth in power: καθ' αὑτῶν αὔξεσθαι τούτους ὑπελάμβανον "*they [the Egyptians] believed that their growth in power was to their own detriment*" (202). As a third factor Josephus mentions the long time that had passed since Joseph's favors to Egypt: "*Those benefits which they had received from Joseph being through lapse of time forgotten*" (202); and a fourth, the change of dynasty: "*and the kingdom having now passed to another dynasty*" (202). (Compare the Septuagint's rendition, ἕτερος, and see note 26 in The Midrash, below.) Only after this lengthy and detailed discussion of the reasons for the enslavement does Josephus mention the Pharaoh's desire to kill off the people, which, because of the nature of Josephus' account, now becomes simply one of many factors. In contrast to the impression of the enslavement given in Exodus, Josephus stresses the length of the enslavement—"*For full four hundred years they endured these hardships*"—and even uses this length of time to facilitate viewing the enslavement as a means of annihilation, which Josephus mentions only after having stated how long the enslavement lasted. The connection between the enslavement and the annihilation is also attenuated by reversing the order in which these motifs appear. In the Bible the enslavement appears after the fear of the Israelites' proliferation and therefore gives the impression of being a direct means to achieving the people's annihilation; whereas in Josephus from the outset the enslavement is attributed to other causes and the desire to annihilate the people only enters as a conclusion drawn from the fact and duration of the enslavement.

The perplexing motif of dealing wisely, which in the Bible is associated with enslaving the people in order to reduce their numbers, in Josephus is associated only with the motif of enslavement. In Josephus, the way in which the Egyptians deal wisely no longer pertains to their plots against the children of Israel, rather it highlights the Egyptians' talent in enslaving the people in a variety of ways: καὶ ταλαιπωρίας αὐτοῖς ποικίλας ἐπενόουν "*and devised [dealt wisely?] for them all manner of hardships*" (202).

The Midrash also grapples with the motif of dealing wisely, but takes the opposite approach to that of Josephus. Instead of removing the motif, the Midrash works it into the story (cf. p. 84). Examples of this approach are *Tanḥuma Buber* (בהעלותך 23) and *Numbers Rabbah* XV.20.[46] Rappaport connects these commentaries to the patriotism of the Jews in Egypt; but such an interpretation has no basis in the Midrash.

Josephus severs the time span of the enslavement from that of the murder decree (204, 205), the latter remaining episodic in nature in contrast to the enslavement, which endured four hundred years. As a result, in Josephus the king who enslaved the people was not the same as the one who issued the decree against the male children.[47] Josephus adds the response of the people (208), so noticeably absent in the Bible, to his account of the murder decree itself; and he paints this response in even darker colors than he used to describe the people's condition after their enslavement (202–204).

Josephus does not mention the names of the midwives, nor does he say how many there were; perhaps because he was perplexed by the question that has plagued later exegetes—how two midwives could oversee the births of a nation of six hundred thousand—although, as far as we can tell, ancient sources do not seem to have been bothered by this question. Josephus believes that the midwives were Egyptian (see above, p. 19; note 32). We cannot concur with Thackeray's unequivocal pronouncement[48] that what Josephus says in this regard is the exact opposite of the plain meaning of the biblical text.

In particular, it should be noted that Josephus does not mention the main point, that the midwives did not do the king's behest. This change in his text is most surprising. Rappaport has a long and obscure note on the subject, which won Schalit's approval.[49] It seems more reasonable to explain the disappearance of the role of the midwives from Josephus'

---

[46] Cited in Rappaport, p. 25, and p. 113, note 125.

[47] The time mentioned here matches what he says in *Ant.*, 1.185. But Josephus, too, inherited the biblical contradiction between the account of the passing generations and the length of time the enslavement endured. (Cf. *Contra Apionem*, 1.299–300. Also see Thackeray's comment there as well as in *Antiquities*, Vol. IV, p. 264; Schalit, *op. cit.*, Vol. 2, p. 52, n. 95; Strack-Billerbeck, Vol. 2, p. 669; and below, The Midrash, note 39.)

[48] *Josephus*, Vol. IV, p. 255, note a.

[49] According to Rappaport (*op. cit.*, p. 25, notes 127, 127a), Josephus hides the fact that the midwives disobeyed the king's edict so that he could make the remark: "*but no man can defeat the will of God, whatever countless devices he may contrive to that end*" (209). Yet it seems to us he could equally well have made this comment even after mentioning the midwives' refusal to comply. Quite the contrary to Rappaport's suggestion, the fact that the midwives—Egyptians according to Josephus—disregarded the king's edict actually fits in well with Josephus' pronouncement. Thus

version in a similar manner to our explanation of the other changes discussed in this section.

Josephus has difficulty with the repetition of the murder decree in the Bible, especially since the first edict, as we recall, was not associated with the birth of the savior. The midwives were not a threat to his survival, nor were their acts of kindness what saved his life. The problem that the midwives play no role in the nativity of Moses is felt all the more keenly in Josephus especially since fear of the birth of Moses, according to him, is the reason for the murder decree. Therefore Josephus omits the story of deliverance which is not connected with the hero of the story.

This conjecture is further supported by one other minor change which can also be explained in a similar way. Josephus reverses the order of the decrees, putting the order to throw the males into the Nile before the instructions to the midwives, and thus essentially turns them into a single decree. Moreover, in his version the king's instructions do not include an explicit order to the midwives to put the children to death; rather, they are instructed *"that the labors of Hebrew women with child should be observed and watch kept for their delivery by the Egyptian midwives"* (206). In this way Josephus obscures even further any independent role the midwives may have played; again, this is possible because the motif has no role of substance in the story. Believing that the midwives were Egyptian, Josephus was facilitated in obscuring the role of the midwives by combining the king's instructions to them with his orders to the Egyptian people in general.

Josephus is not the only one who has difficulty with the dual structure of the biblical narrative. Not only is passing over the midwives not exceptional, it actually is typical of most later sources. We have already noted that the story of the midwives is altogether absent from the Book of Jubilees, Ezekiel the Tragedian, Biblical Antiquities, and Philo. Moreover, we shall see below that it is also absent from Stephen's speech in Acts of the Apostles 7 and from many midrashim, especially those that include annunciation of the birth of a savior (p. 96). The few sources (such as *Tanḥuma Buber* and the *Asatir*, see below) that do maintain the double structure grapple with the difficulties that this structure raises, and even these sources gloss over the specificity of the

---

it is altogether incomprehensible how the desire to make this statement could serve as sufficient foundation for such a marked change in the story. Rappaport offers the following explanation of the fact that Josephus combines the edict to cast the sons into the Nile with the instructions given the midwives: "Through the cooperation of the Egyptian midwives, Pharaoh assured the success of his program of annihilation." We cannot fathom what he meant by this remark, but it seems to indicate that Rappaport sensed that the problem facing Josephus involved the structure of the biblical story.

instruction to the midwives. The parallel structure found in the Samaritan version, *Molad Mosheh*,[50] is instructive. There, too, the narrator inserts the midwives into the edict to throw the children into the Nile: ואמר מלך מצרים למילדות דאתקדם לון המדכר, כל הבן הילד לעברים תשליכון ביאר וכל הבת תחיון. "*And the king of Egypt said to the midwives mentioned previously, 'Every son that shall be born to the Hebrews ye shall throw into the Nile and every daughter ye shall let live.'*" As we see from the continuation of the text there, one cannot assume direct influence here, but more likely a uniform response to a problem posed by the structure.

Josephus explains that Moses was saved firstly because his mother's delivery went unnoticed by the watch, due to her easy labor (218). One must consider whether Josephus perhaps sought to associate Moses' deliverance with both expressions of the annihilation decree—throwing the sons into the Nile and the watch kept by the midwives—since Yocheved's easy labor, which enabled her to escape the vigilance of the watch (218)[51] may actually be an allusion to the midwives, who were ordered to keep watch on the births of the Hebrew women.

Since the structure of the story in Josephus essentially separates the murder decree from the enslavement and ties it only to the prediction of the astrologer, the change made by Josephus creates a lucid structure, logically consistent, and built as follows: the annunciation by the astrologer of the birth of a savior; the king's murder decree (throwing the sons into the Nile and the instruction given the midwives); the impact of the decrees on the people; Moses' deliverance due to his mother's easy labor, his clandestine delivery, his concealment, and the construction of the ark.

The story in Josephus still has an element of tension between the story of the individual and that of the nation. Josephus, in contrast to the Bible, explains the murder decree only as motivated by fear of the individual's birth; yet, again in contrast to the Bible, he describes its effect on the entire nation. Nevertheless, it should be noted that, like the Bible, Josephus refrains from stating explicitly that the edict was carried out, and leaves the reader to learn of the edict's implementation from the reaction of the people.

As we have noted, the biblical story belongs to the genre of legend, whereas Josephus' account is a history. Nevertheless, the changes re-

---

[50] Miller, *The Samaritan Molad Mosheh*, p. 14, lines 3-9.

[51] Compare Rashi's commentary on the homily of Jose b. R. Haninah: שלש גזירות גזר, בתחילה אם בן הוא והמתן אותו ולבסוף כל הבן הילוד היאורה תשליכוהו ולבסוף אף על עמו גזר. " '*He issued three edicts: first*, if it be a son, then ye shall kill him; *then every son that is born ye shall cast into the river; and lastly, he even imposed the same decree upon his own people*' (*Sotah* 12a). With respect to 'ye shall cast,' this refers to his setting up guards and inquisitors to oversee the matter."

viewed above indicate how deeply Josephus was influenced by the Jewish legend. This paradox shows us, firstly, how blurred the critical distinction is in Josephus between legend and history. Josephus' heritage gives him a double burden, stemming on the one hand from his Jewish upbringing, and on the other from his Hellenistic education; for the critical distinction mentioned above was not yet sharply defined in Greco-Roman history writing. Secondly, we see how deep an impact Jewish legend had on Josephus, who like his contemporaries already found it difficult to distinguish clearly between what was written in Scripture and what belonged to the oral tradition that accompanied Scripture through the ages. A detailed discussion of the aggadic sources that can be identified in Josephus may be found in Rappaport, in Schalit's supplementary notes, and of course in Ginzberg's invaluable compendium.

Our objective is limited to examining the development of the nativity prototype, and therefore we shall only note the midrashic additions that pertain directly to our subject. First, a general remark: the expansive nature of the aggadah goes well with Josephus' desire to enlarge upon his subject. Specifically, such extensive treatment goes well with the general tendency to draw out nativity stories. In parallel to the Midrash, Josephus enlarges upon Moses' childhood and, besides describing his birth and recounting the story of the ark, also includes the legend of the crown, which redoubles the motif of the threat to the life of the destined savior (233–237).[52] In his description of Moses' childhood itself, Josephus incorporates the legend of Moses miraculously reaching manhood. This, too, is a typological motif and also appears in the Midrash[53] and in legends about Abraham[54]

A most remarkable passage in Josephus' version is the line in which Thermuthis,[55] Pharaoh's daughter, tells her father about her *"bringing up a boy of divine beauty* (παῖδα μορφῇ τε θεῖον) *and generous spirit, and by what a miracle she had received him of the river's bounty, 'and methought,' she said, 'to make him my child and heir to thy kingdom.'"* (232). What did Josephus have in mind here, in this far-reaching statement? Was he embellishing on his description of Moses' beauty, or are we to take his words at face value? On the description of Moses' beauty, see line 231: *"When he was three years old, God gave wondrous increase to his stature; and none was so indifferent to beauty as not, on seeing Moses, to be amazed at his comeliness. And it often happened that persons meeting him as he was borne along the highway turned,*

---

[52] Cf. Rappaport, p. 27; p. 116, nn. 136, 137; also see The Tale of the Crown, p. 129, below.
[53] Cf. Rappaport, p. 27; p. 115, n. 133
[54] Cf. Ginzberg, Vol. 5, p. 401, n. 64.
[55] On the origins of her name, see Schalit, *op. cit.*, Vol. 2, p. 53, n. 103.

attracted by the child's appearance, and neglected their serious affairs to gaze at leisure upon him. ... Such was the child whom Thermuthis adopted as her son, being blessed with no offspring of her own."[56] What were Josephus' sources for this statement? Jewish sources? myths? or his own invention? This needs to be examined. Whatever the source, perhaps Thermuthis' remarks are a throw-back to the archaic character of the pattern, a pattern originally designed to point out the divine progenitorship of the hero. This throw-back in Josephus must be viewed in parallel to the return of the river to the pattern, and perhaps is a further indication of the vitality of the pattern, always aspiring to return to its original form, no matter what the sources on which Josephus relied.[57]

Stephen's Oration

A brief and consecutive account of the birth of Moses is found in the historic oration of Stephen in Acts of the Apostles 7:17-23. In Stephen's account, as well, the national elements of the story are pushed aside by the legend of the individual. Indeed, the story mentions the proliferation of the people (v. 17), which serves to introduce the edict, but the enslavement, which even in the Exodus version is not related to the birth, is not described. The absence of the enslavement should be compared with the account given in verses 6 and 7, where Stephen does not deviate from the Old Testament source (Gen. 15:13-16) which only describes the enslavement; and with verse 23 and following, where the enslavement provides the setting for all that transpires. Mentioning the enslavement before the nativity story and after it shows clearly that its absence in verses 17-22 must be attributed to the force of the legend of the individual pushing aside the enslavement motif. As in the Old Testament, Stephen does not attribute the hardships of the exile to transgression.[58] Moreover, the redemption is associated solely with the predetermined length of time having elapsed. According to Stephen, as well, the chain of transgression and retribution only begins after the exodus, with the episode of the golden calf. Stephen, too, does away with the double structure of the nativity story, and arranges his account in the simple structure of a

---

[56] On the parallel in Philo and the Midrash, cf. Rappaport, p. 27; *ibid.*, p. 115, notes 133 and 134; especially, cf. the source cited there from *Pirke R. Eliezer* 48, which refers to תארו של משה כמלאך אלהים "*Moses' aspect as an angel of God.*" Cf. also *Torah Shelemah*, p. 57, n. 16; *ibid.*, p. 69, nn. 68-69.

[57] Cf. our remark at the end of the section on Dura-Europos on the suggestion advanced by E. R. Goodenough.

Scaliger proposes an interesting emendation, namely, that one read ὑδογενής (born of the water) instead of ὑλογενής (born of the clay) as the epithet for Moses in the poems of Orpheus, according to Aristobulus as cited in Eusebius, *Praep. Evangel.*, XIII.12.

[58] As in the Septuagint, the new king is a different (ἕτερος) Pharaoh.

single decree and deliverance from that decree. In his version, too, this simplification leads to omission of the midwives.⁵⁹ Stephen retains the motif of dealing wisely—οὗτος κατασοφισάμενος τὸ γένος ἡμῶν ἐκάκωσεν τοὺς πατέρας [ἡμῶν]—but, by omitting the enslavement and the story of the midwives, he relates it to the special way in which he handles the motif of the murder of the male sons. His description of the edict itself is remarkable: οὗτος κατασοφισάμενος τὸ γένος ἡμῶν ἐκάκωσεν τοὺς πατέρας [ἡμῶν] τοῦ ποιεῖν τὰ βρέφη ἔκθετα αὐτῶν εἰς τὸ μὴ ζῳογονεῖσθαι "*He dealt craftily with our race and did evil unto our fathers to expose their infants, that they might not be kept alive.*" Does this reflect the influence of the legends describing the deliverance of the many, inspired by the account of the prophet Ezekiel?⁶⁰ This is apparently the view held by Delitzsch (or Ehrlich, reputedly the ghost writer of the Hebrew translation), who renders the text as: "*to cast out their babes over the field, that they might not live*" (although the rendition in the Septuagint, Ezekiel 16:5, is different). It should be noted that Herodotus uses the Greek verb ἐκτίθημι to describe the abandonment of Cyrus (I.112) on dry land; also, the same root appears in the accounts of Ezekiel the Tragedian and Philo, both of whom omitted the ark motif, as does this version which notes that Moses was abandoned (ἐκτεθέντος) and makes no mention of an ark. On the other hand, this root also appears in the Wisdom of Solomon 18:5, and from the parallel drawn there to the Egyptians perishing in swelling waves it would seem that the word was meant to refer to casting the son into the water. One must also consider the possibility that under the influence of the fate that befell Moses the account of abandonment may indeed have been transferred to the masses; yet the intention remains, as in the Wisdom of Solomon, to casting into the Nile. As far as we can tell from the formulation of the edict, the children of Israel (and not necessarily the mothers) were ordered to carry out the king's edict themselves.⁶¹ The edict appears in proximity to the description of the people's proliferation, and thus we may suppose that, as in the Bible, Stephen assumes a causal connection between the two; but it must be noted that he does not state this explicitly. In Stephen's account there is no annunciation of the hero's birth and the edict is directed at all the newborns, without singling out a specific gender; thus there is no need to explain an edict directed only at the sons. Perhaps this should be viewed as a further evolution of the story's motifs. Af-

---

⁵⁹ Compare the cancellation of the dual structure of rise and fall in his version of the Joseph story (vv. 9–10). Stephen skips over the first stage, the rise and fall of Joseph in Potiphar's house, which is of lesser importance.

⁶⁰ Cf. pp. 110–115, below.

⁶¹ On the vestiges of this tradition in the Book of Jubilees and in Ezekiel the Tragedian, see above, pp. 31, 34, and below, note 1 in the chapter on the *Asatir*.

ter the annunciation of the savior's birth dropped out, doing away with the distinction between male and female infants followed in due course. The later versions that read males—αρρενα (E gig)—apparently can be explained in terms of the influence of the original story in Exodus.[62]

Be that as it may, one should view Stephen's version as the most far-removed from the Babylonian source. He brings the evolutionary process which began in Exodus with the ark being laid "**in the flags by the river's brink**" to its logical conclusion. This takes his version even further than Philo's. Although Philo did away with the ark, he retained the setting of the river's edge. In Stephen's Oration, in contrast, the element of the river drops out along with the ark. Again, similar to the evolution we have observed in Philo, variants of Stephen's Oration[63] restore the river and contain the interesting formulation that Moses was abandoned by (in!) the river (παρα (εις E) τον ποταμον).

Perhaps Stephen's choice of words, ἐκάκωσεν τοὺς πατέρας [ἡμῶν] (19), stems from his desire to associate Pharaoh's deeds with God's prediction in Genesis 15:13, which Stephen cites in verse 6—καὶ δουλώσουσιν αὐτὸ καὶ κακώσουσιν ἔτη τετρακόσια ("**would enslave them and do them evil four hundred years**")—despite the fact, as we have noted above, that the plain sense of these words makes no reference to slaying the sons. See our remarks on p. 67 ff., below on the sources that find a reference to the murder of the sons in the accounts of the enslavement elsewhere than Exodus.

Stephen uses the two verbs ἀνετράφη and ἐκτεθέντος, whose agent is not known, to describe what happens to Moses until the Pharaoh's daughter appears. Therefore we cannot say who played the crucial role in his rescue. In any event, the way he presents the story blurs the special role of the mother. The sister standing guard and the mother being called to be the child's nurse are not mentioned. Slurring over these details puts the status of the mother further into the shadow. The mother's disappearance from the story is not matched by a rise in the father's prominence, although it should be noted that Stephen mentions in passing that Moses grew up in his father's house. On Moses being educated in Egyptian wisdom and on his age when he received the calling to go out unto his brethren, see Ginzberg, Vol. 5, p. 404, n. 69. Apparently Stephen's choice of words in v. 22—δυνατὸς ἐν λόγοις καὶ ἔργοις αὐτοῦ "**and was mighty in words and in deeds**"—alludes to other traditions about Moses, perhaps stories relating to his heroic deeds as a military commander. (Perhaps this passage from Stephen's oration should be

---

[62] Note the profound principle stated by Allgeier: *Eine Übersetzung kann niemals losgelöst vom Originaltext textkritisch beurteilt werden* (*Biblica*, 19, 1938, 4).

[63] Cf. the variants in Nestle-Aland.

added to the list of sources compiled by Ginzberg, *op. cit.*, p. 407, n. 80.)

THE FRESCO AT DURA-EUROPOS

Among the frescoes, dating to the middle of the third century, discovered in the ancient synagogue at Dura-Europos is a portrayal of Moses and the ark (shown on the title page of this book).[64] Various scholars have already noted the relationship between the Dura frescoes and ancient aggadic traditions.[65]

The fresco has no caption describing its content. Therefore, for all that our identification of the details in the picture is quite plausible, such identification remains in the realm of conjecture. Accordingly, we shall make no attempt to conceal any uncertainty regarding our reading of the fresco.

Our discussion is based on the following description of the fresco: at the right Pharaoh, enthroned, orders the midwives to kill all male Jewish babies, and a woman stoops, apparently to put Moses into the ark. In the center of a group of figures at the left, Moses is being taken out of an ark by a naked woman (apparently the daughter of Pharaoh) standing knee-deep in the river. She holds the baby up, while three women (apparently her maidens) stand on the bank behind her. At the far left we see a woman (apparently the sister) handing Moses to the woman next to her (apparently his mother).[66]

Moses alone is the hero of the story. As far as one can tell, the fresco gives no hint of the murder decree applying to the masses, even though the picture includes the episode of the midwives, which in its present biblical form concerns only the masses. As we have seen, the fate of the masses is commonly omitted in ancient versions. This is most likely the reason the theme of enslavement, as well, was not included in the picture. Kraeling[67] indeed suggests that the city gate be seen as an allusion to Pithom and Raamses; but the fact that the picture does not portray any people doing forced labor or make any other allusion to the enslavement does not support his conjecture. We have already noted that in ancient versions of the story the enslavement motif is separated from the nativity story. Recall that we viewed these factors as showing

---

[64] Reasonable quality photographs of these frescoes may be seen in the Encyclopedia Judaica, Vol. 6, as well as in Kraeling, *The Synagogue (The Excavations at Dura-Europos).*

[65] For example, see Lieberman, מדרשי חימן, p. 11 on the remarkable example of the drawing of the snake attacking Hiel, who had hidden in the altar of the priests of Baal in order to kindle a fire there. This fresco is shown in EJ, Vol. 6, p. 289, Fig. 22.

[66] Compare this description to that given in the EJ, p. 295.

[67] *op. cit.*, p. 173.

the pattern's inherent striving to return to its origins. Unlike the case in Philo and Josephus, but similar to the version of Ezekiel the Tragedian, the figure of the father is absent.

Scholars have already noted the great similarity between the figures of the two women standing near the king, in the scene on the right, and the two women on the far left. It is indeed difficult to say definitively whether this similarity was deliberate or was simply the result of a formalized portrayal of female figures. Therefore, we confine ourselves to the more cautious statement that one should consider the possibility advanced by various scholars that the artist was adhering to the midrashic identification: "*Shiphrah is Yocheved and Puah is Miriam.*"[68] In weighing this possibility one must not ignore the fact that this midrashic identification is not found in Hellenistic sources. It seems likely that the woman bending down over the river is Moses' mother, placing down the ark. Since the picture's details are blurred, we cannot say for certain, yet it seems that the figure of the woman kneeling at the river's edge is not the same as that of the midwife to the left of the king or that of the woman receiving the child in the left-most scene of the fresco. (The same conclusion follows from Kraeling's reading of the picture, *op. cit.*) If we are to uphold the suggestion that the midwives standing to the left of the Pharaoh are the same figures as the mother and sister of Moses in the scene on the far left, we must note that perhaps the proximity of these drawings may have led the artist to shy away from the problematic structure according to which the midwife is expected to put her very own son to death. Moreover, painting the figure identically would have led to the most unusual structure, one in which the midwife is the person who places down the ark and is also the wet-nurse—a combination of details which, while it does exist in the legends, is not found in a single continuous form. If there is no real substance to identifying Shiphrah with Yocheved and Puah with Miriam, it is hard to understand why the artist did not portray Moses' mother in the scene on the far left in the same way as the figure placing the ark. Perhaps the artist was not sensitive to these details, or was simply prisoner to certain artistic templates.

The river is the central link of the painting. It extends the length of the painting and unites the two main scenes (the midwives with Pharaoh, and Moses in the ark), which are a reflection of the two literary patterns underlying the nativity story in Exodus. The river flows from right to left, so presumably the ark floated from the first scene to the second. The ark's situation to the left of the figure drawing Moses out of the

---

[68] *Sifre* בהעלותך 78 (*Torah Shelemah*, Vol. 8, p. 37, n. 158).

water is also evidence of this.[69]

Obviously the Dura fresco must be ascribed to the early sources that restored the ark to the river, its original location in the ancient pattern. Moreover, the painting's unusual structure, giving the river a crucial role, brings out this development even more than the parallel literary texts; probably this emphasis on the river motif stems from the artistic media of painting as opposed to literature. We can appreciate the full force of the latent pattern, hidden beneath the surface of the Exodus story and giving the reader the illusion that the ark is floating down the Nile, from the fact that precisely this detail has been overlooked by the scholars who have analyzed this fresco.

Above (p. 13) we discussed the serious difficulties raised by the biblical structure, in which the episode of the midwives serves as the introduction to the Moses nativity story, despite the fact that this episode is actually not related to the birth itself in any way. The Dura fresco is one of the few sources that maintain a connection between the birth of Moses and the instructions given the midwives. The artist chose not to show the deliverance of the masses at the hands of the midwives, but rather juxtaposed the deliverance of Moses to the instruction to the midwives, and even further stressed his point by portraying Moses being placed in the river in the first scene of the fresco. There is a surprising similarity between the structure of the painting and the literary patterns found in Josephus, the *Tanḥuma*, and *Sirāj al-'uqūl*, discussed above (p. 94 ff.). What all these sources have in common is that they chose to skip over the deliverance by the midwives and thus connected the instructions given the midwives with Moses' deliverance by means of the ark.

The naked figure of Pharaoh's daughter drawing Moses out of the river is indeed most remarkable. It is an audacious portrayal, even likely to arouse doubts as to the correctness of identifying the figure as Pharaoh's daughter. Many conjectures have been advanced on this question.[70]

---

[69] Kraeling notes quite justifiably that the picture of the mother kneeling to the right, in the center of the panel, hints that the river flows from left to right, contrary to the dominant direction of the river in the painting. He is inclined to attribute this contradiction to carelessness on the part of the artist or to constraints imposed by spatial considerations (?). Perhaps we have not fully understood his explanation; nevertheless, we would like to advance a closely related conjecture. For the artist to portray the woman facing with the flow of the river, he would have had to paint her with her back to Pharaoh, and this most likely was distasteful to him.

[70] If we accept this identification, then the one who draws Moses out of the water is Pharaoh's daughter herself, contrary to the formulation in the Bible: she sent her maid (אמתה) to fetch it. It has been suggested that this discrepancy be connected with the Aramaic translations of the Bible and the midrashic tradition, according to which אמתה here means her arm. Cf. Targum Onkelos: ואושיטת ית אמתה ונסיבתה "She reached out her arm and took him" (*Torah Shelemah*, Vol. 8, p. 64, n. 43, 44).

Mention must be made of Goodenough's bold suggestion[71] according to which the artist portrayed Moses being drawn out of the water on the basis of elements drawn from myths of the birth of divine infants. The woman drawing Moses out is a goddess, and the women on the shore are nymphs responsible for caring for divine infants. His comparison, especially to the nymphs and the objects they are holding, is impressive[72]; nevertheless, extreme caution must be taken here. It is doubtful whether one may take the liberty of attributing such far-reaching conclusions to a stylistic heritage based on the acceptance of pictorial templates.[73] We prefer the more circumspect statement that the implicit parallelism between the biblical pattern and the myth evoked mythological pictorial parallels in the artist's mind. If this conjecture has substance, then we may say that we have a further example of the recurrent desire of the pattern to return to its roots; for, as we have shown above, in its original form the literary pattern pointed to the divine origins of the hero (cf. Chapter 1, p. 8, and the end of the section on Josephus).

Gutmann in his article in *Eretz-Israel* sees the influence of Ezekiel the Tragedian here (see p. 35 above); but, as we recall, it is precisely in Ezekiel's version that the ark is altogether absent. The sister is portrayed as facing Pharaoh's daughter while handing the infant to his mother, who is situated on her other side. Kraeling's explanation (*op. cit.*), that this confusion stems from the condensation of the picture—i.e., from the fact that the artist had to include many scenes in a single panel—seems reasonable. Condensation also provides a good explanation of why the artist did not portray Pharaoh's daughter on the shore, beside Moses' sister.

[71] *Jewish Symbols in the Greco-Roman Period*, Vol. 9, pp. 197-226.

[72] Cf. *ibid.*, especially p. 204.

[73] For an apt criticism of Goodenough's approach see Bickerman, "Symbolism in the Dura Synagogue," *Harvard Theological Review* LVIII, 1965, or *Studies in Jewish and Christian History*, Vol. 3, pp. 225-244.

CHAPTER THREE

THE MIDRASH

In this chapter we have no intention of providing a comprehensive description of all the themes developed in the *Midrash* or of describing all the trends of thought expressed in this body of literature; rather, we seek to describe the development of the literary model and to investigate its origins. Therefore we shall only take up elements that have already been described in our discussion of the biblical story. The main thrust is to show that interweaving the legend of the birth of Moses with the biblical account of the exile was indeed an important stage in the evolution of the model, but did not seal its further development.[1] The abundance of motifs in the *Midrash* reflects the complexity of the biblical story.

DIFFERENTIATION OF THE STORY

The differentiation and independence of the story of the birth of Moses finds expression, among other things, in the fact that the biblical sources do not know this story (see above, p. 6). Due to its episodic nature, tending to elaborate isolated points and not present a continuous narrative, the *Midrash* does not bring out the differentiation of the story in a prominent way. Nevertheless, the differentiation of this narrative unit can still be sensed in the *midrashim* that seek to interpret references to

---

[1] Cf. the Introduction. The *Midrash* comprises the lion's share of post-biblical Moses nativity stories, as is evident from the length of this chapter. The *Midrash* also presents the greatest methodological difficulties. Clearly it is somewhat artificial to gather together all midrashic works into a single chapter, because the *midrashim* were assembled from many and varied sources, both in terms of their nature and their dates. Our ability to date each and every *midrash* is quite dubious. Moreover, often we cannot even determine the relationship of the various versions of the same legend one to another, and any such determinations are so speculative as to pose a threat to philological exactitude. Not wishing to have the conclusions of this chapter rest on such shaky ground, we have generally foregone any attempt to describe the development of the motifs in the *midrash*, aside from those instances in which parallels with external sources (such as Josephus, the Septuagint, etc.,) provide more solid grounds for dating. For a book dealing with the development of motifs, having to forego tracing this evolution in the very richest source is a considerable drawback. Our decision to forego such an analysis is also related to our preference for citing the most clear, and not necessarily the most ancient, version of any given *midrash*; of course citing all the known versions would not have been feasible.

the exile that appear elsewhere in the Bible than Exodus 1 and 2 in such a way as to infer from them descriptions of the verdict passed against the sons.

Thus, *Sifre* (כי תבא, par. 301) comments on the verse: **and the Lord ... saw our affliction, and our toil** (Deut. 26:7), which in its most straightforward sense describes the period of slavery (cf. Exodus 1:11–14, where we see that "our affliction" refers to the Israelite's bondage) as follows: וירא את עניינו, כמה שנאמר וראיתן על האבנים. ואת עמלינו, כמה שנאמר כל הבן הילוד היאורה תשליכוהו וכו׳. "*and (the Lord) saw our affliction, as it is said, 'ye shall look upon the birthstool: [if it be a son, then ye shall kill him ...],' and our toil, as it is said, 'Every son that is born ye shall cast into the river.'*"

Midrash ha-Gadol on Deut. 23:8 (according to the version cited by Hoffman in *Midrash Tannaim*) comments on the verse: **thou shalt not abhor an Egyptian, because thou wast a stranger in his land**: אמר ר׳ יהושע בן קרחה גדולה היא הטובה שאדם עושה עם חבירו, בדין היה שלא יבא מצרי בישראל לעולם, אמרת מפני מה נתרחקו עמון ומואב, אלא על ידי שלא קדמו בלחם ובמים, והרי הדברים קל וחומר, מה אם מי שנאמר בהן על דבר אשר לא קדמו אתכם בלחם ובמים (דב׳ כג, ה) אמרה תורה לא יבאו בכם לעולם, מי שנאמר בהן כל הבן הילוד היאר׳ה תשליכהו בדין הוא שלא יבאו בישראל לעולם, מה ת״ל לא תתעב מצרי להודיע מה גרם. "*R. Joshua ben Korḥa said: The kindness which man shows his fellow is of great importance. It should have been the law that an Egyptian never enter the assembly of Israel; for why were Amon and Moab to be kept away, if not because they did not meet [the children of Israel] with bread and water? If for not meeting with bread and water (Deut. 23:5) the Torah enjoins that they not come into their midst forever, then all the more so one would expect the law to have stipulated regarding those who said, 'every son ye shall cast into the river,' that they not come into the assembly of Israel forever! Thus, what does the Torah seek to teach us by saying* **thou shalt not abhor an Egyptian [because thou wast a stranger in his land]**? *It is to inform us of the reason [for this injunction, i.e., that we are not to abhor an Egyptian because of the kindness they showed us when we were strangers in their land].*" For R. Yehoshua the notion of being a stranger, expressed in the text, "**thou wast a stranger in his land**," clearly subsumes not only the Israelites' enslavement, but also the murder of their sons; therefore he has difficulty coming to terms with the text.[2] In Nachmanides' commen-

---

[2] Cf. Kasher's comment in *Torah Shelemah*, Vol. 8, p. 243, supplement to n. 209, in which he too has difficulty with the Toraic injunction, "**Thou shall not abhor an Egyptian, because thou wast a stranger in his land**," and resolves the problem in his own way.

The *midrash* cited finds something to Pharaoh's credit in comparing his sin with the deeds of other enemies of Israel. In this it reminds us of the well-known and

tary on Genesis 15:14 we see that the silence of the biblical text on the murder of the sons did not escape his critical eye: "*And it is clear that casting their sons into the Nile is not subsumed by* 'and shall serve them; and they shall afflict them.'" Josephus provides an interesting formulation of the verse—κακοπαθήσαντας (to be in plight, distress) (*Antiquities*, 1.185)—which could also subsume the murder decree.[3]

Nevertheless, we cannot say that the silence of the biblical sources has had no effect on the *midrashim*; however, it is evident in the *midrashim* only to a limited extent. The details of the story that deal with the individual himself, from "**And there went a man of the house of Levi**" (Ex. 2:1) until "**and he became her son**" (Ex. 2:10), are not dwelled upon by the *Midrash*; even when we might expect a reference to this passage (Ex. 2:1–10), we do not find one. For example, it is surprising that the *Midrash* does not lend expression to Moses having had a prior acquaintance with Pharaoh (aside from Moses' association with Pharaoh's daughter, cf. pp. 126–127, below) and only bothers in a few places to connect later events in the narrative with the beginning of the story. In contrast, *Tībat Marqe* (14.1, p. 59)—a Samaritan *Midrash*—is one of the few sources where Moses explains his reason for refusing to go

---

enigmatic *midrash* found in the *Passover Haggadah*: צא ולמד מה בקש לבן הארמי לעשות ליעקב אבינו. שפרעה לא גזר אלא על הזכרים ולבן בקש לעקור את הכל. "Go and learn what Laban the Aramean sought to do to our father Jacob. For Pharaoh ordered that only the male children be put to death, but Laban planned to uproot all, ..." Kasher, (*op. cit.*) goes to great effort to show by casuistry that Laban's great sin was that he wished to divert Jacob from following in the ways of his fathers; whereas to Pharaoh's credit it may be said that he did not force our ancestors to be idolaters and therefore, in the opinion of the homilist, Pharaoh's wickedness was not as great as Laban's. It is interesting to compare this argument with Seeligmann's suggestion, following Finkelstein (*The Septuagint*, p. 85), that the *midrash* from the Haggadah identifies Laban the Aramean with Antiochus IV who issued repressive decrees against the Jews. However, even his suggestion is no more than a far-fetched conjecture.

[3] The hymn *Ma'oz Ẓur* (Rock of Ages) has a remarkable passage—רעות שבעה נפשי, ביגון כחי כלה, חיי מררו בקשי, בשעבוד מלכות עגלה. "Full sated was my soul with ills, my strength was spent with sorrow; they embittered my life by hardship during my subjection to the dominion of Egypt"—which only mentions the enslavement and reminds us, once more, of the dangers of *argumentum e silentio*. However, recall that our argument on the independence of the nativity story and its late incorporation into accounts of the enslavement has much other evidence to support it. Also cf. the alternate versions in Targum Yerushalmi (Genesis 40:12,18): תלתא סליא תלתי שעבודיא ... בטינא ובליבנא ובכל פולחנא באנפי ברא. "Three baskets [as against] three enslavements ... in mortar, and in brick, and in all manner of service in the field"; whereas a parallel text goes further, adding: ורמי בניהון לנהרא "and he will cast their sons into the river" (Cf. *Additions and Variants of Targum Yerushalmi on the Pentateuch*, Ginzburger ed.; also cf. Neophyti Targum (Genesis 40:12,18) and *Torah Shelemah*, Vol. 6, pp. 1515,1521).

to Pharaoh: ועם פרעה מלכה לית בי מימר כי מסגי נפקת ... ולא לי רגילו בהדה שלטנותה "I am ממצרים אל מדין ומה דהוה בידי מן רזיון נשית בבית פרעה רבית והגמלת ונפקת רבי. not accustomed to the ways of this government, ... and am not able to speak with Pharaoh, the king. For I left Egypt for Midian a long time ago, and whatever I knew of their secrets I have since forgotten. In Pharaoh's house I grew up, was weaned, and left as a young man."

In contrast, the *midrashim* dwell on the murder decrees that involved the masses, and especially stress the principle of measure for measure in the death of the Egyptian firstborn sons on the night of the exodus and in the drowning of the Egyptians in the Red Sea. This principle is already evident in the Book of Jubilees 48:14: "*And all of the people whom he brought out to pursue after Israel the Lord our God threw into the middle of the sea into the depths of the abyss beneath the children of Israel. Just as the men of Egypt cast their sons into the river he avenged one million. And one thousand strong and ardent men perished on account of one infant whom they threw into the midst of the river from the sons of your people.*"

The Wisdom of Solomon 18:5, in its unique approach, embellishes on the principle of measure for measure by adding the principle that the righteous is saved by that which causes the downfall of the wicked.[4] A notable example from the *Midrash* is provided by *Tanḥuma Buber* (בא 5):

כל מה שחשבו המצרים על ישראל הביא [הקב״ה] עליהם מה שחשבו להם וכו׳, הם חשבו לשקע אותם במים, אף הקב״ה שקען במים, שנאמר (תה׳ קלו, טו) ונער פרעה וחילו בים סוף וגו׳.

"*Whatever the Egyptian's thought to do to Israel, [the Holy One, blessed be He,] brought on them; they [the Egyptians] thought to drown them in water, so the Holy One, blessed be He, drowned them in water, as it is said:* **But overthrew Pharaoh and his host in the Red Sea** (Ps. 136:15), etc.*"*[5]

Exceptions to the rule that details of the nativity story are not men-

---

[4] In the Wisdom of Solomon the drowning of the Egyptians is the seventh plague. Cf. Loewenstamm, *Evolution*, p. 45 in the Hebrew, pp. 106–107 in the English translation.

[5] Also cf. Targum Onkelos and Targum Yerushalmi on Exodus 18:11: for in the thing wherein they dealt proudly he was above them (כי בדבר אשר זדו עליהם); and Rashi's and Nachmanides' commentaries on this verse (*Torah Shelemah*, Vol. 15, p. 21, n. 78). Also cf. Ginzberg, Vol. 5, p. 427, n. 172; and *Torah Shelemah*, Vol. 8, p. 47, n. 206. To these sources one can add the legend that returns to the single hero and remarks that the water of the Nile was not struck by Moses because the Nile had protected him, as in *Mishnat Rabbi Eliezer* 19: ... אמר הק״בה למשה המים ששמרוך בשעה שהושלכת לים (!) ... איני דן, שילקו על ידך. "The Holy One, blessed be He, said to Moses: ... The water that protected you when you were thrown into the sea [!] ... I shall not pass judgment that they be struck by you" (*Torah Shelemah*, Vol. 9, p. 44, n. 80). We conjectured above that the development of the murder motif around throwing the sons into the Nile actually stemmed from the ark pattern. Here the *Midrash* has further refined the structure by adding a third level—in addition to

tioned elsewhere than in the nativity narrative itself are provided by the legends dealing with the "join" between the legend of the individual and the national tradition: "**And it came to pass in those days, when Moses was grown, that he went out unto his brethren, ...** " (Ex. 2:11 ff.). Yet even there the references to details of the nativity are rather restrained: ‏ויהי מניח דריגון (דרגון) שלו והולך ומיישב להן סבלותם.‏ "*So he left his retinue*[6] *and rearranged their burdens.*"[7]

Reasons for the Exile and the Decrees

Above (p. 26) we mentioned Loewenstamm's perceptive analysis of the unusual place held by the Egyptian exile in biblical historiography, in that this exile is not viewed through the rigid biblical scheme of sin and retribution. Even in the Bible itself one can detect a bias towards fitting the exile into such a scheme.[8] The most far-reaching example of this bias is found in Ezekiel 20:5–9, which incorporates the element of sin in its account of the exile—"**But they rebelled against me, and would not hearken unto me: they did not every man cast away the abominations of their eyes, neither did they forsake the**

---

throwing the sons into the water and having the deliverance be by means of the water, there is also a reward given to the water. Cf. Rashi, who discusses the ambiguity of the biblical text (Ex. 7:20) as to who struck the water. In the wake of the *Midrash*, he finds for Aaron even though it would actually have been more appropriate for it to have been Moses. (Deciding in favor of Aaron apparently dates back to the Septuagint, version A, which reads "with his staff" in verse 20.)

[6] Shinan (*Exodus Rabbah*, p. 85), following Krauss (*Griechische und lateinische Lehnwörter*, p. 194), interprets ‏דריגון‎ as coming from the Greek δροῦγγος and meaning a military unit of about 1,000 to 3,000 men. A similar explanation of the word is given by Kasher. But perhaps ‏דרגון‎ should be emended to ‏ארגון‎, following the Oxford Manuscript of the *Tanḥuma* (cf. *Tanḥuma Buber* (‏ואר"א‎), p. 32, n. 151). After explaining Ex. 2:11, the *midrash* continues to recount that Moses addressed Pharaoh: ‏מבקש אני ממך להעשות על ארגון שלך.‎ Lieberman (*Greek in Jewish Palestine*, p. 8) interprets this to mean that Moses requested to be appointed ἐπὶ τῶν ἔργων σου, in other words, that Moses wanted to be made ἐπιστάτης τῶν δημοσίων ἔργων (the superintendent of the public works). Indeed, this is how the Septuagint renders Ex. 1:11, and this formulation recurs in Philo, *Moses* 1.37.

[7] *Exodus Rabbah* I.27; *Torah Shelemah*, Vol. 8, p. 75, n. 89. Also see the continuation of these passages, *Exodus Rabbah* I.28 and *Torah Shelemah*, Vol. 8, p. 75, n. 93 (cited on p. 91, below).

[8] In addition to the most ancient illustration of this tendency, concerning the sin of the Amorites (cf. p. 26), see the examples cited by Loewenstamm, *Evolution*, pp. 7–8 in the Hebrew, pp. 24–28 in the English translation.

The biblical bias towards giving the tradition a theological interpretation is well-established. For example, note that the reason given in the Book of Joshua for ceasing the conquest of the land is neither retribution for the people's sins, nor as a trial, but rather the natural reason of Joshua's old age; whereas the Book of Judges, chapters 2 and 3, attributes cessation of the conquest to a trial and to the people's sins.

idols of Egypt" (Ez. 20:8)—but does not view the exile as stemming from this sin. Moreover, contrary to his attitude towards the punishment decreed on the generation of the desert (Ez. 20:14-17), Ezekiel does not present the enslavement as an alternative punishment meted out to the Israelites in Egypt, in place of the punishment of total annihilation which, according to his approach, God should have decreed on the Israelites in Egypt. It is also noteworthy that Joshua 24:14 reads: "**and put away the gods which your fathers served on the other side of the flood, and in Egypt,**" but does not connect this to the reason for the exile.[9] The full force of the pattern can be appreciated if we consider I Maccabees 1:11, which innocently attributes the following verse to the Hellenizers(!): "*because disaster upon disaster has overtaken us since we segregated ourselves from them [the Gentiles]*."[10] Little wonder, therefore, that the *Midrash* imposes this pattern even when it is altogether absent from the biblical story itself. For example, we read in *Midrash Abba Gorion*:[11] מדארגיזי בנייא חבייא קדם אבוהון דבשמייא העמיד עליהם מלך חנף ופרע מהן. ואיזה זה מלך אחשורוש. "*When his favorite sons angered their Father in Heaven, He placed a hypocritical king over them and he punished them; and what king was this? Ahasuerus.*" This bias is even more strongly felt in legends about the exodus from Egypt.

A measure of circumspection in associating the hardships of the exile with events of the past may be found in *Sotah* 46b: אמר רבי יהושע בן לוי בשביל ארבעה פסיעות שלוה פרעה לאברהם, שנאמר (בר' יב, כ) ויצו עליו פרעה אנשים וג' נשתעבד בבניו ארבע מאות שנה, שנאמר (בר' טו,יג) ועבדום וענו אותם ארבע מאות שנה. "*R. Joshua b. Levi also said: Because of four paces with which Pharaoh accompanied Abraham, as it is said,* **And Pharaoh gave men charge concerning him** *(Gen. 12:20), he enslaved the latter's descendants for four hundred years, as it is said,* **And shall serve them, and they shall afflict them four hundred years** *(Gen. 15:13).*" The legend indeed associates the hardship with what happened to our forefathers, but does not say that it was due to sin.[12]

Some legends blame the exile on sins of the patriarchs: ואלה שמות בני ישראל, הלכה, הגוזל והאכיל את בניו מה שיהא חיב לשלם, שנו רבותינו הגוזל ומאכיל את בניו מניח לפניהם פטורין מלשלם, ואם היה דבר שיש לו אחריות בניו חייבין לשלם. בוא וראה בשעה שאמר האלהים לאברהם שהוא מוריש לבניו את הארץ, התחיל אברהם מוציא דבר לפני הא' ואומר במה אידע (ברא' מו, ח) אמר לו הא' את הוא [שאני] מתהלל בך ואמרתה לי במה אדע, חייך שאני מודיעך ידע תידע, ושלמה צוח בכל עצב יהיה מותר (משלי יד, כג) כל דבר שאדן

---

[9] The relationship between the passage in Joshua and that in Ezekiel merits further study.

[10] Cf. Kahana's note, הספרים החיצוניים. Our rendition of ἐχωρίσθημεν is after Geiger, *Urschrift und Übersetzungen der Bibel*², p. 71.

[11] *Bet ha-Midrash*, Vol. 1, p. 1.

[12] On the enslavement lasting four hundred years, see below, p. 78 ff.

[שאדם] מיצטער בו הוא מתויר בו, אברהם שניצטער כל אותו הצער השליך עצמו לאש, עקד את בנו על גבי המזבח, השלים עצמו ומל, לפיכך יהיה מותר, הרי בניו חיים בזכות אותו הצער שניצטער, ומהוא ודבר שפתים אך למחסור (שם), ניתחסר הימנו שאמר לו הא' ידע תידע וג', וכיון שניגזרה הגזירה היה יצחק סבור שמיהימנו הגזירה מתחלת, מת יצחק ולא התחילה הגזירה הימנו, כיון שעמד יעקב והוליד שנים עשר שבטים התחיל מתירא מן השטר, למה, יעקב היה לו אחריות, והתחיל משמר את עצמו שלא יתקיים בו השטר, ותידע לך שכן אלא כיון שבא הרעב לכל העולם היו יושבי הארץ כנען יורדין להם לארץ מצרים שנ' וכל הארץ באו מצרימה, ויעקב היה מתירא מן השטר ולא ירד, למה הדבר דומה, לפרה שהיו מבקשין ליתן עליה עול שתחרוש בשדה ולא היתה רוצה לצאת, מה עשו לה, משכו את בנה לשדה והיה גועה ואמו שמעת ויוצאה לה מעצמה, כך היה יעקב מתירא מן הגזירה שניגזר על זקינו, מה עשה הא', משך את יוסף למצרים כדי שישמע יעקב שהוא שן [שם] וירד. "**Now these are the names of the children of Israel**. There is a rule of Halakhah concerning a man who steals and feeds his children; what restitution must he make? Our Rabbis taught: If a man steals and feeds his sons, and places [what he has stolen] before them [and then dies], they are exempt from paying; but if it was something for which one bears legal responsibility, his sons are obliged to pay. For example, when God said to Abraham that He would give the land as an inheritance to his sons, Abraham began to challenge God, asking, '**whereby shall I know ... ?**' (Gen. 15:8). God answered him: 'You are the one through whom I am praised, and you dare say to me whereby shall I know? By your life, I will let you know, **know of a surety** (Gen. 15:13).' Also Solomon cried out, '**in all sorrow there is profit**' (Prov. 14:23). Anything that a man regrets, he may profit by; Abraham, who experienced all the sorrow of throwing himself into the fire, binding his son on the altar, perfected and circumcised himself, therefore will have profit, for his sons live by virtue of the very sorrow which he experienced. And what is the meaning of '**but the talk of the lips tendeth only to penury** (מחסור; Prov. 14:23)? He paid the price (ניתחסר הימנו), in that God had told him, '**know of a surety**, ... ' As soon as the decree was issued, Isaac was sure that it would begin with him; but Isaac died, and the decree did not begin with him. When Jacob became prominent and begot twelve tribes, he began fearing he would have to pay off the debt. Why? Because Jacob had responsibility; and he began to protect himself so that the debt would not be demanded from him. And it would have been so; except that when famine plagued the entire world, the residents of the land of Canaan went down to Egypt, as it is said, '**and all countries came into Egypt**' (Gen. 41:57); but Jacob was afraid of having to repay the debt, and did not go down. This may be likened to the case of a cow on whom people sought to put a yoke to make her plow a field, but the cow refused to come out. So what did they do? They dragged her calf into the field; the calf lowed, and his mother heard and came out of her own accord. Thus, Jacob was afraid of the decree that had been passed on his elder; so God drew Joseph down to Egypt so that Jacob would hear that he was there and would go there too."[13] Following Scripture, this *midrash* sees the beginning of the exile in God's words to Abraham, but adds to the biblical connection an element of sin, namely the sin of primordial man.[14] In *Tībat Marqe* we read: זרען משכון במצרים מסני על מלה דשנו בה אברהם באור כשדים. "Their seed were a pledge in Egypt, long due for Abraham's misdeed in Ur of the Chaldeans."[15]

Some *midrashim* attribute the events of the exile to the sins of the children of Israel themselves: רבנן פתחי לה פתחא להאי פרשתא בה' בגדו כי בנים זרים ילדו עתה יאכלם חדש את חלקיהם (הושע ה, ז). ללמדך, כשמת יוסף הפרו ברית מילה. אמרו נהיה כמצרים. מכאן אתה למד שמשה מלן ביציאתן ממצרים. וכיון שעשו כך הפך הקב"ה אהבה שהיו המצריים אוהבים אותם לשנאה, שנאמר הפך לבם לשנא עמו [להתנכל בעבדיו] (תה' קה, כה). לקיים מה שנאמר עתה יאכלם חדש את חלקיהם. אל תיקרי חדש אלא חדש שחידש עליהם גזירותיו. "Hence it is written: **Now there arose a new king**. **The Rabbis commenced this discourse with this verse: They have dealt treacherously against the Lord, for they have begotten strange children; now shall the month devour them with their portions** (Hos. 5:7). This teaches that when Joseph died, they abolished the covenant of circumcision, saying: 'Let us become like the Egyptians.' You can infer this from the fact that Moses had to circumcise them on their departure from Egypt. As soon as they had done so, God converted the love with which the Egyptians loved them into hatred, as it is written: **He turned their heart to hate His people, to deal craftily with His servants** (Ps. 105:25), to fulfill that which is said: **Now shall the month devour them with their portions**. Do not read this as *ḥodesh* (month), but as *ḥadash* (new), for he renewed his decrees against them."[16] Jewish historiography is presented here stage after stage. In Exodus the fears of the new king who did not know Joseph are given as the reason for the decree. The psalmist sees the enslavement as stemming from God's will (cf. I Kings 18:37; and note 34 in The Moses Nativity Story in the Bible).[17] The *Midrash*

---

[13] *Yelammedenu ha-Kadmon*, cited in *Ginze Schechter*, Vol. 1, p. 45; *Torah Shelemah*, Vol. 8, p. 3, n. 11, and Kasher's note there.

[14] Also cf. *Midrash Abkir*, cited in *Yalkut Shimoni*, n. 162; the Oxford manuscript gives the source. See the editor's notes there, p. 3; also cf. *Torah Shelemah*, Vol. 8, p. 3, n. 10.

[15] 6.1; p. 45. See *Genesis Rabbah*, XLIII (p. 421), and the *Minḥat Yehudah* commentary there; also cf. *Torah Shelemah*, Vol. 3, p. 614, n. 106.

[16] *Exodus Rabbah* I.8.

[17] Spinoza makes an interesting comment, cited by Seeligmann in "Menschliches Heldentum und göttliche Hilfe," p. 386, n. 2: *In Psalm 105 vs. 24 dicitur, quod Deus Aegyptiorum animum mutavit, ut odio haberent Israelitas, quae etiam mutatio naturalis plane fuit, ut patet ex cap. 1. Exodi, ubi ratio non levis Aegyptiorum narratur, quae eos movit, Israelitas ad servitutem redigere* (from *Tract. Theol.*

adds the element of sin to explain why this was the will of God.[18] *Ginze Schechter*, Vol. 1, p. 63 cites a parallel *midrash*, found in a manuscript,[19] built on the verse "**And the children of Israel were fruitful, and increased abundantly, and multiplied, and waxed exceedingly mighty**" (Ex. 1:7), which adds to the sin of non-circumcision the sin of growing their forelocks: "*It is written, 'And the children of Israel were fruitful, and increased abundantly'* (וישרצו). [עשם] עשה[. שרצים בשביל שמשכו להם ערלה וגידלו [להם] בלור[יות]. *Scripture describes them as swarming things* (שרצים) *because they drew out their foreskins and grew their forelocks.*"[20]

In *Tanḥuma Buber* (שמות 6) we read as well: ותמלא הארץ אתם, שנתמלאו בתי טרטיאות ובתי קרקסיאות מהם, מיד גזרו עליהם לפרוש מן המטה שנאמר ותמלא הארץ אותם וגו'. "**And the land was filled with them**—*When they began to fill the theatres and circuses, they immediately passed a decree against them that they desist from going to bed, as it is written, 'and the land was filled with them.'*" A more explicit statement is found in *Exodus Rabbah* I.30: ויאמר אכן נודע הדבר (ב, יד) ר' יהודה בר' שלום בשם ר' חנינא הגדול ורבותינו בשם ר' אלכסנדרי אומרים היה משה מהרהר בלבו ואומר מה חטאו ישראל שנשתעבדו מכל האומות. כיון ששמע דבריו, אמר לשון הרע יש ביניהם, היאך יהיו ראויים לגאולה. לכך אמר אכן נודע הדבר, עתה ידעתי באי זה דבר הם משתעבדים. "**And he said: Surely the thing is known** (Ex. 2:14)—*R. Judah, son of R. Shalom, said in the name of R. Ḥanina the Great, and our Sages*

Politici, Ch. 6, p. 164). Gunkel, however, in his commentary on Psalms, views הֵפֵךְ, turned, as an intransitive verb; however Seeligmann *op. cit.* refutes this interpretation. Let us point out, however, that the principal argument against Gunkel is provided by Psalms 105:24: **And he increased his people greatly; and made them stronger than their enemies**, which is structured according to the same principle, attributing to God the actions described in Exodus as *mutatio naturalis*. It is also interesting that in Chapter 5 (p. 148) he writes: *dum enim inter alias nationes ante exitum ex Aegypto vixerunt, nullas leges peculiares habuerunt*... Furthermore, his remark, "*homines superstitionibus Aegyptiorum assueti rudes*," perhaps reveals the influence of the *midrashim* that impute idolatry to the children of Israel. Compare this with Ibn Ezra's (long) commentary on Exodus 2:23. Of course Spinoza, unlike the *midrash*, does not associate their hardship with their behavior.

[18] We have already noted that the tendency to associate exile with sin is already evident in Genesis 15:16 (cf. p. 26 above); there, however, in contrast to the *Midrash*, the exile is tied to the sinfulness of the Amorites. *Lekaḥ Tob* has an interesting *midrash* on this verse, which turns the explanation given in the Bible back towards the Hebrews by tying it in with Abraham's transgression, mentioned in the *midrash* from *Yelammedenu* which we cited above: "For the iniquity of the Amorites (האמורי) is not yet full. *The iniquity of the utterance* (האמירה) *uttered by Abraham, as it is written*, And he said, Lord God, whereby shall I know that I shall inherit it? *(Gen. 15:8).*" (*Torah Shelemah*, Vol. 3, p. 666, n. 194).

[19] The *Tanḥuma* according to Ginzberg, *op. cit.*

[20] Also see Sforno's comment on this verse, and Kasher's note, *op. cit.*, Vol. 8, p. 19, n. 86.

said in the name of R. Alexandri: Moses was meditating in his heart, 'Wherein have Israel sinned that they should be enslaved more than all the nations?' When he heard his [Dathan's] words, he said: 'Talebearing is rife among them, and how can they be worthy of salvation?' Hence he said, '**Surely the thing is known**, for now I know the cause of their bondage.'"[21]

The sin of not keeping the rite of circumcision befits Toraic literature which is not yet familiar with the theme of moral turpitude as deciding the fate of the nation.[22] By *Exodus Rabbah* the theme of immorality, of man's duty to his fellow man, as in the outlook of the Prophets, has already been added.

In conclusion, the exile is not set in a religious vacuum, devoid of any relationship to God's dominion and will. From the psalmist' view, "**He turned their heart to hate His people**" (Ps. 105:25), the *Midrash* necessarily concludes that sin was the cause of the enslavement—the sins of the fathers and the sins of the sons.

Redemption

Let us proceed from the motif of exile to its opposite and complementary motif, redemption. In Exodus the people's redemption from exile is not explained in terms of righteousness or repentance of the sons, because the ancient story does not attribute the exile to the sons' wickedness or sin. Moreover, there is also no appeal to God to redeem the people from the hardships of exile, because events take place without any direct connection with God (cf. p. 26). What happened to the story of the exile also happened to the story of the redemption from exile. Above we saw that in Exodus 2:23 the author was careful not to say that the Israelites cried out to God. By the time we get to Deuteronomy, however, where a person bringing an offering of the first of all the fruits of the earth pronounces the requisite formulation, we find that the cry in Exodus, which was not specifically directed, has become: "**we cried unto the Lord**

---

[21] Also compare the parallel versions listed there. *Exodus Rabbah* begins with a long homiletical interpretation of Proverbs 13:24: He that spareth his rod hateth his son: but he that loveth him chasteneth him betimes. *Yefeh To'ar*, a commentary by the 16th century exegete Shemu'el Yafeh Ashkenazi, comments on the way this midrashic work begins: "Perhaps the homily, "But he that loveth chasteneth him betimes—*this refers to the Holy One, blessed be He*," is cited here [introducing *Exodus Rabbah*], to give the reason they were enslaved in Egypt, namely that they went down to Egypt so that they would thereby merit receiving the Torah and the land of Israel, ... therefore He had them first suffer the exile in Egypt, so that their spirit would be subdued by the bondage in Egypt and it would be easier for them to bear the burden of the Torah." It is interesting, however, that the *midrash* itself does not note this.

[22] See Kaufmann, *Toledot*, Vol. 1, Bk. 1, p. 27.

God of our fathers" (Deut. 26:7).²³ A similar formulation appears in Numbers 20:15–16: "**and we have dwelt in Egypt a long time; and the Egyptians vexed us, and our fathers: And when we cried unto the Lord, he heard our voice ....**" Also see I Samuel 12:8. The *Midrash* continues further in this direction. The numerous homilies attached to this verse add an an element that does not appear in the verse: a direct appeal to God. For example, see *Midrash Tehillim* (Ps. 22.20): .אליך זעקו, כמו שנאמר ויאנחו בני ישראל מן העבודה ויזעקו "They cried unto thee *(Ps. 22:6)—As it is written,* **And the children of Israel sighed by reason of the bondage, and they cried.**"²⁴

The way the redemption from Egypt has been perceived through the generations is a subject which exceeds the scope of this work. However, we wish to note briefly that the *Midrash* shows strong vacillation regarding the essence of the redemption, and all the various approaches

---

²³ G. von Rad discusses the extreme antiquity of the entire unit in *Das formgeschichtliche Problem des Hexateuch*. However, see Seeligmann's reservation, "מסורת פולחנית," p. 52. In our opinion, having considered Seeligmann's comments, we find Von Rad's position unassailable. It is true that this unit is strongly marked by a deuteronomistic linguistic style, however this does not give us leave to view this style as clear proof of a late date. In Deuteronomy one must draw a fundamental distinction between ancient material and its reworking in the spirit of centralization of ritual worship; it is only this last stratum which should be ascribed a late date. Similarly, in our opinion, here too one must distinguish between ancient material and its later reworking.

Note how this formulation evolved in later sources that allude to God's words at the burning bush, Exodus 3:7–9: **I have surely seen the affliction of my people which are in Egypt, and have heard their cry, ... Now therefore, behold, the cry of the children of Israel is come unto me.** This text (Ex. 3:7–9) preserves the ancient feature of not mentioning that the cry was directed towards God; yet, in contrast to Exodus 2:23, it states that the children of Israel are God's people. Exodus 3:7–9 echos in I Samuel 9:16: **for I have looked upon my people [their affliction = עני]** (in the Septuagint), **because their cry is come unto me.** But by Isaiah 19:20 the formulation changes, and the cry is directed to God: **for they shall cry unto the Lord because of the oppressors, and he shall send them a savior, and a great one (ורב), and he shall deliver them.** Most likely one should emend this text from Isaiah to read as in the Qumran scrolls, **And he shall come down (וירד)** and shall deliver them, paralleling the formulation in Exodus (3:8), **And I am come down to deliver them.** In other words, God is the subject of all the verbs in the verse. Kutscher (*The Language and Linguistic Background of the Isaiah Scroll*, pp. 185(83) and 271 in the Hebrew, pp. 245(89) and 354 in the English translation) holds a different opinion. Regarding the combination of the motifs of God hearing a cry not specifically directed towards Him, and God coming down, see Genesis 18:20–21: "**I will go down now, and see whether they have done altogether according to the cry of it, which is come unto me,**" as well as Gen. 19:13. Also see the instructive remarks by Ehrlich (*Die Psalmen*) on the words אל הסלע in Psalm 137:8.

²⁴ Also compare what Abraham, son of Maimonides, said: "We may presume this to have been a cry of prayer to the Almighty."

are brought into play. Just as the exile was explained as having resulted from sin, of fathers or of sons, so too the redemption is explained as having been due to the merits of the fathers and the righteousness of the sons, or alternatively to their repentance. The arbitrary view of the exile as having taken place "for no apparent reason" or as stemming from some prior decree (Gen. 15:13–16), is balanced by a similar perception of the redemption. This can be seen in further depth in the *midrashim* cited in *Torah Shelemah*, Vol. 8, pp. 103–110, and in Ginzberg's note (*op. cit.*, Vol. 5 p. 413, n. 106). Here we shall only cite the terse statement: אמר ר"א כשנגאלו ישראל ממצרים לא נגאלו אלא מתוך חמשה דברים אלו, מתוך צרה, ומתוך תשובה, ומתוך זכות אבות, ומתוך רחמים, ומתוך הקץ. מתוך צרה דכתיב ויאנחו בני ישראל, מתוך תשובה דכתיב ותעל שועתם, מתוך זכות אבות דכתיב ויזכור אלהים את בריתו, ומתוך רחמים דכתיב וירא אלהים את בני ישראל, מתוך הקץ [דכתיב] וידע אלהים וכו'. "R. Eleazar said: Israel were redeemed from Egypt only because of the following five reasons: (i) Distress, (ii) Repentance, (iii) The Merits of the Fathers, (iv) God's Mercy, (v) The Term [of their redemption]. Because of Distress, as it is written, **And the children of Israel sighed** (Ex. 2:23); because of repentance, as it is written, **And their cry came up** (ibid.); because of the Merits of the Fathers, as it is written, **And God remembered His covenant** (ibid. 24); because of God's Mercy, as it is written, **And God saw the children of Israel** (ibid. 25); and because of the Term, as it is written, **And God took cognizance of them** (ibid.)"[25]

The Length of the Enslavement

Since the enslavement was associated in Exodus with the murder of the sons, it was portrayed as coinciding with the murder decrees (cf. p. 16, above), and consequently the duration of the enslavement was foreshortened to match this overlap. Most of the *midrashim* preserve this quality of the biblical story and plainly view the Pharaoh of the enslavement as the Pharaoh who issued the decrees against the sons.[26]

---

[25] *Deuteronomy Rabbah* II.23 [Vilna ed.]; *Torah Shelemah*, Vol. 8, p. 103, n. 182 of the commentary and the parallel versions listed there.

[26] The apogee of viewing these various events as having taken place during the reign of a single king is seen in those legends of the Sages that identify the Pharaoh who issued the decrees with the Pharaoh who suffered the plagues: תנא הוא התחיל "It בעצה תחילה דכתיב ויאמר אל עמו לפיכך לקה תחילה כדכתיב ובכה ובעמך ובכל עבדיך. is taught: He [Pharaoh] originated the plan first, as it is written, and he said unto his people (Ex. 1:9); therefore he was punished first, as it is written, **Upon thee, and upon thy people, and upon all thy servants** (Ex. 7:29)" (*Sotah* 11a). The enslavement, the murder decrees, and the plagues are all included within the reign of a single king. This view, however, is hard to reconcile with Exodus 2:23: **And it came to pass in process of time, that the king of Egypt died.** Perhaps this approach holds, as does Targum Yerushalmi, that the king did not actually die, but that

he became afflicted with leprosy: "ואיתכתש מלכא דמצרים" *He became a leper, who is deemed as one dead, as it is said: Let her not I pray, be as one dead (Num. 12:12; Aaron's prayer for Miriam after her leprosy), and it says: In the year that King Uzziah died (Isa. 6:1.* According to the Sages, Isaiah began to prophesy on the day that Uzziah became leprous; cf. II Kings 15:5)" (*Exodus Rabbah* I.34 and variants; cf. also *Torah Shelemah*, Vol. 8, p. 101, n. 177; Ginzberg, Vol. 5, p. 412, n. 101). The leprosy legend, however, does not appear in *Sotah*. There, the legend identifying the Pharaoh of the decrees with the Pharaoh of the plagues comes immediately after the controversy between Rab and Samuel: ויקם מלך חדש וגו׳. רב ושמואל, חד אמר חדש ממש וחד אמר שנתחדשו גזירותיו. מאן דאמר חדש ממש דכתיב חדש, ומאן דאמר שנתחדשו גזירותיו דלא כתיב ומת וימלוך. אשר לא ידע את יוסף דהוה דמי כמאן דלא ידע ליה כלל. "*Now there arose a new king, ...* Rab and Samuel differed in their interpretation. One said he was really new, while the other said that his decrees were made new. He who said that he was really new did so because it is written 'new'; and he who said that his decrees were made new did so because it is not stated that [the former king] died and he reigned [in his stead]. *Who knew not Joseph—who comported himself as though he did not know him [Joseph at all]*" (*Sotah* 11a). According to the one who argued that his decrees were made new, the Joseph story and the descent of his brethren to Egypt also occurred during the reign of a single Pharaoh. It should be noted, however, that in spite of the superficial similarity, the compression of these various events into the reign of a single king is hard to view as continuing the biblical approach. In Scriptures, compression of the enslavement stems from its association with the nativity legend; whereas in the works of the Sages, this compression stems from the desire to view the plagues on Egypt as meting out measure for measure—"*He [Pharaoh] originated the plan first, . . . therefore he was punished first*"—and from a tendency to view the black as blacker and to amplify the villany of Pharaoh's evil. Although this *midrash* has puzzled scholars, early and late, it is clear to us that the remark, "*that his decrees were made new*," was prompted by the desire to emphasize Pharaoh's villany. Not only was Pharaoh a villain, he was also an ingrate, as we see in *Lekaḥ Tob*, which enumerates Joseph's favors to Pharaoh—"*Joseph, after all, brought riches into Pharaoh's home, purchased all the land of Egypt for Pharaoh, and levied taxes upon them*"—and concludes, "*Cursed are the evil ones who are ungrateful and do not repay those who have done them favors*" (cf. variants cited in *Torah Shelemah*, Vol. 8, p. 20, n. 88). This ungratefulness is all the more impressive when the Pharaoh who is the ingrate was himself the one who received the favors. Compare *Genesis Rabbah* XC.2 (p. 1100), where the homilist infers backwards and finds even the Pharaoh who was beneficent to Joseph to have been evil.

It is interesting that the Septuagint renders "new" (v. 8) as ἕτερος, i.e., "other." Also of interest is the choice of the word *alius* in Biblical Antiquities 9:1, a rendition which appears to deny the homiletical sense. Compare this with *Antiquities* (2.202) and Acts 7:18. In the *Gemara*, *Sotah* 11a and *Erubin* 53a, there is a difference of opinion between Rab and Samuel. If the Septuagint's rendition here is indeed polemical, then the controversy mentioned between Rab and Samuel must actually date to a far earlier period.

Nevertheless, there are a fair number of *midrashim* that preserve the length of the enslavement. Generally, however, they do this by adjusting the length of the enslavement to match the reckoning of the number of generations the Hebrews dwelled in Egypt (which by the Sages' calculations is 210 years. See note 39, below.) For example, we read in *Genesis Rabbah* LXI.7:[27] בימי אלכסנדרוס מקדון באו בני ישמעאל ליעור על ישראל על הבכורה, ובאו עימהם שתי משפחות רעות כנעניים ומצריים... אמרו מצרים מתורתן אנו למדין ובאים עליהם. ששים ריבוא בני אדם יצאו מאצלינו טעונים כלי כסף וזהב דכת׳ וינצלו את מצרים (שמ׳ יב, לו) יתנו לנו את זהבינו ואת כספינו, אמר לו גביעה בן קוסם אדני המלך ששים ריבוא בני אדם עבדום ר״י שנים מהם כספים ומהם זהבים יתנו לנו מדינר דינר בכל יום. "In the days of Alexander of Macedon the Ishmaelites came to dispute the birthright with Israel and they were accompanied by two evil families, the Canaanites and the Egyptians.... Then said the Egyptians: 'We base our suit against them on their own Torah. Six hundred thousand left us, laden with silver and gold utensils, as it is written, **And they despoiled the Egyptians** (Ex. 12:36). Let them return us our silver and gold.' Said Gebiah the son of Kosem: 'Your Majesty! Six hundred thousand men served them two hundred and ten years, of whom some were silversmiths and some goldsmiths. Let them pay us at the rate of a *dinar* per day.'"[28]

According to *Midrash ha-Gadol* (Ex. 4:13) Moses cites the length of the enslavement as the reason for his reluctance to go to Pharaoh: אלו התרית בהן שנה או שתים לפני הדבר כבר עשיין, אלא שנשתעבדו בהן מאתים ועשר שנים. יאמר לי פרעה מי שעבדו עבד עשר שנים ולא מיחה בו כל בריה יבוא אחר ויוציאו מתחת ידו או מי שעבד את הכרם עשר שנים ולא מיחה בו כל בריה יבוא אחד ויוציאו מתחת ידו. "It would be one thing if you had warned them a year or two before the deed had been done. But they [the Israelites] have been enslaved to them for two hundred and ten years. Pharaoh will say to me that if someone has been a slave to a certain master for ten years and not a soul has protested, how could another person come and take that slave away from him? or if someone has worked a vineyard for ten years and not a soul has protested, how could another person come and take it away from him?"[29]

Genesis Rabbah XCVI.1 (p. 1192) retains the length of the enslavement and even extends it beyond its biblical limits: כיון שנפטר אבינו יעקב התחיל שעבוד מצרים על ישראל. "As soon as the Patriarch Jacob died, the Egyptian servitude commenced for Israel."

Also note the attitude towards the length of the bondage in Ezekiel

---

[27] P. 666.
[28] *Torah Shelemah*, Vol. 12, p. 43, n. 569.
[29] Compare the *Mekilta of R. Simeon b. Yoḥai*, p. 7; *Torah Shelemah*, Vol. 8, p. 173, n. 44.

the Tragedian (cf. p. 33, above) and in Biblical Antiquities 9:3.[30] *Tanḥuma* (וישב 3), interprets Genesis 15:13 according to its plain sense: "א״ר יהודה בר שלום שיהיו גרים ותושבים בארץ לא להם משתעבדים ת׳ שנה. *R. Judah b. Shalom said they would be strangers residing in a land that was not theirs and would be enslaved for four hundred years.*"[31] Compare this to the following intricate homily in *Pesikta de R. Kahana*,[32] which is mostly about the question of redemption alluded to above, and which also is based on a similar understanding of Genesis 15:13:[33] קול דודי הנה זה בא מדלג על ההרים מקפץ על הגבעות (שה״ש ב, ח) ר׳ יודה א׳ קול דודי הנה זה בא, זה משה. בשעה שבא משה וא׳ לישר׳ בחדש הזה אתם נגאלין אמרו לו, רבינו משה, היאך אנו נגאלין, לא כך אמ׳ הקב״ה לאבינו אברהם ועבדום וענו אותם ארבע מאות שנה (ברא׳ טו, יג) והלא אין בידינו אלא מאתים ועשר, א׳ להם, הואיל והוא חפץ בגאולתכם אינו מביט בחשבונותיכם אלא מדלג על ההרים מקפץ על הגבעות מדלג על הקיצים ועל החשבונות ועל העיבורים, ובחדש הזה אתם נגאלין, החדש הזה לכם ראש חדשים (שמ׳ יב, ב)... "**The voice of my beloved! behold, he cometh leaping upon the mountains, skipping upon the hills.** *(Song 2:8)—According to R. Judah, the words 'the voice of my beloved' refer to the coming of Moses. When he came and said to Israel, 'You are to be redeemed this month,' they replied: 'Moses, our master, how can we expect to be redeemed now? Did not the Holy One say clearly to our father Abraham,* **Thy seed ... shall serve them; and they shall afflict them four hundred years** *(Gen. 15:13)? According to our reckoning, we have served only two hundred and ten years. Moses replied: Since He desires your redemption, He does not heed your reckonings. Instead* **He leaps upon the mountains, He skips upon the hills** *(Song 2:8)—that is, he skips over the end span and over your reckonings of years and times, saying, 'It is My will that in this month you shall be redeemed.* **This month shall be unto you the beginning of months** *(Exod. 12:2), [the beginning of your redemption].*'"

In the biblical narrative, forcing the period of enslavement into the narrow time span of the decrees against the sons creates an element of tension which naturally is felt most strongly at the beginning and end points of the story. The join at the end is not smooth because the enslavement continues, whereas the murder decree disappears as soon as it has served its purpose of introducing the birth of Moses. This tension is resolved in the *midrashim* that separate the enslavement from the murder decrees. An extreme example of such separation may be found

---

[30] Additional opinions dating the enslavement from the death of Joseph, the death of Levi, the birth of Miriam, etc., are cited in the commentary in *Torah Shelemah*, Vol. 8, p. 12, n. 49.
[31] *Torah Shelemah*, Vol. 3, p. 655, n. 140.
[32] *Pesikta de R. Kahana* 5 (בחדש הזה), p. 88.
[33] *Torah Shelemah*, ibid., p. 657, n. 150.

in *Pirke Rabbi Eliezer*, where the enslavement actually comes after the edicts against the sons:[34] ר׳ ינאי אומר והלא לא העבידו המצרים את ישראל אלא שעה אחד מיומו של הקב"ה שמונים ושלש שני ושליש שנה, עד שלא נולד משה, שאמרו החרטומים לפרעה עתיד נער לילד והוא יוציא את ישראל ממצרים, וחשב ואמר בלבו ישליכו את כל הילודים הזכרי ליאורה והוא מושלך עמהם שנאמר כל הבן הילוד היארה תשליכהו ונמצא הדבר בטל. שלש שנים ושליש [השליכום ליאור] עד שנולד משה ולאחר שנולד אמרו לו הנה נולד והוא כמוס מעינינו. אמר להם הואיל ונולד מכאן ואילך אל תשליכו הילדים היארה אלא תנו עליהם עול קשה למרר חיי אבותיהם שנאמר וימררו את חייהם. "R. Yannai said that the Egyptians actually did not enslave the Israelites but for one hour in the Holy One's reckoning of a day—that is, eighty-three years and a third of a year.[35] Prior to Moses' birth the magicians told Pharaoh that a son would be born who would take Israel out of Egypt; so Pharaoh thought to himself, 'Let them cast all the male newborns into the Nile, and this son will be cast into the water along with them, and then their prediction will come to naught,' as it is written, **Every son that is born ye shall cast into the river**. For three and a third years [they cast the sons into the Nile] until Moses was born. After he had been born they [the magicians] said to him [Pharaoh], 'Lo, he has been born but is hidden from our sight.' He [Pharaoh] answered them, 'Since he has already been born, henceforth do not cast the sons who are born into the Nile, but rather put a heavy burden on them to embitter their fathers' lives,' as it is said, **and they made their lives bitter (Ex. 1:14)**."[36]

---

[34] *Pirke Rabbi Eliezer* 48; *Torah Shelemah*, Vol. 8, p. 48, n. 212.

[35] According to Psalms 90:4—**For a thousand years in thy sight are but as yesterday when it is past**—a day in the reckoning of the Holy One, blessed be He, is equal to a thousand years. Following the Babylonian method, if we divide this divine day into twelve hours, we obtain that each hour is eighty-three and a third years. R. Yannai arrives at this total by adding eighty years—the age of Moses when he addressed Pharaoh (Ex. 7:7)—to the three and a half years that preceded the birth of Moses. For Ginzberg (*op. cit.*, Vol. 5, p. 399, n. 56) the duration given here for the edict to cast the sons into the Nile was problematic. Aside from the primary object of these calculations—to arrive at a total of eighty-three and a third years—perhaps another factor which came into play was the view that casting the sons into the Nile began during the pregnancy preceding the birth of Aaron, who was three years older than Moses (Ex. 7:7). Cf. *Dibre Yeme Moshe Rabbenu*: "And she called him Aaron (אהרן), for during the pregnancy (הריון) Pharaoh began to spill the blood of their males upon the earth and some of them he cast into the Nile." Aaron's name is associated with the travails of pregnancy perhaps as early as the Testament of Levi 17.3 (Charlesworth, *op. cit.*, p. 794; cf. Ginzberg, *op. cit.*, Vol. 5, p. 396, n. 36). On the omen preceding Aaron's birth, cf. note 205, below.

[36] Radal (R. David Luria) has an interesting commentary on this *midrash*: "It appears that [the *midrash*] wishes to interpret **and they made their lives bitter** ... as coming after the decree **ye shall cast into the river**." The beginning of this *midrash* is indeed problematic. Instead of ... *eighty-three years and a third of a year. Prior to Moses' birth the magicians* ... Radal proposes reading "eighty-three

A similar remark is found in *Dibre Yeme Moshe Rabbenu* (Jellinek ed.). There, after the murder decrees, Balaam recommends: ועתה אם תשמע בקולי אל תהרגם בחרב רק תרבה עליהם עוויים קשים שיהיו כלים מאליהם וייטב הדבר בעיני פרעה ובעיני עבדיו. " 'Now, if you take my advice, you won't kill them by the sword, but only impose a multiplicity of hardships on them, so that they die out of their own accord.' And his words pleased Pharaoh and his servants."[37]

In *Seder Olam*, which only includes the list of generations and a chronology of events, the tension between the time of the enslavement and the timing of the decrees is not felt for the simple reason that this work does not relate to the murder decrees at all. We read there:[38] וימת יוסף וכל אחיו. יוסף מת בן ק"י שנה. אין לך בכל השבטים שקצר ימיו פחות מיוסף, ואין לך בכל השבטים שהאריך ימים יותר מלוי, וכל זמן שהיה לוי קים לא נשתעבדו ישראל למצרים שנאמר וימת יוסף וכל אחיו וגו'. ומשמת לוי התחילו המצריים לשעבדם. מכאן אמרו אחד מן

---

years and a third of a year. Three and a third years prior to the birth of Moses, the magicians said, ..." This does not solve the problem, however, for if the bondage was not decreed until after Moses was born, then it could only have lasted eighty years, i.e., less than an hour in the reckoning of the Holy One, blessed be He, which equals eighty-three and a third years. Therefore, we suggest emending the text to read "not even one hour (אפלו שעה אחת)" instead of "but for one hour (אלא שעה אחת)." In other words, this *midrash* ought to begin as follows: "R. Yannai said that the Egyptians did not enslave Israel even one hour in the reckoning of the Holy One, blessed be He, which equals eighty-three and a third years. Prior to Moses' birth the magicians told Pharaoh that a son was destined to be born who would take Israel out of Egypt, ... "

The continuation of Radal's commentary is instructive with respect to the subsequent evolution of this *midrash*. On the *midrash* cited above (p. 68), taken from *Sifre* (כי תבא, par. 301) and also appearing in the *Passover Haggadah* he notes, "It follows from the Sages' interpretation of the verse, The Lord ... looked on our affliction, and our labor, and our oppression—*our labor refers to the sons, as it is written, every son* ..., *and our oppression refers to the oppression expressed in the words* the oppression wherewith the Egyptians oppressed them (Ex. 3:9), *which is the bitter hardship of bondage*—that the bondage came after the decree against the sons.

[37] In this work, which combines quite freely a number of legends of the Sages, postponing the enslavement does not go well with the opening of the unit. There Miriam's name is interpreted after the Sages' homily: ותקרא שמה מרים כי בעת ההיא החלו המצריים בני חם למרר חיי בני ישראל. "*And she was called Miriam* (מרים) *because at that time the Egyptians, the descendents of Ham, began to make bitter* (למרר) *the lives of the children of Israel.*" This interpretation of her name was associated, at least originally, with the enslavement. The version cited by Shinan does not include Balaam's words. Perhaps they were added by someone sensitive to the surprising lack of reference to the enslavment in the version published by Shinan. (This remark is only appropriate if Shinan's conjecture is true, that his version represents an early stage in the text's evolution.) The relationship between the legend of the individual and the story of the enslavement in the various versions of this work and *Sefer ha-Yashar* merits further investigation, but is beyond the scope of this work.

[38] *Seder Olam Rabbah* 3.

האחים שמת ידאגו כל האחים. אחד מן החבורה שמת תדאג כל החבורה. ובני ישראל פרו
וישרצו וגו' ויקם מלך חדש וגו'. נמצא משמת לוי ועד שיצאו ישראל ממצרים קט"ז שנה ואין
השעבוד יותר על כן ולא פחות מפ"ז שנים כשנותיה של מרים. ולמה נקרא שמה מרים על שם
מירור. "And Joseph died and all his brethren. *Joseph died at the age of 110. No one in all the tribes lived fewer years than Joseph, nor did anyone in all the tribes live longer than Levi. As long as Levi was alive, Israel was not enslaved to Egypt, as it is written:* **And Joseph died and all his brethren.** *But once Levi had died, the Egyptians began to enslave them. Hence it is said that if one of the brothers has died, all the brothers should worry. If one of the group dies, all the group should worry.* **And the children of Israel were fruitful, and increased abundantly, ... Now there arose up a new king** ... *From Levi's death until the Israelites' exodus from Egypt was 116 years; therefore the period of bondage was neither more nor less than 87 years, coinciding with the age of Miriam. Indeed, why was she called Miriam? Because of making bitter* (מירור).[39]

DEALING WISELY

We noted above (cf. p. 14) that the motif of dealing wisely in Exodus 1:10 finds its expression and continuation in the Pharaoh's words to the midwives (v. 15) and not in the enslavement. This structure gave rise to the many *midrashim* that go to pains to insert the motif of dealing wisely into the story of enslavement: הבה נתחכמה לו, עשה פרעה בערמה שנ' הבה נתחכמה
לו פן ירבה, אמר פרעה כל מי שיעשה י' לבנים אתן לו כל יום י' כספים, מ' אתן לו מ'.
ישראל הלכו אחד הממון ועשו יום ראשון הרבה, כתבו פלוני עשה כך, אמר פרעה כל אחד
כתבו עליו עשה כך וכך, וכל מי שאינו עושה [מה] שעשה ביום ראשון היו מכים אותו הנוגשים.
"**Come on, let us deal wisely with them.** *Pharaoh dealt wisely, as it is written:* **Come on, let us deal wisely with them; lest they multiply**. *Pharaoh said: 'Whoever shall make ten bricks, I shall give him ten coins every day, forty bricks, I shall give him forty*

---

[39] Compare the sources cited in Ginzberg, *op. cit.*, Vol. 5, p. 420, n. 126, and *Torah Shelemah*, Vol. 8, p. 12, n. 49. These sources grapple with a problem which does not concern us here, namely, that the length of the enslavement does not match the accounting of the generations that came down to Egypt and those who left in the exodus. Moreover, in *Seder Olam* (*op. cit.*) it says further: יכול כל ד' מאות שנה היו
ישראל במצרים והלא קהת מיורדי מצרים היה וכתיב ושני חיי קהת קל"ג שנה ושני חיי עמרם
קל"ז שנה ופ' שנים של משה הרי ש"נ שנים וכו'. "Could it be that the Israelites were in Egypt the entire four hundred years? For Kohath was among those who descended to Egypt, and it is written, **and the years of the life of Kohath were an hundred thirty and three years** (Ex. 6:18). **And the years of the life of Amram were an hundred and thirty and seven years** (Ex. 6:20). Add to this the eighty years of Moses, and you have 350 years. ..." See note 47 in Josephus, and p. 183 below, on the approach taken by Ibn Ezra to this question, who, in sharp contrast to *Seder Olam*, relates the interest taken in geneology to the murder decree.

coins.' The Israelites were enticed by the riches, and the first day they made many [bricks], and wrote down, 'So and so made so many.' Pharaoh said: 'Record how many bricks each person made.' And whoever did not make as many bricks as he had made the first day, the taskmasters smote."[40] Similarly in *Tanḥuma Buber* we have: בשעה שאמר פרעה הבה נתחכמה, קיבץ פרעה את כל ישראל, אמר להם בבקשה מכם עשו עמי היום בטובה, היינו דכתיב ויעבידו מצרים את בני ישראל בפרך, בתחילה בפה רך. פרעה נטל סל ומגריפה, וכל מי שהיה [רואה פרעה] נוטל סל ומגריפה ועושה בלבנים היה עושה, מיד הלכו ישראל בזריזות ועשו אומנות עמו כל היום לפי כחן, לפי שהיו בעלי כח וגבורים, כיון שהחשיך העמיד עליהם נוגשים, אמר להם חישבו את הלבנים, מיד עמדו ומנו אותן, אמר להם כזה אתם מעמידין לי בכל יום ויום. "Come on, let us deal wisely with them. When Pharaoh said 'let us deal wisely with them' he gathered together all the Israelites and said: 'Please work with me today as a favor.' This is the meaning of the verse, **And the Egyptians made the children of Israel to serve with rigour** (בפרך); they began by sweet-talking them (בפה רך). Pharaoh took up a basket and hoe, and whoever [saw Pharaoh] taking up a basket and hoe and making bricks did the same. The Israelites were quick to follow his example and toiled with him the entire day, working with all their strength, since they were mighty and heroic. When it grew dark, Pharaoh placed taskmasters over them and told them to calculate how many bricks had been made. They immediately counted all the bricks, then Pharaoh said: 'You shall make this many bricks for me every day.'"[41]

According to some of the *midrashim*, Amram (or the entire tribe of Levi) realized the wily designs of the king and managed to escape enslavement.[42] Perhaps by excluding Amram and the tribe of Levi from the rest of the people, the *midrash* sought to explain how, in the continuation of the story, it was that Moses and Aaron were apparently not in bondage but could come and go freely before Pharaoh.

Not all the *midrashim* associate dealing wisely with enslavement: אמר ר' ברכיה בשם ר' לוי ארורים הן הרשעים שהן מקיימין עצה על ישראל, וכל אחד ואחד אומר עצתי יפה מעצתך, עשו אמר שוטה היה קין, שהרג את אחיו הבל בחיי אביו, ולא היה יודע שאביו פרה ורבה והוליד את שת, אני איני עושה כן, אלא יקרבו ימי אבל אבי ואהרגה את יעקב אחי (בר' כז, מא), ואירש חלקו. פרעה אמר שוטה היה עשו שאמר יקרבו ימי אבל אבי, ולא היה יודע שאחיו פרה ורבה בחיי אביו, אני איני עושה כן, אלא עד דאינון דקיקין תחת כורסיא

---

[40] From a Kurdistan manuscript, cited in *Torah Shelemah*, Vol. 8, p. 22, n. 99.
[41] *Tanḥuma Buber* (בהעלותך 23); *Torah Shelemah*, Vol. 8, p. 30, n. 135. The Gemara (*Sotah* 11b) cites R. Eliezer's remark: "בפרך, 'with rigor,' means בפה רך, 'by sweet-talking,'" but does not explain the play on words. Rashi, however, comments on this *gemara*, "They drew them along with words and pay, until they were accustomed to labor."
[42] Cf. *Torah Shelemah*, Vol. 8, p. 22, n. 99 and p. 30, n. 136; Ginzberg, *op. cit.*, Vol. 5, p. 391, n. 6.

דאמהון, אנא מחינא להון, הדא הוא דכתיב הבה נתחכמה לו, ניהוי חכימין יתיר מן קדמוי, מיד כל הבן הילוד היאורה תשליכוהו. "R. Berechiah said in the name of R. Levi: Cursed be the wicked who contrive dark counsel against Israel, each one boasting: 'My counsel is better than thine.' Esau said: 'Cain was a fool, for he slew his brother Abel while his father was still alive. Did not Cain know that his father would be fruitful and multiply and would beget Seth? I shall not do so. When **the days of mourning for my father are at hand, I will slay my brother Jacob** (Gen. 27:41) and inherit his portion.' Pharaoh said: 'Esau was a fool in saying, **Let the days of mourning for my father be at hand**. Did he not know that while his father was alive, his brother Jacob would be fruitful and would multiply? I shall not do so. While they are yet small and frail, under the very birth-stools of their mothers, I shall smite the children of Israel.' So in saying '**Let us deal wisely**' (Ex. 1:10) Pharaoh meant: 'Let us be smarter than those who preceded us.' Immediately [Pharaoh charged all his people]: **Every son that is born ye shall cast into the river**."[43] It is hard to view this *midrash* as illustrating the return of the motif of dealing wisely to its original location. In Scriptures, according to our conjecture (cf. p. 14), this motif was originally associated with the instruction given the midwives to put the sons to death in secret; whereas the element of dealing wisely in the *midrash*—"*While they are yet small and frail, under the very birth-stools of their mothers*"—is appropriate to the murder of the newborns in general. Moreover, from the very mention of "**Every son that is born ye shall cast into the river**" we see that the second murder decree is foremost in the consciousness of the *midrash*. This decree, in Scripture itself, is actually characterized by foregoing the element of deviousness that went along with the first murder decree. Note that the main thrust of "dealing wisely" in this *midrash* is not directed at the Children of Israel, but rather at the haters of Israel who came before Pharaoh: "*Let us be smarter than those who preceded us.*"

Another *midrash*, which interprets the idea of dealing wisely as directed specifically against the Holy One, blessed be He, the Redeemer of Israel, also associates dealing wisely with throwing the sons into the Nile: הבה נתחכמה לו, להם מיבעי ליה, א״ר חמא בר׳ חנינא באו ונחכם למושיען של ישראל במה נדונם, נדונם באש כתיב (יש׳ סו, טו) כי הנה ה׳ באש יבא וכתיב (שם שם, טז) כי באש ה׳ נשפט וגו׳, בחרב כתיב ובחרבו את כל בשר, אלא בואו ונדונם במים, שכבר נשבע הקב״ה שאינו מביא מבול לעולם שנאמר (שם נד, ט) כי מי נח וגו׳, והן אינן יודעין שעל כל העולם כולו אינו מביא, אבל על אומה אחת הוא מביא, אי נמי הוא אינו מביא אבל הן באין ונופלין בתוכו וכה״א (שמ׳ יד, כז) ומצרים נסים לקראתו. "**Come let us deal wisely with him**—It should have said, 'with *them*.' R. Ḥama b. Ḥanina said:

---

[43] *Midrash Tehillim* 2.4; *Torah Shelemah*, Vol. 8, p. 23, n. 100.

[Pharaoh meant,] Come and let us outwit the Savior of Israel. With what shall we afflict them? If we afflict them with fire, it is written, 'For, behold, the Lord will come with fire,' (Isaiah 66:15), and it continues, 'For by fire will the Lord plead' (ibid. 16). [If we afflict them] with the sword, it is written, 'and by His sword with all flesh' (ibid.). But come and let us afflict them with water, because the Holy One, blessed by He, has already sworn that he will not bring a flood upon the world; as it is said, 'For this is as the waters of Noah unto me' (Is. 54:9). They were unaware, however, that although He would not bring a flood upon the whole world, He would bring it upon one people; or alternatively, He would not bring [the flood], but they would go and fall into it. Thus it says, 'And the Egyptians fled towards it' (Ex. 14:27)."[44] This *midrash* also answers the question why the murder was done by throwing the newborns into the Nile (cf. p. 107).

Thus we see that there is much variety in the way the motif of dealing wisely is handled in the *midrash*. This variety applies to the content (the way the Egyptians dealt wisely), to the object against whom this contriving was directed (be it Israel or the Holy One, blessed be He), and to the component of the narrative with which it is interwoven (the enslavement or the murder decrees). This wealth of treatment of the subject emerges from that which is lacking: the *midrash* completes and illumines an element that was shrouded in shadow in the biblical narrative.

Targum Yerushalmi takes a different approach, rendering the text as: איהון כדון נחיעט עליהון בהלין דינין נוערא יתהון. "*Let us take counsel regarding them, how we shall reduce their numbers.*" The problematic absence of any wile is solved by the Targum by rendering this idea as "let us take counsel." Compare this to the Neophyti Targum: איתון ונסב עליהון עצן בישן. "*Come let us take evil counsel against them.*"[45] Also see *Sekel Tob*, which presents a sort of hybrid, preserving the motif of dealing wisely along with that of taking counsel: אמר לעמו תנו עצה נתחכמה לו לעם בני ישראל. "*He said to his people: Advise us, how shall we deal wisely with this people, the children of Israel?*"

Rashi interprets Exodus 1:10 in the manner of Targum Yerushalmi: "*Let us deal wisely with them (more literally, with him)—i.e., with the people. Let us consider wisely what to do with them.*" Also see Biblical Antiquities, p. 37, above.

LEST THEY MULTIPLY AND THE ENSLAVEMENT

Also Jewish legends had difficulty understanding the connection between the fear lest the people multiply and the means used against them:

---

[44] *Sotah* 11a; *Torah Shelemah*, Vol. 8, p. 23, n. 102.

[45] The translation, עצן בישן, was probably influenced by the root עצ׳, meaning to oppress.

hard labor. *Exodus Rabbah* I.12 tries to explain this connection: תחלה גזר וצוה לנוגשים שיהיו דוחקים בהם כדי שיהיו עושין סכום שלהם ושלא יהיו ישנים בבתיהם, והוא חשב למעטן מפריה ורביה. אמר מתוך זה אינן מולידין. אמרו להם הנוגשים אם אתם הולכין לישן בבתיכם עד שאנחנו משלחים אחריכם בבקר היום הולך לשעה לשתים ואין אתם משלימין הסכום שלכם. והנגשים אצים לאמר כלו מעשיכם [דבר יום ביומו] (שמ׳ ה, יג) והיו ישנים על הארץ. אמר האלהים אני אמרתי לאברהם אביהם שאני מרבה את בניו ככוכבים, שנאמר (בר׳ כב, יז) כי ברך אברכך [והרבה ארבה את זרעך ככוכבי השמים] ואתם מתחכמים להם שלא ירבו נראה אי זה דבר עומד שלי או שלכם מיד וכאשר יענו אתו כן ירבה וכן יפרץ (א, יב). "At first, he made a decree commanding the taskmasters to insist upon their making the prescribed number of bricks and commanded that they should not be allowed to sleep in their homes, thinking thereby to limit their natural increase, saying to himself, 'This way they will not bear children.' The taskmasters said to them, 'If you go home to sleep, by the time we send for you in the morning, the day will have advanced an hour or two and you will not be able to complete your quota.' **And the taskmasters hasted them, saying, Fulfil your works, [your daily tasks]** *(Ex. 5:13). So they used to sleep on the ground. Whereupon God said: 'I promised Abraham their father that I would multiply his children like the stars, as it is written:* **That in blessing I will bless thee, [and in multiplying I will multiply thy seed as the stars of the heaven]** *(Gen. 22:17), and now you are cunningly planning that they not increase. Well, we shall see whose word shall prevail, yours or Mine.' At once we are told:* **But the more they afflicted them, the more they multiplied and grew** *(Ex. 1:12).*"[46] Above, in note 23 of Chapter 1, we considered the possibility that the motif of dealing wisely was originally formed due to the difficulty in understanding the enslavement as a means of annihilation. This internal connection can also be seen in the present homily in the formulation, "and now you are cunningly planning." One cannot say definitively whether the difficulty in understanding the enslavement gave rise to the motif of dealing wisely or whether, inversely, the difficulty in understanding the idea of dealing wisely gave rise to the way in which the enslavement is presented here.

In *Midrash Abkir*, cited in *Yalkut Shimoni*, n. 163, we read: ובכל עבדה בשדה, וכי בשד׳ היו עובדין ולא בעיר, אלא שנזרו עליהן אנשים ילינו בשדה והנשים בעיר כדי למעטן מפריה ורביה, ונשיהם היו מחממות להם חמין ומביאות להם כל מאכל ומשתה ומנחמות אותן ואומ׳ לעולם לא משתעבדין בנו, סוף שהק׳ גואל אותנו. ומתוך כך באין עליהן ופרין ורבין כו׳. "**And in all manner of service in the field**—*Could it have been that they were working in the fields and not in the city? Rather, it was decreed that the men should sleep in the field and the women in the city in order to reduce their being fruitful and multiplying. But the wives would prepare them hot dishes and bring their husbands all sorts of food*

---

[46] *Exodus Rabbah* I.12; *Torah Shelemah*, Vol. 8, p. 29, n. 129.

and drink and console them, saying, 'They shall not enslave us forever; in the end the Holy One will redeem us.' And during these times they would have intercourse and were fruitful and multiplied."[47] A similar legend is found in *Sotah* 11b and *Exodus Rabbah* I.12, where there are also other parallel versions. (In *Exodus Rabbah* the legend about the wives follows directly after the legend from *Exodus Rabbah* cited above, i.e., after "At first, he made a decree ... ")

In a Kurdistan manuscript[48] the homilist associates the reason for the plague of hordes of beasts[49] with the scriptural verse here: ובכל עבדה בשדה, שהיו אומרים להם הביאו לנו דובים ואריות מן היער עד שהיו הולכים לצוד אותם היו טורפים אותם. "**And in all manner of service in the field**—For they used to tell them, 'Bring us bears and lions from the forest,' so that by the time they went to hunt the animals, the animals would kill them." This legend originates from *Seder Eliyyahu Rabbah* (7)8: ערוב מפני מה בא עליהן, אמרו להן לישראל צאו והביאו לנו זאבים ואריות והכניסו לבית מלחמתינו ונעשה בהם קינגיאות כמה שאנו רוצים, כדי שיהו במדברות החיצונות ולא יכנסו בתוך בתיהן ויבואו זה על (זה) [זו] ויפרו וירבו. "Hordes of beasts—why did this plague come upon the Egyptians? Because they ordered the Israelites, 'Go out and get us wolves and lions and bring them into our arenas so that we can stage contests as we wish.' But the Egyptians' purpose was to get them off to the most distant parts of the desert, so that they could not readily return to their homes where they might couch with their wives and be fruitful and multiply."[50]

The above *midrash* bears an affinity to others which similarly exaggerate the severity of the bondage and reduce the distance between the enslavement and the murder decrees, as we have already noted in Philo. For example, in *Pirke Rabbi Eliezer* we read: וישמע אלהים את נאקתם ר' עקיבא אומר סקלטורי [י״ג ספקלוטירי] פרעה היו מחנקים את ישראל בקירות הבית בין לובן הלבנים לפיכך היו צועקים מתוך הקידות והקב״ה שמע את נאקתם שנאמר וישמע אלהים את נאקתם ויזכור אלהים את בריתו. "**And God heard their groaning** (*Ex.* 2:24). R. Akiba said: Pharaoh's advisors [executioners] used to suffocate the Israelites within the walls of their homes, among the lime used on the bricks. Hence, they would cry out from within the walls and the Holy One, blessed be He, would hear their groaning, as it is written: *And*

---

[47] *Ibid.*, p. 35, n. 151.
[48] Cited in *Torah Shelemah*, Vol. 8, p. 35, n. 152.
[49] Later commentaries have understood ערוב to refer to hordes of beasts of prey. Loewenstamm (*Evolution*, p. 37, n. 38 in the Hebrew original; p. 91, n. 43 in the English translation) discusses the semantic evolution of this word and its original meaning, which apparently was some sort of bothersome insect. See Z. Ben-Ḥayyim's article, "מלת שוא יונית במילונים לעברית," *Leshonenu* 50 (1986), pp. 119–121, for an interesting correction to Loewenstamm's remark.
[50] See Kasher's remark.

God heard their groaning, and god remembered his covenant (Ex. 2:24)."[51]

This development is probably due not only to the obvious aggadic trend towards hyperbole and the desire to make the enslavement more closely related to the purpose it purported to serve, but also to the proximity in Scripture of the enslavement to the murder decrees. This can be seen from the legends that transfer the murder of the sons from the next two decrees and interweave it with the enslavement. For example, see the *Mekilta of R. Simeon b. Yoḥai*, Exodus, p. 1: ומה ת״ל ראה ראיתי שני פעמים. מאחר שהיו משקיעין את בניהם במים היו חוזר׳ וכובשים אותן בבנין. "What does the Torah seek to teach us by the emphatic 'I have surely seen' (Ex. 3:7)? After drowning their sons in water, they also immured them [the babes] in the construction work."[52] Compare the *piyyut* of Yannai, which balances the enslavement against the murder decree: שמו למולידים תחת אבנים—עוד ליאור השליכו וולדי בנים. "They did in the begetters under stones—while casting newborn sons into the Nile."[53]

Midrash ha-Gadol attempts to explain the narrative in a way which is closer to the plain sense of the text: בנוהג שבעולם שכל זמן שמשעבדין באדם הוא תושש וזרע מתמעט אבל כאן כן ירבה וכן יפרוץ. "Generally, when a person is enslaved he becomes weakened and his seed decreases; but here the more they multiplied and grew."[54] Compare this to Abarbanel: "Scriptures tells us that their dealing wisely was 'to afflict them with their burdens' so that, suffering many hardships, they would not have time to be fruitful and multiply."

Deuteronomy Rabbah combines both approaches:[55] א״ר יהושע מלמד שחזרו מצריים על כל האומניות לראות איזה אומנות ממעטת מפריה ורביה ולא מצאו אלא מלאכת חרישה... אעפ״כ היו נכנסין לבתיהם וישים בבתיהם ונזקקין לפריה ורביה, אמרו המצריים כמו שלא גזרו כלום, אלא בכל מקום שעשין מלאכתן שם יהו ישראל ישנים וכך עשו. "R. Joshua said, this teaches us that the Egyptians reviewed all the crafts, to see which craft reduces natural increase, and they found that the most effective was plowing, ... Nevertheless, they used to return to their homes and sleep there and occupy themselves with being fruitful and multiplying. The Egyptians said to themselves, 'It is as if we had not passed any decree'; so they insisted that wherever the Israelites worked, there they should sleep. And so they did."[56]

---

[51] Chapter 48.
[52] Also cf. Ginzberg, *op. cit.*, Vol. 5, p. 392, notes 9, 10; *Torah Shelemah*, Vol. 8, p. 27, n. 123; *ibid.*, p. 30, n. 136 of the commentary; *ibid.*, p. 106, n. 195.
[53] *Kerobah* for the first day of Passover. Zulai ed., 261; Rabinovitz ed., Vol. 2, p. 252.
[54] *Torah Shelemah*, Vol. 8, p. 28, n. 128.
[55] Lieberman ed., p. 15.
[56] *Torah Shelemah*, Vol. 8, p. 33, n. 146.

The following *midrash* is interesting for the light it sheds on the paradox that a slaveowner should want to have as many slaves as possible, yet Pharaoh desired to reduce their numbers. The *midrash* innocently recounts: דבר אחר, וירא בסבלתם (ב, יא) ראה שאין להם מנוחה, הלך ואמר לפרעה מי שיש לו עבד אם אינו נח יום אחד אינו מת, ואלו עבדיך הם אם אתה מרויח להם יום אחד בשבוע אינם מתים. אמר לו לך ועשה להם במו שאמרת. הלך ועשה להם משה כך ותקן להם את השבת לנוח. "**And he looked upon their burdens** *(Ex. 2:11)—Another interpretation: He saw that they had no rest, so he went to Pharaoh and said: 'If one has a slave and he does not rest one day a week, will he not die? But these are your slaves, and if you give them one day of rest a week, they will not die.' Pharaoh replied: 'Go and do with them as you say.' Moses did so, and ordained for them the Sabbath day for rest.*"[57] The homilist's concern about relating the Sabbath to the background of enslavement made him forget that the king of Egypt desired precisely to kill off his slaves.

A different approach is taken by David ha-Nagid. He naively separates the enslavement from the desire to annihilate the people and thus restores the motif to its former place. "*The wicked Pharaoh enslaved them and afflicted them more than the four kingdoms [that oppressed the Jews]; for, after enslaving them with hard labor, he then wished to kill them off and wipe out their memory, as it is said:* **And the king of Egypt spake to the Hebrew midwives.**"[58]

Lest They Multiply and Murder of the Sons

Just as the aggadah had difficulty understanding how imposing hard labor on the Hebrews related to the fear lest they multiply, so too it had difficulty understanding exactly how murdering the newborn sons would serve as a means for the Egyptians to accomplish their malicious ends. For example, we read in *Seder Eliyyahu Rabbah* (7)8: ועם בת הוא וחיה, זו עיצה טובה שגזרו עלינו, אילו אמרו, אם בת היא והמן אותה ואם בן הוא וחי, כבר נתמעטו ישראל באותה שעה. דרכו של איש שישא עשר נשים ויהיו לו בנים נימולין. ואין דרכה של אשה שתינשא אפילו לשני בני אדם. "**If it be a daughter, then she shall live** *(Ex. 1:16). This was a fortunate plan that they decreed upon us, for if they had said: 'If it be a daughter, then ye shall kill her; and if it be a son, then he shall live,' the number of Israelites would have decreased immediately. It is the way of man to marry ten wives and have his sons circumcised. But it is not the way of woman to marry even as many as two men.*"[59] *Midrash Tehillim* 2.4, cited above (p. 86), works Pharaoh

---
[57] *Exodus Rabbah* I.28; Ginzberg, *op. cit.*, Vol. 5, p. 405, n. 72; *Torah Shelemah*, Vol. 8, p. 75, n. 93.
[58] *Midrash R. David*, p. 10.
[59] *Torah Shelemah*, Vol. 8, p. 41, n. 177.

into its homily: המן אמר שוטה היה פרעה שאמר כל הבן הילוד וגו׳ וכול הבת תחיון, ולא היה יודע שהבנות נישאות לאחרים, והן פרות ורבות. "Haman said: 'Pharaoh was a fool when he charged all his people, saying: Every son that is born ye shall cast into the river, and every daughter ye shall save alive. Did he not know that the daughters would marry others, would be fruitful, and would multiply?'"

In contrast to the above *midrashim*, which view Pharaoh's letting the daughters live as a sign of his folly, other *midrashim* view this as further proof of the Egyptians' wickedness: וכל הבת תחיון, וכי מה צורך היה לפרעה לקיים הנקבות, אלא כך היו אומרים נמית הזכרים ונקח הנקבות לנשים לפי שהיו המצריים שטופי זמה. "And every daughter ye shall save alive— What need did Pharaoh have to save the girls? What they said in fact was: 'Let us kill the males so that we may take unto ourselves the females for wives,' for the Egyptians were steeped in immorality."[60] This interpretation allows the idea of attacking the male children to be separated from the idea of reducing the Hebrews' numbers. Note what is said in Biblical Antiquities on the subject: "*Let us kill their males, and we will keep their females so that we may give them to our own men as wives. And whoever is born from them will be a slave and will serve us.*"[61] Also in *Sefer Yeraḥmiel* (p. 104) we read: "*We shall slay the males that they may not increase, and allow the females to live to be our servants and our wives, and the males that we beget from them shall be our slaves.*"[62]

THE HEBREW MIDWIVES

The homiletical tradition which holds that the midwives were Egyptian (which in our opinion is the plain sense of the text) can be found in the *Midrash*, but in quite a limited fashion. This tradition is far less evident than the one which views the midwives as Hebrews. Recall that, according to Samuel David Luzzatto, this view appears in the Septuagint, the Vulgate, and Josephus. To this list Ginzberg[63] adds *Imrei No'am* and *Midrash Tadshe* 21:[64] כ״ב נשים ישרות גדולות בצדקות היו בישראל כו' ועוד יש גיורות מן הגוים כי במילדות פועה ושפרה נאמר [המצריות], ותיראן המילדות את האלהים. "There were twenty-two upright and greatly righteous women in Israel, ... and

---
[60] *Exodus Rabbah* I.18; *Torah Shelemah*, Vol. 8, p. 49, n. 214.
[61] Biblical Antiquities 9.1; Charlesworth, p. 315.
[62] Cf. Ginzberg, *op. cit.*, Vol. 5, p. 393, n. 14. Also compare this to Wellhausen's much later midrashic interpretation, referring to Exodus 1: "Wo der Versuch, Israel zu entnationalisieren, dargestellt wird als Versuch es zum Weibe zu machen" (*Der Text der Bücher Samuelis*, p. 172, n. 1). This is an instructive remark, indicating how little understood the murder of the sons was by commentators not yet familiar with Gressman's interpretation.
[63] *op. cit.*, Vol. 5, p. 393, n. 17.
[64] *Bet ha-Midrash*, Vol. 3, pp. 190–191.

also converts from among the gentiles, ... It is said of the (Egyptian) midwives Puah and Shiphrah, **'but the midwives feared God.'**"[65]

The trend towards separating the story of the midwives, which originally served to introduce the birth of the savior (cf. p. 13, above), from the birth of Moses, continues in the *Midrash*. This occurs in the numerous *midrashim* that identify Shiphrah and Puah with Yocheved and Miriam, according to the prevailing trend in the *aggadah*, and especially in legends of the Sages that attempt to make specific that which is oblique.[66] Of note in the development of this tradition is the *midrash* in *Sifre* where, taking the Jewish origin of the midwives as a certainty, they are compared with Ruth the non-Jew: ומה אם מי שהיתה מן העם ש׳ בו (מל״א יא, ב) לא תבואו בהם והם לא יבואו בכם על שקירבה את עצמה כך קירבה המקום, ישראל שעושים את התורה עאכ״ו. ואם תאמר בישראל לא היה כן והרי כבר נאמר ויאמר מלך מצרים למילדות העבריות וגו׳ שפרה זו יוכבד פועה זו מרים. *"If it is true of a woman who belonged to the nation of whom it is said,* **'Ye shall not go in to them, neither shall they come in unto you'** *(I Kings 11:2), that for bringing herself close, the Omnipresent brought her close; then all the more so does it hold for Israel, who obey the Torah. And should you claim that such never happened in Israel, remember that it is written:* **And the king of Egypt spake to the Hebrew midwives. Shiphrah was Yocheved and Puah was Miriam."**[67] Apparently in *Midrash ha-Gadol* the homilist's sureness that the midwives were Hebrews led him to choose precisely this verse to juxtapose with R. Meir's remarks from the *Gemara*, *Abodah Zarah* 26a: נכרית לא תיילד את בת ישראל מפני שחשודין על שפיכות דמים. *"A heathen woman may not act as midwife to an Israelite woman because heathens are suspected of murder."*[68] The mother of the redeemer, whose son the midwife was supposed to rescue, herself becomes the midwife and rescues others. Indeed, compare *Exodus Rabbah* I.25: ותקח האשה את הילד ותציקהו. באותה שעה נתן לה הקב״ה מקצת שכרה. היא

---
[65] Also cf. *Torah Shelemah*, Vol. 8, p. 38, n. 166. Ginzberg (*op. cit.*) also cites Philo, *Quis Rerum Divinarum Heres*, 26, and notes that Philo calls them "midwives of the Egyptians"; but in the passage under discussion, it says μαίας Ἑβραίων, as in the Septuagint's rendition, μαίαις τῶν Ἑβραίων. We could not find the formulation cited by Ginzberg even in the variant readings. Ginzberg's Hebrew translator adds to the original that "Philo generally speaks of these two women as being 'midwives of the Egyptians.' " We have not, however, been able to find the source for this remark.

[66] Cf. Heinemann, דרכי האגדה, p. 28. The *aggadah*, in its trend against anonymity, identifies anonymous figures, whose names were not given in Scripture, with famous individuals. For example, the "man of Benjamin" who fled out of the army (I Samuel 4:12–17) is identified in *Midrash Samuel* 11.1 (p. 78) as Saul. Alternatively, as in the case of Shiphrah and Puah being identified as Yocheved and Miriam, an unknown name is identified with a figure of renown.

[67] *Sifre* (בהעלותך 78); Ginzberg, *op. cit.*, Vol. 5, p. 393, n. 17; *Torah Shelemah*, Vol. 8, p. 37, n. 158.

[68] *Torah Shelemah*, Vol. 8, p. 36, n. 156.

היתה מחיה את הילדים, אף הקב"ה החזיר לה בנה ונתן לה שכרה. "**And the woman took the child and nursed it.** *It was then that God granted her part of her reward, for because she helped to keep other children alive, God restored her own child unto her and gave her a reward.*"

Another indication that the sensitivity to the connection between the instruction to the midwives and the birth of Moses had been lost may be seen in the legends that associate the instruction with Aaron: ולא שקטתי מגזירה שניה אם בן הוא והמתן אותו, והעמיד הקב"ה גואל זה אהרן על שם ההריון. "**Neither was I quiet** *(Job 3:26) on account of the second decree,* **If it be a son, then ye shall kill him**; *but the Holy One, blessed be He, produced a redeemer, namely Aaron* (אהרון), *after the pregnancy* (הריון)."[69]

Few *midrashim* draw a connection between the birth of Moses and the instruction to the midwives. In *Tanḥuma Buber* (ויקהל 5) we read: מה כתיב (ויקרא) [ויאמר] מלך מצרים למילדות, מה אמר להן, וראיתן על האבנים, למה עשה כן, אלא שהיו האיסטרולוגין אומרים להן ביום הזה גואל של ישראל נולד, ואין אנו יודעים אם מצרי ואם לאו, באותה שעה כינס כל המצרים ואמר להם השאילו לי בניכם יום אחד, שנאמר כל הבן הילוד, של ישראל אין כתיב כאן, אלא כל הבן, בין ישראל ובין מצרי. "*Why is it written:* **And the king of Egypt (called for) [spake to] the midwives?** *What did he say to them?* '**And see them upon the stools,** ...' *Why did he do so? Because his astrologers had said:* '*Today Israel's redeemer has been born, but we do not know whether he is an Egyptian or not.*' *At that moment he assembled all the Egyptians and said to them:* '*Lend me your sons for one day.*' *For it is said:* '**Every son that is born ye shall cast into the river**' *without specifying 'of the Israelites'; i.e., every son, whether Israelite or Egyptian.*" Attention should be paid to the special sequence of events here—the tidings of the savior's birth come after the instruction to the midwives—contradicting the natural sequence. In so ordering the narrative, despite the fact that the legend mentions the instruction to the midwives, it succeeds in associating the annunciation primarily with the instruction to cast the sons into the Nile. Even the words "at that moment," which introduce the sentence which includes the decree to cast the sons into the Nile, blurs the perception of the instruction to the midwives as the primary response to the annunciation, and thus diverges from the time sequence in the Bible, where the instruction to cast the sons into the Nile follows the instruction to the midwives to kill the sons at birth (cf. Josephus, p. 55 ff.). In the introduction to this *midrash*, it is assumed that the midwives

---

[69] *Exodus Rabbah* XXVI.1, Vilna ed.; *Torah Shelemah*, Vol. 8, p. 33, n. 145; also cf. *Dibre Yeme Moshe Rabbenu*; *Torah Shelemah*, Vol. 8, p. 54, n. 11. In the *midrashim* about the midwives Aptowitzer and, following him, also Joseph Heinemann, imagine there to be echoes of anti-Hasmonean polemics. This matter, however, goes beyond the scope of our study.

are Yocheved and Miriam. Thus the *midrash* distances the midwives as far as possible from their Egyptian origins, which origins provide the explanation of why the king of Egypt could expect them to collaborate with him. Identifying them as Yocheved and her daughter leads to the paradoxical structure in which the midwife is expected to put her very own son to death. *Sirāj al-'uqūl*[70] goes even further and includes the midwives but does not mention the instruction to them: ויאמר מלך מצרים למילדת, ומה אמר להם, אלא בשעה שנתעברה אמו של משה באותו הלילה חלם פרעה שנפלו כוכבי מצרים מן השמים וכנס אחד מישראל לחיקו והשליכן לים, ומיד אמר פרעה לחרטמי מצרים ונבהלו ועשו באסטגנינותם ואמרו זה בן במעי אמו ואינו נלקה אלא במים. והם לא ידעו שעל מי מריבה הוא נידון ומיד גזר פרעה כל הבן הילוד היארה תשליכוהו. "**And the king of Egypt spake to the midwives**—*What did he say to them? On the very night that Moses' mother conceived, Pharaoh dreamed that the stars of Egypt had fallen from the heavens, and that one of the Israelites had gathered them in his arms and cast them into the sea. Pharaoh told Egypt's magicians forthwith. The magicians were alarmed, and investigated with their astrology. Then they said: this son is already in his mother's womb, and he will not come to harm except by water. But they did not know that it was by the water of Meribah that he would be judged. So Pharaoh immediately ordered* **every son that is born ye shall cast into the river.**"[71] In this *midrash* the purpose of the instruction to the midwives is to prevent the birth of Moses, and therefore, as in Josephus' version, the *midrash* obscures the uniqueness of the instruction to the midwives—"**and see them upon the stools, if it be a son, then ye shall kill him**"—and combines it with the edict "**every son that is born ye shall cast into the river**," which in the biblical story is the only decree connected with the birth of Moses.

The Annunciation

As in Scripture, the above two *midrashim*—*Sirāj al-'uqūl* and *Tanḥuma Buber* (ויקהל 5)—mention the instruction to the midwives first; but, unlike Scripture, the reason they give for this instruction is the king's fear of the individual savior. The king's instruction to the midwives is intended to prevent the birth of this savior, although, according to the usual formulation in the typological pattern, the king's murder attempt is destined to fail and the savior is destined to be born despite the king's attempt to prevent his birth. Naturally the midrashic instruction to the

---

[70] Cited in *Torah Shelemah*, Vol. 8, p. 36, n. 155.

[71] The *midrash* is apparently addressing itself to the repetition of "and he said" in verses 15 and 16. Cf. *Torah Shelemah*, Vol. 8, p. 36, n. 155 of the commentary, citing Rashi's remarks on Esther 7:5: "**Then the king Ahasuerus answered** [lit. said], **and said unto Esther the queen**—Wherever we find 'and said' repeated twice, it is for no other purpose than to indicate a *midrash*."

midwives is associated with the edict to cast the sons into the Nile, whose failure leads to the birth of the hero; and this instruction to the midwives is not associated with the biblical instruction, "**If it be a son, then ye shall kill him**," whose failure in implementation does not affect the fate of Moses in any way (cf. p. 13, above). Thus the annunciation of the savior's birth, directed at a single individual alone, is the decisive factor that compelled the *Midrash* to associate the instruction to the midwives with the edict which in the Bible leads to the birth of the single individual.

Examining the evolution of the pattern is instructive. According to the approach advanced above (p. 12), the *aggadah* restored to the story the original motif of annunciation of the hero's birth, which in the biblical narrative had disappeared from the murder pattern (the story of the midwives); but since in the course of time the story of the midwives had lost its connection with the birth of the savior, when the annunciation—an original motif of the story—was restored, it brought in its wake the loss of the king's original response to the midwives ("**If it be a son, then ye shall kill him**").

Those *midrashim* that associate the annunciation with the instruction given the midwives without obscuring the singularity of that instruction (such as Targum Yerushalmi, *Lekaḥ Tob* 1:16, *Sekel Tob* 1:16, *Yalkut Shimoni* 164, and others) inherited the difficulty of the biblical text, namely that the midwives' refusal to comply with the decree actually has no bearing on the fate of Moses. However, due to the episodic nature of the *Midrash*, in that it relates to an isolated moment and does not present a narrative continuum, this difficulty is not felt as poignantly here as in the Bible.

The vast majority of the *midrashim* that begin with the annunciation resolve the tension between the motif which focusing on the individual and the story of the midwives (which is not related to that individual) in a very simple yet drastic manner: they make no mention whatsoever of the story of the midwives. For example, in *Sotah* 12b we read: "ראו שמושיען של ישראל במים הוא לוקה עמדו וגזרו כל הבן הילוד היאורה תשליכוהו. *They saw that Israel's savior would suffer misfortune through water; so they arose and decreed,* **Every son that is born ye shall cast into the river**." Also compare *Pirke Rabbi Eliezer* 48:[72] "*Prior to Moses' birth the magicians told Pharaoh that a son would be born who would take Israel out of Egypt; so Pharaoh thought to himself, 'Let them cast all the male newborns into the Nile, and this son will be cast into the water along with them, and then their prediction will come to naught,' as it is written,* **Every son that is born ye shall cast into the river**."

---

[72] *Torah Shelemah*, Vol. 8, p. 48, n. 212.

On Exodus 2:2 *Midrash ha-Gadol* writes: ותהר האשה ותלד בן, באותה הלילה שנתעברה ראה פרעה החלום. "**And the woman conceived, and bare a son**—*On the very night that she conceived, Pharaoh had a dream.*"[73]

R. David ha-Nagid separates the decrees. He associates the instruction to the midwives with Pharaoh's desire to annihilate the people: "*He wished to annihilate them and wipe out their males, as it is written,* **And the king of Egypt spake to the Hebrew midwives**." He explains the decree to throw the sons into the Nile, however, in terms of the fear of the individual savior: "*But when Pharaoh saw that he could not achieve his ends through the midwives, he invoked his entire people to exercise his governance over them, and ordered that they [his people] take every male son that would be born to the Israelites and throw him in the Nile. All this he did because his magicians had informed him that Israel's savior would be born in that year and that he would suffer misfortune by water; therefore it is said,* **And Pharaoh charged all his people,** . . ." Note that by saying "all this" R. David ha-Nagid nevertheless leans towards juxtaposing the reason given for the decree to throw the sons into the Nile with the instruction to the midwives. In terms of its literary genre, Midrash R. David ha-Nagid, although it bears the title Midrash, comes closer to biblical exegesis and differs from most other *midrashim* in the degree of continuity to which the author aspires. This quality of R. David ha-Nagid's *midrash* weakens its episodic nature and apparently led to its particular structure. (The most striking example of a cross between exegesis and *midrash* is provided by Rashi, to whose commentary we devote a separate chapter.)

Dibre Yeme Moshe Rabbenu also preserves the continuity of the narrative. The structure there (annunciation, instruction to the midwives, decree to throw the sons into the Nile, and the birth of Moses) suffers the drawback that the actions of the midwives bear no relationship to the fate of Moses, on whose account the decree was issued in the first place. However, as is characteristic of the author, he does not pay close attention to such details.

The *midrashim* that begin with the annunciation automatically provide an answer to the question of why the decree was directed only at the male children. Nevertheless, one should note the unusual combination of both approaches in *Lekah Tob* and *Sekel Tob*, which, by using the approach of question and answer, bring out the connection between the singularity of the decree concerning the male newborn and the annunciation:[74] וכל כך למה, לפי שראו איצטגניני פרעה שמושיען של ישראל עתיד להוולד באותו פרק, לפיכך גזר מיתה על הזכרים. "*And why was this done? Be-*

---

[73] Cf. the variants given in *Torah Shelemah*, Vol. 8, p. 47, n. 207.
[74] *Sekel Tob* 1:16; *Torah Shelemah*, Vol. 8, p. 41, n. 176.

cause *Pharaoh's magicians had seen that Israel's savior was destined to be born during that period, so he decreed death on the male children.*" However the text appends the gratuitous comment, ולפי שהיו מצריים שטופי זימה גזר ואם בת הוא וחיה. "*But since the Egyptians were imbued with wickedness, he ordered* **but if it be a daughter, then she shall live**."

In the beginning of this section (p. 95) we noted that the annunciation forces the *Midrash* to separate the story of the midwives from the instruction, "**If it be a son, then ye shall kill him**" and instead to associate the instruction to the midwives with the edict to cast the sons into the Nile. This leads to the paradox that restoring the ancient element of annunciation to the narrative actually forces the narrative to give up a different ancient element. The innovation introduced by restoring this ancient element is even more prominent in those *midrashim* that include the annunciation but completely omit the story of the midwives. Although in these works the legend retains the original motivation for murder of the sons—the fear that arises due to the annunciation—it associates the failure of the murder attempt with Moses' deliverance in the ark, a motif which is taken from a story pattern that orginally was not at all cognizant of the murder motif (cf. p. 12, above). In other words, the ark pattern appropriated the annunciation from its original setting—the story of the midwives—clearly because it is precisely the ark pattern that Scripture associates with Moses. As we noted above, casting the sons into the Nile provides the transitional link between the various patterns. The emphasis on the homicidal nature of this act originates in the murder pattern (the story of the midwives), whereas the specific choice of the river as the means of perpetrating the deed comes from the ark pattern.

The *midrashim* that include the annunciation also provide an answer to the problem that the motif of killing the male sons disappears from the story even though the enslavement continues. Recall that combining the episodic legend of the individual with the more extensive tradition of prolonged bondage created an element of tension between the various time settings of the narrative. We have already noted that this tension is felt primarily at the beginning and end points of the narrative units, and have seen how this tension manifests itself in the *aggadah*. We must add, noting after Loewenstamm,[75] that legends which include the annunciation are likely to alleviate this tension. Viewing the edict as resulting from the annunciation of the savior's birth—regardless of whether the legend thereby preserves the original structure or reconstructs it—inverts the relationship in the biblical account between the fate of the nation and the fate of the individual. In the legend the nation

---

[75] Loewenstamm, "Die Geburtsgeschichte Moses."

suffers on account of the individual, whereas in the Bible the individual suffers on account of the nation. Restoring the edict to its original cause—the individual savior—separates its setting in time from that of the enslavement (which bears no causal relationship with the individual savior) and makes it possible to sever the concurrence of the two motifs. Killing the newborns has its origins in the story of the individual, and therefore the length of time the edict applied is determined solely by what happens concerning the individual. The fate of the individual determined when the edict began, as we read in *Midrash ha-Gadol*: ולא יכלה עוד הצפינו, כששלמו תשעה חדשים מליל חלומו שלפרעה יצאו לחפש בכל המקומת. "**She could not longer hide him**—*When a full nine months had passed since the night of Pharaoh's dream, they set out to search everywhere.*" A similar explanation is given in *Sotah* 12a, which connects the timing of the edict's initiation with the mistake made by the Egyptians (see p. 108). Likewise, in *Sotah* 12b, the individual determined when the edict ceased being carried out: ותאמר מילדי העברים זה וכו׳ א״ר יוחנן מלמד שנתבבאה שלא מדעתה זה נופל ואין אחר נופל. "**Of the Hebrews' children is this** ... *R. Joḥanan said, it teaches that she unwittingly prophesied that this one will fall [into the river] but no other will fall (with him).*"[76] ראו שמושיען של ישראל במים הוא לוקה עמדו וגזרו כל הבן הילוד היאורה תשליכוהו כיון דשדיוה למשה אמרו תו לא חזינן כי ההוא סימנא, בטלי לגזירתייהו. ... *They saw that Israel's savior would suffer misfortune through water; so they arose and decreed,* **Every son that is born ye shall cast into the river.** *After Moses had been thrown [into the water], they said, 'We no longer see the sign'; thereupon the decree was rescinded.*" Likewise, in *Exodus Rabbah* I.21 we read: ולמה השליכתו ביאור שיהו חושבים האצטגנינין שכבר הושלך במים ואל יחפש אחריו. "*Why did she cast him into the river? So that the astrologers might think that he had already been cast into the water, and would not search for him.*" Compare this with *Dibre Yeme Moshe Rabbenu*:[77] וקהת אבי אביו קרא לו אבינדור כי בעבורו גדר אלהים פרץ בית יעקב ולא יספו להטיל אותם למים. "*Kohath, his father's father, called him Abigdor because for his sake God sealed (גדר) the breach of the house of Jacob and they ceased casting them into the water.*"

Severance from the enslavement is even greater in the *midrashim* that infer from the verse "**And Pharaoh charged all his people**" that he issued the decree even against his own people (as in *Sotah* 12a). *Tanḥuma Buber* (ויקהל 5) provides another example: "*Because his astrologers had said: 'Today Israel's redeemer has been born, but we do not know whether he is an Egyptian or not.' At that moment he assembled all the Egyptians and said to them: 'Lend me your sons for one*

---

[76] According to Rashi's commentary, the reason for this was that the decree to drown the males was rescinded on that very day.

[77] *Torah Shelemah*, Vol. 8, p. 54, n. 11.

day.' For it is said: '**Every son that is born ye shall cast into the river**' without specifying 'of the Israelites'; i.e., every son, whether Israelite or Egyptian." In these *midrashim* the death of the newborns is no longer connected with the desire to wipe out the Israelites, or with fear of them, or even with hostility towards them; rather, it is directed solely against the individual. As Loewenstamm notes,[78] the *Tanḥuma* could do without the rescission of the decree, since from the very outset it was restricted to a specific day. A parallel motif appears in *Exodus Rabbah*,[79] except that here it is not associated with the birth itself, but with the conception: גואל ישראל נתעברה בו אמו, ואין אנו יודעים אם מישראל הוא או מצרי הוא. "Pharaoh's astrologers told him, 'The mother of Israel's savior is already pregnant with him, but we do not know whether he is an Israelite or an Egyptian.'" Therefore Pharaoh extended the decree: השאילו לי בניכם לט׳ חדשים שאשליכם ליאור. "'Lend me your children for nine months that I may cast them in the river.'" According to this interpretation the Egyptian sons as well were thrown into the river over a prolonged period. Perhaps this is the reason the *midrash* adds there, ולא רצו לקבל ממנו. אמרו לו בן מצרי לא יגאל אותן אלא מן העברים. "But they would not agree, saying: 'An Egyptian son would not redeem them; he must be a Hebrew.'"[80] This approach is opposed by the Septuagint, the Samaritan Targum, Targum Onkelos, and Targum Yerushalmi, and the Neophyti Targum, all of which render the verse as "born to the Jews." A similar wording is found in Josephus (*Antiquities*) and in Biblical Antiquities (cf. p. 47, above). It seems that we may infer from the Septuagint's opposition that this homily should be ascribed an earlier date (cf. our remark above, p. 79, on rendering חדש, "new," as ἕτερος). *Sekel Tob* 1:22 attempts to arrive at a compromise solution: ויצו פרעה לכל עמו, שגור גם על המצרים. לאמר. מאי לאמר כיון שיאמרו להם מצריים הללו שכיני ישראל, שתינוק נולד בבית ישראל, יהי׳ כל עמו מסייעין אותן ליטול התינוק. כל הבן הילוד, בן ישראלי. "**And Pharaoh charged all his people**—*he also decreed on the Egyptians*. **Saying**—*why does the text specify 'saying'? So that the Egyptians, who were the Israelites' neighbors, would say to them that a baby had been*

---

[78] "Die Geburtsgeschichte Moses," p. 202.
[79] *Exodus Rabbah* I.18; *Torah Shelemah*, Vol. 8, p. 46, n. 202; also see our remark in Chapter 2 note 2 with regard to the conjectured reading in Jubilees.
[80] On the various approaches to calculating how long the edict applied, cf. Ginzberg, *op. cit.*, Vol. 5, p. 399, n. 56. For Ginzberg's suggestion that the text in Jubilees should read "until the day you were cast" instead of "until the day you were born," see our section on Jubilees, n. 2. Also cf. Abarbanel's approach in citing legends regarding the annunciation (in his commentary on Exodus). He cuts off his citation of the *midrash* from *Pirke Rabbi Eliezer* (cited above, p. 82) after the passage, "henceforth do not cast the sons who are born into the Nile," apparently because he could not accept the inverted order of events, in which the enslavement came later.

born in an Israelite house, and thus all his people would help him seize the baby. **Every son that is born**—*this refers to Israelite sons.*"[81]

Annunciation of the savior's birth appears in the sources in a wide variety of forms. Sometimes it is ascribed to the king's astrologers or magicians, i.e., to his advisors, as in *Antiquities* 2.205, *Pirke Rabbi Eliezer* 48,[82] *Exodus Rabbah* I.18,[83] and *Asatir* 8. Sometimes Pharaoh has the dream, but his astrologers interpret it; as in Targum Yerushalmi on Exodus 1:15, *Sirāj al-'uqūl*,[84] and *Dibre Yeme Moshe Rabbenu*.[85] Occasionally the annunciation is attributed to Amram, as in *Antiquities* 2.215, or to Miriam, as in *Megillah* 14a,[86] *Dibre Yeme Moshe Rabbenu*,[87] and *Midrash ha-Gadol* 2:1.[88] This list is not exhaustive and may be supplemented by the references given below.

The content of the annunciation is delivered according to two patterns. The first includes only a prediction of what is destined to happen in the future; the second includes the initial appearance of an omen and its subsequent interpretation. Naturally those *midrashim* in which Pharaoh has a dream, and sometimes indirectly also those in which the magicians perceive an omen which they do not know how to interpret, belong to the second pattern. (Cf. pp. 106ff., below.)

The visions themselves are also varied. In Targum Yerushalmi 1:15 we read: ואמר פרעה דמך הוה חמי בחילמי והא כל ארעא דמצרים קיימא בכף מודנא חדא וטליא בר אימרתא בכף מודנא חדא והות כרעא כף מודנא דטליא בגוה. "*And Pharaoh said: I was sleeping and in my dream I saw that all the land of Egypt hung in one scale, and a lamb in the other scale; and the side with the lamb outweighed the opposite scale.*" According to *Sirāj al-'uqūl*,[89] "*On the very night that Moses' mother conceived, Pharaoh dreamed that the stars of Egypt had fallen from the heavens and that one of the Israelites had gathered them in his arms and cast them into the sea.*" In *Dibre Yeme Moshe Rabbenu*,[90] ופרעה חלם והנה . . . זקן אחד עמד לנגדו ובידו מאזנים ממאזני הסוחרים. ויקח האיש הזקן את המאזנים ויתלם לפני פרעה ויקח את כל זקני מצרים ושריה וכל גדוליה ויאסרם ויתנם יחד בכף מאזנים האחת, ואחרי כן לקח טלה חלב אחד ויתנהו בכף מאזנים השנית ויכרע הטלה את כולם. "*Pharaoh dreamed and behold . . . an*

---

[81] *Torah Shelemah*, Vol. 8, p. 46, n. 203. "In other words, he charged even his own people to help him carry out his decree to kill every newborn son of the children of Israel," as Kasher explains in his commentary, *ibid.*
[82] *Ibid.*, p. 48, n. 212.
[83] *Ibid.*, p. 46, n. 202; p. 47, n. 207; p. 41, n. 176.
[84] *Ibid.*, p. 36, n. 155.
[85] *Ibid.*, p. 49, n. 215.
[86] *Ibid.*, p. 61, n. 34.
[87] *Ibid.*, p. 54, n. 11.
[88] *Ibid.*, p. 50, n. 1.
[89] *Ibid.*, p. 36, n. 155.
[90] *Ibid.*, p. 49, n. 215.

old man was standing before him, holding a merchant's balance. The old man took the balance and hung it in front of Pharaoh. Then he took all the elders of Egypt, all her ministers and great men, and bound them together and placed them in one of the scales. Afterwards he took one suckling lamb and placed it in the other scale, and the lamb outweighed them all." In *Midrash ha-Gadol* 1:22 we read:[91] ראה פרעה הרשע בחלומו, רחל רבוצה וילדה שה, והיה רואה מאזניים תלויים בין הארץ לרקיע. ומביאין את השה ומניחין בכף מאזנים ומביאין כל כסף וזהב שלמצרים ומניחין בכף שניה והיתה מכרעת על כולם. ועדיין היו מביאין כלי זיין שלמצרים והיו מוסיפין על הכסף ועל הזהב והשה מכריע. "In his dream the wicked Pharaoh saw a ewe couching, and she bore a lamb. And he also saw a balance hanging between heaven and earth; and the lamb was brought and placed in one of the scales, and all the silver and gold of Egypt was brought and placed in the other scale, but the lamb outweighed it all. And even when they brought the Egyptians' weapons and added them to the silver and gold, still the lamb tipped the scales." The *Asatir* 8 says, "Israel's star had risen." The origin of the imagery found in these visions—an old man, scales, a ewe, and especially a lamb (compare the Revelation of John)—is interesting in its own right, although this is not the place to discuss it. However, it seems that there has been some borrowing of an existing pattern.

The annunciation motif grew on the soil provided by the universal faith in man's ability to discover the future by means of a dream or other omens. According to this outlook, an arcane order governs the universe, and everything, even the gods, is subject to this order. It is this order that determines the future, hidden from man's sight; but sometimes it is revealed to man through a dream or other sign, and sometimes man himself can disclose it by witchcraft or occult wisdom, primarily through the agency of witches, magicians, astrologers, and the like, whose art is to make such disclosures.[92] Clearly this motif did not originate in the Israelite faith; for the motif includes recognition of an occult system operating in the universe and of occult wisdom that can disclose this system—notions that can hardly be associated with monotheistic biblical faith. This characteristic of the annunciation is preserved to a certain extent in the *midrashim* that attribute the deliverance of the newborn to the astrologers' failure to identify the child or to their error[93] ("He shall suffer misfortune by water") and thus they remain within the realm of the magical.

It is interesting that Josephus, in contrast to the *Midrash*, actually

---

[91] Also cf. the variants which Margulies lists there, and *Torah Shelemah*, Vol. 8, p. 50, n. 215 of the commentary.

[92] In the *Asatir* 9, we read: "Palti [the magician] comprehended the secret of the book of omens."

[93] Cf. p. 106–108, below, on the astrologer's mistakes.

attributes Moses' deliverance directly to God. It is instructive that at the same times as the element of foreknowledge is transferred to Amram or Yocheved, the element of the dream is replaced by revelation and the word of God; God, who reveals the future to His prophet, takes the place of the occult that determines the future. This is already evident in *Antiquities*. In Josephus the annunciation appears doubly. The somber future is disclosed to the king by one of his astrologers, practicing his art as a person *"with considerable skill in accurately predicting the future"* (2.205). Amram, on the other hand, learns of the annunciation from the fact that *"God had compassion on him and, moved by his supplication, appeared to him in his sleep, ... and told him ... this child, whose birth has filled the Egyptians with such dread that they have condemned to destruction all the offspring of the Israelites, shall indeed be thine; he shall escape those who are watching to destroy him"* (2.212–215).

With respect to Miriam, in *Megillah* 14a we read:[94] ז' נביאות וכו' מרים דכ' (שמ' ט"ו, כ) אחות אהרון ולא אחות משה, אר"נ אמר רב שהיתה מתנבאה כשהיא אחות אהרן, ואומרת, עתידה אמי שתלד בן שיושיע את ישראל. " 'Seven prophetesses.' Who were these? ... Miriam, as it is written, **And Miriam the prophetess the sister of Aaron** *(Ex. 15:20)—the sister of Aaron and not the sister of Moses.*[95] *R. Naḥman said in the name of Rab: [She was called thus] because she prophesied when she was the sister of Aaron [only] and said: My mother is destined to bear a son who will save Israel."*

By and large in the *Midrash* the annunciation directly precedes the birth. The sources that place the annunciation before the birth usually associate it with the king's decree, **Every son that is born ye shall cast into the river**, because the realization of the danger foretold is intricately bound up with the failure of precisely this decree, as we have explained above. This is the case in *Antiquities*, the *Mekilta* on בשלח (Tractate *Shirata* 10, p. 151),[96] the *Mekilta* of R. Simeon b. Yoḥai (בשלח 15:20, p. 100; Miriam's prophecy), *Sanhedrin* 101b,[97] *Midrash ha-Gadol* 1:22, *Exodus Rabbah* I.18,[98] *Pirke Rabbi Eliezer* 48,[99] *Midrash ha-Gadol* 2:1,[100] *Sefer ha-Yashar*[101] *Dibre Yeme Moshe Rabbenu*,[102]

---

[94] *Torah Shelemah*, Vol. 8, p. 61, n. 34; also cf. the parallel versions listed there.

[95] According to Rashi's commentary, at the time of her prophecy, before Moses was born, she was identified as the sister of Aaron.

[96] Miriam's prophecy; *Torah Shelemah*, Vol. 8, p. 51, n. 1 of the commentary.

[97] *Ibid.*, p. 47, n. 207 of the commentary.

[98] *Torah Shelemah*, Vol. 8, p. 46, n. 202; p. 47, n. 207.

[99] *Ibid.*, p. 48, n. 212.

[100] Miriam's prophecy, *Ibid.*, p. 51, n. 1 of the commentary.

[101] Pages 286–287 (Balaam's counsel and Miriam's prophecy). Cf. also *Torah Shelemah*, Vol. 8, p. 51, n. 1 of the commentary.

[102] Miriam's prophecy, *Torah Shelemah*, p. 54, n. 11.

Midrash ha-Gadol on "**And the woman conceived,**"[103] and the *Ḥem'at ha-Ḥemdah* manuscript.[104]

Relatively few sources associate the annunciation with the instruction given the midwives. These sources have the advantage of providing a good explanation of why the decree was issued from the outset against the male children: **If it be a son, then ye shall kill him**. Examples are Targum Yerushalmi, which most likely was influenced by the fact that it adheres to the sequence of the biblical text, *Sirāj al-'uqūl*,[105] *Dibre Yeme Moshe Rabbenu*,[106] *Lekaḥ Tob* 1:16, and *Sekel Tob* 1:16.[107]

Some sources obscure the distinction between the two orders which Pharaoh issued—to the midwives and to all his people—as in *Tanḥuma* (ויקהל 4) and *Tanḥuma Buber* (ויקהל 5).[108] Also see *Dibre Yeme Moshe Rabbenu*.

Of course Miriam's prophecy appears before the birth, although the specific decree which it precedes is not always mentioned. (Indeed, the most likely association is with the edict to cast the sons into the Nile, which naturally concerns Miriam.) Illustrations are provided by *Megillah* 14a, *Sotah* 13a,[109] and Biblical Antiquities.

Aside from the literary pattern which places the annunciation prior to the birth, there is also a pattern which presents the annunciation twice, repeating it at the moment of birth itself. In these stories the content of the annunciation is that the savior has already been born. In all the *midrashim* of this type the first annunciation is associated with the edict to throw the sons into the Nile, for the reasons discussed above.[110] For example, consider *Pirke Rabbi Eliezer* 48,[111] and *Sotah* 12a: א״ר יוסי בר׳ חנינא אף על עמו גזר. "*R. Jose son of R. Ḥanina said: He imposed the same decree upon his own people.*" Rashi comments on this, "*R. Tanḥuma expounded that the day Moses was born the astrologers said, 'Today the savior of Israel has been born,' ...*"

Rashi's commentary on Exodus is unique in that it cites the annunciation before both of the king's decrees—the instruction to the midwives and the edict to throw the sons into the Nile. The second annunciation comes after the birth and is different in content from the first (cf. Rashi, below). The structure of the story in the *Asatir* is discussed later on.

---

[103] *Ibid.*, p. 56, n. 13.
[104] *Ibid.*, p. 56, n. 13 of the commentary.
[105] *Ibid.*, p. 36, n. 155.
[106] *Ibid.*, p. 49, n. 215.
[107] *Ibid.*, p. 41, n. 176.
[108] *Ibid.*, p. 46, n. 202.
[109] *Ibid.*, p. 61, n. 34; also cf. the variants listed there.
[110] We have not encountered a single example of a literary pattern which is only cognizant of the annunciation made at the time of birth.
[111] *Ibid.*, p. 48, n. 212.

ABRAHAM

The legends dealing with the annunciation of the birth of Moses, which we have described above, bear great affinity to the legends of the birth of Abraham, which include a similar annunciation motif. Actually, the Abraham legends should be viewed as a variation on the theme of the Moses legends. Therefore, a brief review of the parallel Abraham nativity legends ought to be included in our study of Moses nativity legends.

The legends of Abraham's childhood provide a typical example of the developmental stages outlined in the Introduction. They express the desire to complete the history of the hero's life from the very beginning, but unlike the legend of the birth of Moses, they did not work their way into the biblical text. Still, it is evident that these legends have been cast in typological forms. Therefore one should not be surprised to find that the legends of the birth of Abraham were cognizant of the annunciation cautioning the ruler of the land about the birth of the savior.[112] Although it is not a hard and fast rule, we may generally ascribe greater antiquity to the Moses legend; in other words, it was the Moses nativity story that influenced the Abraham legend. We assume this relationship between the Moses and Abraham traditions for the following reasons: firstly, the Moses nativity legend appears as far back as the Bible and other ancient sources. The earliest evidence of it is in *Jewish Antiquities* (and perhaps even in Jubilees, as mentioned above); moreover, most of the other sources on the Moses legend are more ancient than the sources on the Abraham legend, all of which are quite late. Of course, one cannot be sure that a late source does not contain an ancient *midrash*, but in the present case the ancient sources supplement the testimony of the later sources. These ancient sources include many legends on Abraham's youth, but the motif of prior annunciation is not among them. That the Abraham legends are dependent on the Moses legends is also indicated by the motif of mass murder which appears in several versions. This motif is not known in other folk literature, and presumably was created in Exodus under the influence of combining the legend of the individual with the tradition of the nation. Also there is no noticeable Christian influence.[113]

With respect to the vision, most versions of the Abraham legend simply note the fact that Nimrod saw signs in the stars. In *Ma'aseh Abraham* Version B[114] the vision is made more explicit: עמד כוכב אחד ממזרח ובלע ד' כוכבים לארבע רוחות השמים. *"One star came out of the East and*

---

[112] Ginzberg, Vol. 5 (*Abraham*), p. 209, n. 13; p. 212, n. 34; p. 216, n. 48.

[113] Cf. Ginzberg, Vol. 5 (*Abraham*), p. 209, n. 8. Nevertheless, see Seeligmann's remarks in "*Voraussetzungen*," p. 155, on Is. 29:22—who redeemed Abraham—as alluding to the above tradition.

[114] *Bet ha-Midrash*, Vol. 2, p. 119; also cf. the *midrash* cited in *Rabbenu Bahya*

swallowed *four stars to the North, South, East and West.*" A similar scene is described in the *Protevangelium of James* (cf. p. 172, below).

Aside from the usual formulation, "Prior to Abraham's birth,"[115] which introduces the annunciation before the birth, one also finds the annunciation at the very moment of Abraham's birth, similarly to Matthew.[116] The Moses legends, in contrast, are familiar with the annunciation at the time of the birth only as a secondary motif to its appearance prior to the birth.

In contrast to the Jesus nativity legend in Matthew 2, the Abraham legend retains the motif of the child's abandonment, which appears in most of the parallels in folk literature. Like the Moses story, although without the accompanying literary charm of the Exodus narrative, the Abraham legend attenuates the motif of abandonment, and his mother returns to the cave where she had left him.

In addition to Nimrod's attempts to hurt Abraham or his mother at the moment of birth, most of the Abraham legends add the famous story of Abraham being cast into the fiery furnace. One cannot assume, however, that this pattern was influenced by the dual structure of the Moses legend, for the tendency to redouble and even treble the motif of danger is not uncommon. For example, see the legends about Cyrus in Herodotus, Book I, 107–122. Unlike the Moses nativity legend, but similar to the Jesus nativity legend in Matthew, in the Abraham legend both murder attempts focus on the individual.

Mistakes of the Magicians

A favorite motif of folk legends is a magician's mistake. For example, see the legend of Cyrus' birth (I,120), where the magicians prophesy very well, but err in their interpretation of the prophecy. In Moses nativity legends the magician's error appears in a variety of contexts and is put to use in several ways. In *Sotah* 12b (cited below) the magician's error leads to the decree being rescinded; so, obviously one should not press the point of why the decree is not evident later on. In addition, their error incidentally provides an explanation of why the king failed to discover the young child with the aid of his magicians. (In Matthew 2 the same function is performed by the magicians' refusal to return to the king after they are cautioned in their dream.)

---

on the verse, "I am the Lord that brought thee out of Ur of the Chaldees" (Gen. 15:7), *Torah Shelemah*, Vol. 3, p. 643, n. 89.

[115] *Ma'aseh Abraham*, Version A, *Bet ha-Midrash*, Vol. 1, p. 25.

[116] For example, in the *midrash* cited by Mann in *The Bible as Read and Preached in the Old Synagogue*, Vol. 2, p. 155; in the *midrash* which appears in *Rabbenu Baḥya*; in *Ma'aseh Abraham*, Version B, *Bet ha-Midrash*, Vol. 2, pp. 118–119; in *Midrash ha-Gadol* on Genesis 11:28, and in other variants which Margulies lists there.

The *aggadah* seeks to explain why the king of Egypt chose to kill all the newborn sons precisely by throwing them into the river and provides a double answer to this question. Firstly in *Sotah* 11a: "**Come, let us deal wisely with him** ... *Come and let us outwit the Savior of Israel* ... *and let us afflict them with water, because the Holy One, blessed be He, has already sworn that he will not bring a flood upon the world,* ... They were unaware, however, that although He would not bring a flood upon the whole world, He would bring it upon one people."

Secondly in *Sotah* 12b: ראו שמושיען של ישראל במים הוא לוקה עמדו וגזרו כל הבן הילוד היאורה תשליכוהו כיון דשדיוה למשה אמרו תו לא חזינן כי ההוא סימנא בטלי לגזרתייהו והם אינן יודעין שעל מי מריבה הוא לוקה והיינו שאמר רבי חמא בר' חנינא מאי דכתיב המה מי מריבה אשר רבו המה שראו איצטגניני פרעה וטעו. "*They saw that Israel's savior would suffer misfortune through water; so they arose and decreed,* **Every son that is born ye shall cast into the river**. *After Moses had been thrown [into the water], they said, 'We no longer see the sign'; thereupon the decree was rescinded. But they knew not that he was to suffer misfortune through the water of Meribah. That is what R. Ḥama b. Ḥanina said, What means the text,* **These are the waters of Meribah, because they strove** *(Numbers 20:13)? These are [the waters] about which Pharaoh's magicians saw and erred.*"[117] Aside from the error itself, these *midrashim* share in common a reference to "Israel's savior," which in the first *midrash* refers to the Holy One, blessed be He, and in the second refers to Moses; and both *midrashim* are attributed to the same source, R. Ḥama b. Ḥanina. It is hard to say whether these two *midrashim* were formed in parallel from the outset; or whether one was created in the wake of the other and is secondary in terms of the history of the tradition. Be that as it may, it is worth noting that some of the tension between the story of the individual and the story of the entire people is also reflected in these parallel *midrashim* about the magicians' error. The malicious intent in the first *midrash* is directed at the many, "to afflict them with water"; whereas in the second it is directed against the individual who "was to suffer misfortune through water."

The first *midrash* also explains wherein the king of Egypt dealt wisely, and thus belongs with the *midrashim* discussed on pp. 84–87 above.

Another mistake made by the Egyptians has to do with erring in determining when the savior would be born. The *midrash* which seeks to account for the births of Miriam and Aaron (cf. pp. 117–121, below)

---

[117] Rashi's comments: "'After Moses had been thrown, ... '—as long as he remained in the river, he could suffer no greater misfortune, and the sign of misfortune disappeared." Kasher, in his commentary in *Torah Shelemah*, Vol. 8, p. 47, n. 207, explains that, "Rashi seeks to expound how, since the magicians had been mistaken, the sign could possibly have vanished. The reason he gives is that as long as Moses was in the Nile, the sign was no longer seen."

views the phrase, **"and took to wife a daughter of Levi,"** as referring to Amram's remarriage to Yocheved after having divorced her; and on this basis the *midrash* explains how it was that she could no longer conceal her son: ותצפנהו שלשה ירחים, דלא מנו מצרים אלא משעה דאהדרה והיא הות מיעברא ביה תלתא ירחי מעיקרא. **"She hid him three months.** *[She was able to do this] because the Egyptians only counted [the period of her pregnancy] from the time that she was restored, but she was already three months pregnant then."*[118]

Some *midrashim* claim that the Egyptians' error was due to Moses having been born prematurely: ותהר האשה ותלד בן, באותה הלילה שנתעברה ראה פרעה החלום, ומנו תשעה חדשים והן לא ידעו שכל הנביאים לא נולדו אלא לשבעה חדשים ומשה אב לנביאים. **"And the woman conceived, and bare a son.** *Pharaoh had a dream the night that she conceived, and [from then] they counted nine months; but they did not know that all the prophets were born at seven months, and that Moses was the proto-prophet."*[119] Also see Targum Yerushalmi: וילידת ביר בסוף שיתא ירחין **"And she bore her son at the end of six months."**[120]

The Fate of the Masses

In the Bible, Pharaoh's order to the midwives, **"if it be a son, then ye shall kill him,"** is not actually implemented, for they **"saved the male children alive."** In contrast, the extent of implementation of the second edict, issued because of the failure of the first order to the midwives, remains obscure. The only son whose deliverance is explicitly mentioned is Moses, whereas the fate of the rest of the people is not explicitly stated, although the general impression obtained from the narrative is that the edict was indeed carried out. The fate of the masses is overlooked in the Bible because, unlike the order given by Pharaoh to the midwives, the edict to throw the sons into the Nile is associated with the story of the individual; and as we have mentioned above, interest in the individual

---

[118] *Sotah* 12a. Cf. *Genesis Rabbah* LXXXV.10, p. 1043: "How do we know that a fetus is not perceptible in its mother's womb until three months?"

[119] *Midrash ha-Gadol*; *Torah Shelemah*, Vol. 8, p. 56, n. 13 and the parallels listed there.

[120] Cf. Rashi on Genesis 25:24: "And when her days to be delivered were fulfilled—*But it is written of Tamar 'And it came to pass in the time of her travail (Gen. 38:27)'* to indicate that she had not reached full term, for she bore them at seven months." Also see *Genesis Rabbah* LXIII.8, p. 686, and Albeck's commentary there. Cf. Ginzberg, Vol. 5, p. 397, n. 44 and p. 399, n. 56. Also Isaac and Samuel were born in the seventh month. Cf. *Rosh ha-Shanah* 11a; Ginzberg, Vol. 6 (*Samuel*), p. 217, n. 13; *Torah Shelemah*, Vol. 3b, p. 763, n. 166. Also see Lieberman, *Greek in Jewish Palestine*, pp. 22–23. According to the Protevangelium of James, Mary too was born in the seventh month. Cf. below, The Protevangelium of James, n. 35.

pushed aside the account of the fate of the masses; or, more likely, since the edict to throw the sons into the Nile was integrally bound up with the story of the individual, from the outset it protected the pattern from permitting the story of the masses to intrude into the narrative. The Bible's obscurity on this point is also reflected in the *midrash*. Most of the *midrashim* that include the motif of annunciation preserve the biblical story line and make no mention of the fate of the masses. This is not surprising, since the reason these legends give for the edict only concerns the individual; therefore, even more so than the in Bible, the scope of vision in these legends only takes in the individual. The fate of the masses is mentioned but rarely, and at that in passing descriptions, without pausing to elaborate or describe the edict's dreadful impact on the nation. For example, see *Pirke Rabbi Eliezer* 48:[121] *"For three and a third years [they cast the sons into the Nile], until Moses was born. After he had been born, they [the magicians] said to him [Pharaoh]: 'Lo, he has been born but is hidden from our sight.' He [Pharaoh] answered them, 'Since he has already been born, henceforth do not cast the sons who are born into the Nile.'"* Also see Wisdom of Solomon 18:5: *"One child had been cast forth and saved."*

It should be noted that even those *midrashim* that did not include the annunciation did not generally expand on the motif of drowning the children in the Nile. Only on rare occasions, as far as we have been able to ascertain, does the *midrash* go into an extensive description of the actual implementation of Pharaoh's decree to throw all the newborn sons into the Nile. For example, in the *Mekilta of R. Simeon b. Yoḥai* (שמות, p. 1) we read: ומה ת"ל ראה ראיתי שני פעמים. מאחר שהיו משקיעין את בניהם במים היו חוזרי׳ וכובשים אותם בבנין. *"What does the text seek to teach us by the emphatic,* **I have surely seen** *(Ex. 3:7)'? After drowning their sons in water, they also immured them [the babes] in the construction work."*[122] In *Yannai* we read: *"while casting newborn sons into the Nile."*[123] Also, note what the *Asatir* says (8): *"The fathers and mothers trembled. And the Hebrew women acted with faith, and cast themselves together with their children."*

Many *midrashim* translate the Bible's silence regarding the fate of the people into deliverance. Sometimes this deliverance is only partial:[124] ד"א למה מצוה זו [ושאלה אשה משכנתה (שמ' ג, כב)] נאמרה לנשים כו', שכיון שגזר פרעה כל הבן הילוד היארה תשליכוהו היו בנות ישראל משחדות מתכשיטיהן לעבדי פרעה ומשחידות למצרים שלא יגלו ומשליכין מבניהם מקצת ומניחין מקצת. לכך לא כפל הכתוב לומר וישליכו כל הבן וצוה הקב"ה ושאלה אשה משכנתה כדי שיחזור הדבר לישאו להחזיר להן מה שנתנו להן.

---

[121] *Torah Shelemah*, Vol. 8, p. 49, n. 212.
[122] Cf. also *Torah Shelemah*, Vol. 8, p. 133, n. 114.
[123] Rabbinovitz ed., Vol. 2, p. 252.
[124] *Ḥemdat Yamim*; cited in *Torah Shelemah*, Vol. 8, p. 163, n. 243.

ואין בזה גניבת דעת אלא החזרת חפץ לבעליו. "Why was this command [every woman shall borrow of her neighbor (Ex. 3:22)] specifically addressed to the women? Since Pharaoh decreed Every son that is born ye shall cast into the river, the Israelite women used their jewelry to bribe Pharaoh's servants and to bribe the Egyptians not to discover [the newborns], so that they threw only some of their sons [into the water], and some they let be. Therefore the text does not recapitulate, saying 'they threw every son.' And the Holy One, blessed be He, commanded every woman shall borrow of her neighbor to restore the former state of affairs, returning what they had given them; and this was not a matter of deceptive persuasion, but rather of returning belongings to their true owners."

Sometimes the deliverance was complete, as we see in *Pesikta Rabbati* 47, p. 189:[125] מהו אלהים אלי אתה (תה׳ סג, ב) בשעה שגזרו המצרים על ישראל כל הבן הילוד וכו׳ היתה בת ישראל בזמן שהיתה מרגשת קרובה לילד היתה יוצאה לאשפה ויולדת שם. מיד היה הקב״ה יורד ומרחיצו (ומנקו) ומלבישו [שנא׳] (יחז׳ טז, ט, י) וארחצך במים ואשטוף דמיך מעלייך ואלבישך רקמה ואנעלך תחש. "What is meant by O God, thou art my God (Ps. 63:2)? When the Egyptians had decreed against Israel that every son that is born ..., the Israelite women used to go out to the refuse heap when they felt they were about to give birth, and would bear their children there. Immediately the Holy One, blessed be He, would descend and wash him[126] and clothe him, as it is said, **Then washed I thee with water; yea, I throughly washed away thy blood from thee [and I anointed thee with oil]. I clothed thee also with broidered work, and shod thee with badgers' skin (Ezek. 16:9–10).**" A similar legend, although somewhat toning down the dramatic anthropomorphism and transferring the act of deliverance to an emissary, is found in *Sotah* 11b: וכיון שמגיע זמן מולדיהן הולכות ויולדות בשדה תחת התפוח, שנאמר (שה״ש ח, ה) תחת התפוח עוררתיך וגו׳ והקב״ה שולח משמי מרום מי שמנקיר ומשפיר אותן כחיה זו שמשפרת את הולד, שנא׳ (יחז׳ טז, ד) ומולדתיך ביום הולדת אותך לא כרת שרך ובמים לא רחצת למשעי וגו׳ ומלקט להן שני עגולין אחד של שמן ואחד של דבש, שנא׳ (דב׳ לב, יג) וינקהו דבש מסלע ושמן וגו׳ וכיון שמכירין בהן מצרים באין להורגן ונעשה להן נס ונבלעין בקרקע ומביאין שוורים וחורשין על גבן, שנאמר (תה׳ קכט, ג) על גבי חרשו חורשים וגו׳ לאחר שהולכין היו מבצבצין ויוצאין כעשב השדה, שנא׳ (יחז׳ טז, ז) רבבה כצמח השדה נתתיך וכיון שמתגדלין באין עדרים עדרים לבתיהן, שנאמר (שם, ז) ותרבי ותגדלי ותבואי בעדי עדיים אל תקרי בעדי עדיים אלא בעדרי עדרים, וכשנגלה הקב״ה על הים הם הכירוהו תחלה שנא׳ (שמ׳ טו, ב) זה אלי ואנוהו. "When their time of childbirth arrived, they went and were delivered in the field beneath the apple tree, as it is said, **I raised thee up under the apple tree (Song 8:5).** And the Holy One,

---

[125] *Ibid.*, p. 48, n. 210.

[126] The first edition reads 'and suckle him'; Ish Shalom emends this to 'and clean him,' but this is unnecessary, as one can learn from the *midrash* taken from *Deuteronomy Rabbah*, below.

blessed be He, sent down someone from the high heavens who washed and straightened the limbs [of the babes] in the manner that a midwife straightens the limbs of a child; as it is said, **And as for thy nativity, in the day thou wast born thy navel was not cut, neither wast thou washed in water to cleanse thee** *(Ezek. 16:4). He also provided for them two round cakes, one of oil and one of honey, as it is said,* **And He made him to suck honey out of the rock, and oil ...** *(Deut. 32:13). When the Egyptians noticed them, they went to kill them; but a miracle occurred on their behalf so that they were swallowed in the ground, and [the Egyptians] brought oxen and ploughed over them, as it is said,* **The ploughers ploughed upon my back** *(Ps. 129:3). After they [the Egyptians] had departed, they [the babes] broke through [the earth] and came forth like the herbage of the field, as it is said,* **I caused thee to multiply as the bud of the field** *(Ezek. 16:7); and when [the babes] had grown up, they came in flocks to their homes, as it is said,* **And thou didst increase and wax great and didst come with ornaments** *(ibid. 7)—do not read* **with ornaments** *(בעדי עדיים) but* **in flocks** *(בעדרי עדרים). At the time the Holy One, blessed be He, revealed Himself by the Red Sea, they recognized Him first, as it is said,* **This is my God and I will praise Him** *(Ex. 15:2)."*

Both approaches are found side by side in the Lieberman edition of *Deuteronomy Rabbah,* p. 14: אמר ר״ל שני מלאכים היה הקב״ה מוסר לאחד מהם אחד להרחיצו וא׳ להלבישו, ונזקק להניקו ולהסך אותו וכו׳ א׳ר חייא הגדול לא המלאכים היו עושין כן, אלא הקב״ה בכבודו, שנא׳ וארחצך, אילו נאמר וארחיצך, הייתי אומר שמא ע״י מלאך, אלא כתי׳ וארחצך ולא ע״י מלאך וכו׳. "*R. Levi said: The Holy One, blessed be He, used to assign each of them two angels, one to wash him and one to clothe him; and he had to suckle him and to anoint him, etc. R. Ḥiyya the Great said, it was not the angels that did these things, but the Holy One, blessed be He, as it is said,* **then washed I thee** וארחצך *(Ezek. 16:9). Had it said* וארחיצך,[127] *I would have said it might have been by an angel; but it said* וארחצך,[128] *indicating that this was not done by an angel.*" Jewish literature through the generations has often toned down anthropomorphism by transferring the action to angels, either partially or completely. For example, see the legends on Moses' burial, which to varying degrees transfer the act of burying to angels, whereas Scripture says "**and he [God] buried him in a valley**" (Deut. 34:6).[129] This approach can be found even in Scripture in several places. For example, see Judges 1:11–24; or the instructive example of Genesis 18:1–15, where anthropomorphism precluded the later reworking of the text which re-

---

[127] *Hiphʻil*—causative form.
[128] *Kal* form.
[129] Ginzberg, *op. cit.*, Vol. 6, p. 161, n. 948.

placed the plural with the singular.¹³⁰

Pirke Rabbi Eliezer 42 also has a legend of deliverance applying to the masses:¹³¹ ר׳ שילא אומר, כל הילדים שהשליכו ליאור לא מתו אלא היאור הפליט אותם ומשליך אותם למדבר מצרים. והיה הקב״ה מביא סלע בפי כל אחד ואחד וסלע מצדו. והסלע שהיה בפיו היה מניק אותו דבש, והסלע שבצדיהם היה מניק אותו שמן, כהיה שהיא מניקה את בנה, שנאמר (דב׳ לב, יג) ויניקהו דבש מסלע ושמן מחלמיש צור. "R. Shela says: All the children that were cast into the Nile did not die; rather, the Nile spit them out and cast them into the desert of Egypt. Then the Holy One, blessed be He, would bring a rock to put in the mouth of each babe, and would place another rock beside each; the rock in the babe's mouth would suckle him with honey and the rock at his side would provide him oil, like an animal that suckles her young, as it is said, **And He made him to suck honey out of the rock, and oil out of the flinty rock** (Deut. 32:13)." Note that Targum Yerushalmi 2:23 implies that many children perished: ופקיד לקטלא בוכריא דבני ישראל בגין למסחי באדמיהון. "And he ordered to kill the firstborn of the children of Israel so that he could bathe in their blood" [to be cured of leprosy]; but, in contrast, *Exodus Rabbah* I.34 adds: אמרו רבותינו נעשה להם נס ונתרפא מצרעתו. "The Sages said that a miracle was wrought for them and he [Pharaoh] was healed of his leprosy."¹³²

An important point in the development of the motif is marked by the legend in *Sotah* 12b, discussed on p. 99 above, in which throwing Moses into the Nile caused the omen to disappear and thus led to the decree's rescission. *Sotah* 12b continues: והיינו דקאמר משה (במד׳ יא, כא) שש מאות אלף

---

¹³⁰ Also cf. Cohen, *Masorot*, pp. 68–69.

¹³¹ Cf. *Torah Shelemah*, Vol. 8, p. 48, n. 210, and the parallel versions listed there, to which *Tībat Marqe* 224.2, p. 281 should be added.

¹³² *Torah Shelemah*, Vol. 8, p. 102, n. 180; also see the wide variety of parallels given there, and Ginzberg, Vol. 5, p. 412, n. 101. The version found in Targum Yerushalmi, according to which Pharaoh's act was directed specifically against the firstborn, surely stems from the tendency to associate this act with the plague of the firstborn, following the principle of measure for measure which we have discussed above (p. 70).

The remark in אהבת יונתן (cited in *Torah Shelemah*, Vol. 8, p. 103, n. 180 of the commentary) that the text ought to be emended to read "sons," is of interest in the development of exegesis. This remark was surely prompted by the perceptive observation that the murder decree in the beginning of the story does not distinguish between firstborn sons and non-firstborns. Also cf. אהבת יונתן on Lev., p. 253.

A similar singling out of firstborns is made regarding Passover. The custom of the firstborn son fasting on the eve of Passover, alluded to as far back as the Jerusalem Talmud (*Pesaḥim* 10 *Halakhah* 1, p. 37a), probably emerged from the desire to counterbalance the plague of the firstborn, even though in the biblical source (Ex. 11, 12) all the children of Israel, not only the firstborn, were in danger on the night that God smote the firstborn of Egypt. Cf. Loewenstamm, *Evolution*, p. 91 in the Hebrew original, p. 211 in the English translation. Finkelstein ("The Oldest Midrash," pp. 306–307) did not sense this.

רגלי וגו' אמר להן משה לישראל בשבילי נצלתם כולכם. "*And concerning this Moses said,* **Six hundred thousand footmen** (רגלי) ... *(Num. 11:21). Moses said to Israel, 'On my account* (לרגלי) *were all of you delivered [from drowning by the edict of Pharaoh].'*" According to the approach which we have set forth, the murder decree subsumed the masses only secondarily and was directed from the outset to kill none other than a specific individual. As we have indicated after Gressmann, extending the decree from the specific individual to the generality is a characteristic feature of Moses nativity stories and stems from the influence of the national tradition of exile, into which the legend of the individual intruded. In the first stage of the decree's extension, still clearly evident in the legends of the Sages, the original nature of the edict is retained to some extent; for in these legends, although the decree is passed against the masses on account of the individual, nevertheless the deliverance of the individual has no impact on the masses. The process reaches its completion in the *midrash* which we have here; just as the plot on the life of the individual is extended to the generality, so too the deliverance of the individual is extended to the generality. Many are saved by virtue of one, and deliverance of one becomes deliverance of all. Thus, see the *Tosafot* on *Sotah* 12b, who wonder at Moses' remark: בשבילי ניצלתם כולכם. תימא אדרבא בשבילו נגזרו הגזירות שראו אצטגניני פרעה וכו'. "'*On my account were all of you delivered.*' Quite the contrary. It was on his account that the decrees were originally issued, since Pharaoh's astrologers saw ... " The *midrash* presented in *Genesis Rabbah* XCVII, p. 1247, and in *Midrash ha-Gadol* on Exodus 1:7 goes even further:[133] אמ' ר' לוי ששים רבוא תינוקת עיברו נשותיהן של ישראל בלילה אחד, וכולן הושלכו ליאור ועלו בזכותו של משה, הוא שמשה אומר שש מאות אלף רגלי העם אשר אנכי בקרבו (במדבר יא, כא) כולן לרגלי עלו. "*R. Levi said: Six hundred thousand babes were conceived by the Israelite women on a single night, and they were all thrown into the Nile and came out by virtue of Moses. That is the meaning of Moses saying,* '**The people, among whom I am, are six hundred thousand footmen** (רגלי) *(Num. 11:21). They all came out on my account* (לרגלי)*.*'" This *midrash* does not simply transfer the act of deliverance from the individual to the generality, but also transfers from one to many the time of conception which, as we recall, was perceived by the astrologers and, as a necessary consequence, entailed the timing of casting the sons into the Nile, as determined by the astrologers on the basis of when Moses' conception occurred. Also recall the *midrashim* describing the rescission of the edict to cast the sons into the Nile, presented on p. 99 above.

Perhaps the Bible's silence on the fate of the masses and the *midrash-*

---

[133] *Torah Shelemah*, Vol. 8, p. 16, n. 69.

im which conclude, due to the influence of this silence, that the children of Israel were untouched are related to the perplexing *midrash* from *Midrash Wa-Yosha'* (or *Abkir*), cited in *Yalkut Shimoni*, Vol. 1, 241:[134]

עמד עוזא׳ שר של מצרים לפני הק ואמ׳ לפניו רבו׳ של עול׳ נקראתה צדיק וישר ואין לפניך לא עולה ולא משא פנים ולא מקח שחד, למה אתה רוצה להטביע את מצרים, כלום הטביעו בניי מבניך או הרגו מהם, בשביל שיעבוד ששיעבדו בהם אתה רוצה לטובען כו׳.

"Uzza, the tutelary angel of the Egyptians, stood before the Holy One and said, 'Lord of the Universe, it is said that you are just and righteous, that you do not brook injustice, show partiality, or allow yourself to be swayed by bribery; so why do you want to drown Egypt? Have my sons as much as drowned one of your sons, or killed any of them? For the bondage with which they enslaved them, you wish to drown them, ...'"

The impact of the fate of the individual on the fate of the nation is expressed in transferal of the concealment and foundling motifs from one to many. Like Yocheved, the Israelite women do not hand their sons over to be killed, but rather hide them and force the Egyptians to seek them out:[135] כל היכא דהוו שמעי מצראי דמתיליד ינוקא ממטי ינוקא התם כי היכי דלישמעינהו ומעי (בהדייהו). "Whenever the Egyptians were informed that a child was born, they would take another child there so that he should hear him [crying] and cry with him." Likewise, note the transition to the plural in *Dibre Yeme Moshe Rabbenu* 4:[136] ותלך האשה ותצפון את בנה מפני מצרים לבלתי דעת מצרים עת לידתנה לבלתי השחיתם . . . ויהי כמשלש חדשים לעת צפון האשה את הילד ויודע הדבר בית פרעה וכו׳. "*And the woman went and hid her son from the Egyptians, so that the Egyptians would not know when they gave birth and would not destroy them . . . Three months after the woman hid her son, it became known in Pharaoh's house.*"

The foundling story in Ezekiel holds a prominent place in the extension of the motif to the generality. Elsewhere[137] we have discussed the motifs shared in common by the Moses nativity story and Ezekiel's parable on Jerusalem (Chapter 16). There we noted that Pharaoh's daughter's deliverance of Moses is paralleled in Ezekiel by God's deliverance of the one "**cast out in the open field.**" This parallel is put to use in the *Midrash*, as can be seen in many homilies. For example, see *Pesikta Rabbati* 47, p. 189 (cited above, p. 110). There, as in Ezekiel, the Holy One, blessed be He, himself performs the deliverance: "*Immediately the Holy One, blessed be He, would descend and wash him [suckle him] and clothe him, as it is said,* **Then washed I thee with water; yea, I throughly washed** . . . *(Ezek. 16:9).*" In *Sotah* 11b (cited above,

---

[134] *Ibid.*, p. 49, n. 212*; also see *ibid.*, the supplements to n. 209, pp. 243–244.
[135] *Sotah* 12a; cf. also *Torah Shelemah*, Vol. 8, p. 58, n. 24, and the parallel versions listed there.
[136] *Torah Shelemah*, Vol. 8, p. 54, n. 11.
[137] Cohen, *Masorot*, pp. 6–7.

p. 110) this bold motif is toned down by having an emissary perform the deliverance: "*And the Holy One, blessed be He, sent down someone from the high heavens who washed and straightened the limbs [of the babes] in the manner that a midwife straightens the limbs of a child; as it is said,* **And as for thy nativity, in the day thou wast born thy navel was not cut, neither wast thou washed in water to cleanse thee** *(Ezek. 16:4)* ..." The detailed description of washing and clothing, which in Ezekiel comes when the young maiden reaches maturity, "**the time of love**" (Ezek. 16:8), is transferred in the *midrashim* to the birth. (Perhaps the motif is thereby restored to its original form.) Even transferring the setting to Egypt works well and is appropriate to the history of the people.[138] The point of connection between Ezekiel 16 and Exodus 1 and 2 is the foundling motif; but from here the parallel spreads to include other motifs, such as the Hebrews' miraculous proliferation:[139] כן ירבה וכן יפרץ. עד היכן, אר׳שב״ל עד ויקוצו מפני בני ישראל, היה המצרי מבקש לעמוד עם חבירו והיה אלף מישראל עד שלא היה רואה את חבירו, עד שהיה נותן ידו על חוטמו ומבקש לשמוט את נפשו, והיה אומר אי מפני האומה הזו מה מרובה היא, הוא שאמ׳ הקב״ה ליחזקאל, רבבה כצמח השדה נתתיך. "**The more they multiplied and grew**—*how much so? According to R. Simeon b. Lakish, until they were grieved because of the children of Israel. An Egyptian would try to stand together with his friend, but he would see a thousand Israelites so that he could not see his friend; until he would hold his nose and seek to end his life, and would say, why is it that this people is so numerous? That is the meaning of the Holy One, blessed be He, saying to Ezekiel,* '**I have caused thee to multiply as the bud of the field** *(Ezek. 16:7).*'"

In this connection perhaps one should mention the remarkable passage in Acts 7:19, discussed above (p. 59). It should be noted that this exceptional passage appears in the same chapter as other traditions that diverge from those presented in the Old Testament. Only some of these traditions have been noted by Strack and Billerbeck. To their list one must add the tradition according to which Jacob is buried in Shechem[140] (v. 16); the tradition of an angel having spoken to our forefathers on Mount Sinai (v. 38); the punishment that God "**gave them up to worship the host of heaven**" (v. 42) after the people had made the golden calf (cf. Ezek. 20:23); and others.

Anonymity of the Parents

The *Midrash* does away completely with the anonymity of Moses' parent-

---

[138] Cf. the parallels cited in *Torah Shelemah*, Vol. 8, p. 48, n. 210.
[139] *Deuteronomy Rabbah*, Lieberman ed., p. 16; *Torah Shelemah*, Vol. 8, p. 29, n. 132.
[140] See n. 29 of our section on Matthew.

age. It is clear to the homilists that the "man of the house of Levi" was Amram and that the "daughter of Levi" was Yocheved. The *midrashim* exaggerate Amram's importance and thereby eliminate the biblical inclination towards emphasizing the singularity of the chosen hero by concealing the identity of his parents. "*Amram was the greatest man of his generation,*" according to *Sotah* 12a; he was the Head of the Sanhedrin, according to *Exodus Rabbah* I.13; and according to *Shabbat* 55b and *Baba Batra* 17a, he was one of "*Four [who] died on account of the snake.*"[141] Still more examples can be found in the *midrashim* cited in the commentary in *Torah Shelemah*, Vol. 8, p. 52, n. 3.

Dibre Yeme Moshe Rabbenu embeds the Bible's terse formulation in a broader statement:[142] איש לוי היה בארץ מצרים ושמו עמרם בן קהת בן יעקב [לוי בן ישראל] וכו' וילך האיש אל יוכבד בת לוי אחות אביו ותהר האשה וכו'. "*There was a man of the house of Levi in the land of Egypt, and his name was Amram son of Kohath son of Jacob [Levi son of Israel] ... and the man went to his father's sister Yocheved, the daughter of Levi, and the woman conceived, ...*"[143]

Two later sources explicitly express surprise that Amram's name was suppressed. *Midrash ha-Gadol*[144] states: וילך איש מבית לוי, למה לא פרסמו הכתוב ולא הזכיר שמו, אלא מפני שאבותיו קיימין והוא קטן שבהם. ד"א שהלך מגזירותיו של הקב"ה וגזר גזירה אחרת. "**And there went a man of the house of Levi.** *Why did Scripture not publicize who he was or mention his name? Because his fathers were still alive, and he was the youngest of them. According to another interpretation, it was because he departed from the decrees of the Holy One, blessed be He, [be fruitful and multiply] and issued a different decree [that the men should leave their wives].*" Similarly, in the *Zohar*[145] we read: וילך איש מבית לוי, מאי טעמא לא נזכר שמו, רבי יהודה אמר בשם רבי אבהו מפני שבצנעה הלך ובצנעה חזר לאשתו, כדי שלא יכירו בו הה"ד וילך איש ולא נאמר וילך עמרם בפרהסיא. ויקח את בת לוי אף היא בצנעה חזרה ולא נזכר שמה. "**And there went a man of the house of Levi.** *What was the reason for not mentioning his name? R. Judah said in the name of R. Abbahu: It is because he left his wife and returned to her in privacy, so that he would not be noticed; thus it says* **and there went a man**, *and does not say that Amram went in public. With respect to the phrase,* **and took to wife a daughter of Levi**, *she too returned to him in*

---

[141] Rashi explains that actually they deserved not to die, but died anyway because it had been so decreed on account of the snake in the Garden of Eden.

[142] *Torah Shelemah*, Vol. 8, p. 54, n. 11.

[143] It is also interesting to compare the formulation in Judges 13:2 with that in I Samuel 1:1.

[144] *Ibid.*, p. 52, n. 4 of the commentary.

[145] *Zohar*, Vol. 2, 19; *Torah Shelemah*, Vol. 8, p. 52, n. 4.

privacy, and hence her name is not mentioned." The *Zohar*[146] also says: רבי יהודה אומר עמרם ממש היה ולא נזכר שמו מפני שהליכה זו לא היתה ממנו להזדווג לאשתו אלא מלמעלה. *"R. Judah says that it was indeed Amram,*[147] *but his name is not mentioned because his act of going to take a wife was not prompted by his desire for intercourse with his wife, but rather was prompted from on high."* *Sekel Tob*[148] derives disclosure of Amram's identity from the Bible's concealment of it: וילך איש, אין איש אלא מגדולי ישראל ומגדולי הארץ, וכה"א (שמ"א י, יב) והאיש בימי שאול [גדול] וזה עמרם. *"And there went a man. Man (איש), here, denotes none other than one of the great men of Israel and great men of the land, as it is used in I Samuel 17:12, 'the man in the days of Saul [was great],' and that man was Amram."*

In terms of the glory and renown given Amram, the *Midrash* is similar to Philo, Josephus, and Biblical Antiquities. It should be noted, however, that despite Amram's exaggerated importance in the *Midrash*, his figure there does not intrude into the story of the ark. In the *Midrash*, as in the Bible, it is the mother who hides her child and who constructs the ark. In this respect the *midrashim* differ from Josephus, the Septuagint, and Philo (in whose version, recall, there is no ark). Note the active role of **"his parents"** in Hebrews 11:23.[149] Also note the switch of father and mother in the variant texts: "Her father stood and patted her head" (*Megillah* 14a; as opposed to "Her mother stood and said to her" (in the Münich manuscript[150]).

The Second Marriage

The appearance of an older sister on the scene (Ex. 2:4) is surprising and contradicts the beginning of the chapter, which describes Moses as a firstborn and only son. We noted above (cf. Chapter 1, note 34) that the main problem here does not stem from the fact that we have not been told of her existence, but from the fact that the narrative pattern has no place for a birth between the Pharaoh's instruction, **"Every son that is born ye shall cast into the river,"** and the birth of the savior, Moses. Aside from the questions raised by the presence of the sister, later generations added problems posed by the existence of Aaron, although he is not actually mentioned in the story itself. This problem, which cannot be solved within the setting of the biblical narrative, led the *Midrash* to go beyond the bounds of the structure of the biblical narrative and to view the marriage of Amram and Yocheved (whose names the *midrash*

---

[146] *Zohar*, Vol. 2, 19; *Torah Shelemah*, Vol. 8, p. 53, n. 5.
[147] Some of the Sages held that "a man" (איש) here refers to the angel Gabriel.
[148] *Torah Shelemah*, Vol. 8, p. 52, n. 3.
[149] Ginzberg, *op. cit.*, Vol. 5, p. 395, nn. 28, 30.
[150] Cf. דקדוקי סופרים by R. Rabbinovicz; also see the commentary in *Torah Shelemah*, Vol. 8, p. 61, n. 34.

וילך איש מבית לוי ויקח את בת לוי, supplied unawares) as a remarriage:[151] חכמים אומרים, אומר לו הקב״ה למשה זכות עמרם אביך עמדה לך שעמד ועשה דבר גדול בישראל, כשהכבידו מצרים עבודה קשה על ישראל והיו מטבעין אותן ביאר, אמרו, אנו נושאים נשים ומולידין בנים, ומצרים מטבעין אותן ביאר, למה אנו מיגעים את עצמנו לחנם, עמד עמרם ועשה דבר גדול בישראל והסכימה דעתו לדעת המקום, גירש את אשתו כשהיא מעוברת שלשה חדשים, בסוף שלשה חדשים חזר ועשה בה קדושין שנאמר וילך איש מבית לוי ויקח את בת לוי והיו מלאכי השרת מקלסים לפניה כחתנים וככלות שנאמר (תה׳ קי״ג, ט) אם הבנים שמחה, וכו׳.

"And there went a man of the house of Levi, and took to wife a daughter of Levi. The Sages said: The Holy One, blessed be he, said to Moses: The merit of your father, Amram, was to your credit; for he had done a great thing in Israel. When the Egyptians oppressed Israel with heavy labor and were drowning their children in the Nile, they said, 'We get married, and have children, and then the Egyptians drown them in the Nile; so why do we exhaust ourselves for nought?' Then Amram came forth and did a great act in Israel, and his opinion was in accord with that of the Omnipresent: he divorced his wife when she was three months pregnant. Three months later he came and remarried her, as it is said, **and there went a man of the house of Levi, and took to wife a daughter of Levi**, and the Ministering Angels sang praises before her like brides and grooms, as it is said, **a joyful mother of children** (Ps. 113:9), etc."

In many *midrashim*,[152] the story centers around Miriam: וילך איש מבית לוי וכו׳, להיכן הלך, א״ר יהודה בר זבינא שהלך בעצת בתו. תנא עמרם גדול הדור היה, כיון שאמר פרעה הרשע כל הבן הילוד היאורה תשליכוהו, אמר, לשוא אנו עמילין, עמד וגירש את אשתו. עמדו כולן וגרשו את נשותיהן, אמרה לו בתו, אבא קשה גזירתך יותר משל פרעה, שפרעה לא גזר אלא על הזכרים ואתה גזרת על הזכרים ועל הנקבות. פרעה לא גזר אלא בעולם הזה ואתה בעה״ז ולעה״ב. פרעה הרשע ספק מתקיימת גזרתו ספק אינה מתקיימת אתה צדיק בודאי שגזרתך מתקיימת שנא׳ (איוב כב, כח) ותגזר אומר ויקם לך. עמד והחזיר את אשתו, עמדו כולם והחזירו את נשותיהן. **"And there went a man of the house of Levi.** Where did he go? R. Judah b. Zebina said that he went in the counsel of his daughter. A Tanna taught: Amram was the greatest man of his generation; when he saw that the wicked Pharaoh had decreed, **'Every son that is born ye shall cast into the river,'** he said, 'In vain do we labor.' He arose and divorced his wife. All [the Israelites] thereupon arose and divorced their wives. His daughter said to him, 'Father, thy decree is more severe than Pharaoh's; because Pharaoh decreed only against the males, whereas thou hast decreed against the males and females. Pharaoh only decreed concerning this world, whereas thou hast decreed concerning this world and the World to Come. In the case of the wicked Pharaoh there is some doubt whether his decree will be

---

[151] *Mekilta of R. Simeon b. Yoḥai, Shemot* (Hoffmann ed., p. 3); *Torah Shelemah*, Vol. 8, p. 51, n. 2.
[152] *Sotah* 12a; *Torah Shelemah*, Vol. 8, p. 50, n. 1.

fulfilled or not, whereas in thy case, being righteous, it is certain that thy decree will be fulfilled, as it is said, **Thou shalt also decree a thing, and it shall be established unto thee** (Job 22:28).' He arose and took his wife back; and they all arose and took their wives back." The prominent role which Miriam plays can be explained by the fact that it is her presence in the biblical narrative that provided the primary reason for creating this *midrash*. Sometimes, as in the *Mekilta*[153] the *Midrash* associates the remarriage with Miriam's prophecy: ותקח מרים הנביאה, וכי היכן מצינו שנביאה היתה מרים אלא שאמרה לאביה סופך אתה מוליד בן שמושיע את ישראל מיד מצרים מיד וילך איש מבית לוי ויקח וגו׳. **"And Miriam the prophetess ... took** (Ex 15:20). But where do we find that Miriam prophesied? From none other than her having said to her father: 'You are destined to beget a son who will save Israel from the hands of the Egyptians.' Immediately **there went a man of the house of Levi and took to wife** . . . ."

In *Sotah* 12a we find that the older children, Miriam and Aaron, are included, appropriately, in the wedding celebration: ויקח ויחזר מיבעי ליה, א״ר יהודה בר זבינא שעשה לו מעשה ליקוחין, הושיבה באפריון ואהרן ומרים מרקדין לפניה ומלאכי השרת אמרו (תה׳ קי״ג, ט) אם הבנים שמחה. **"The text should have read 'and took back'!** R. Judah b. Zebina said: He acted towards her as though it had been their first marriage; he seated her in a palanquin, Aaron and Miriam danced before her, and the Ministering Angels proclaimed, **A joyful mother of children** (Ps. 113:9)."

The problematic element of the biblical text which led to the creation of the *midrash* is put explicitly in *Midrash ha-Be'ur*:[154] וילך איש מבית לוי ויקח את בת לוי וכי היום נשאה והלא כבר ילדה לו אהרן ומרים אלא כשגזר פרעה כל הבן וכו׳. **"And there went a man of the house of Levi, and took to wife a daughter of Levi**. How could it be that she was only married on that day; for she had already born him Aaron and Miriam? The explanation is simply that when Pharaoh decreed **'Every son that is born'** . . . ."

Daube[155] exposes the contradiction inherent in the assertion of the *Midrash* that Amram divorced his wife when she was already three months pregnant in order to prevent his son being born and drowned in the Nile. The conclusions which he draws from this contradiction, however, are incorrect, since they do not take into account the literary genre of the sources.[156] Rashi, nevertheless, may have been influenced

---

[153] *Mekilta*, Tractate *Shirata* 10, p. 151; *Torah Shelemah*, Vol. 8, p. 50, n. 1.
[154] From the manuscript cited in *Torah Shelemah*, Vol. 8, p. 51, n. 1.
[155] *The New Testament and Rabbinic Judaism*, p. 7.
[156] On Daube's remarks, see Loewenstamm's note in "Die Geburtsgeschichte Moses," p. 212, n. 36. Also cf. our note 34 in Chapter 1.

by this contradiction.[157] *Sekel Tob* 2:2 notes: "She was pregnant with Moses at the time he divorced her, but it was not yet evident to him."

The historical setting for the *midrashim* about Amram's decision can be seen in the *Gemara*, *Baba Batra* 60b:[158] מיום שפשטה מלכות שגוזרין עלינו גזירות כו' דין הוא שנגזור על עצמנו שלא לישא אשה כו'. "*From the day that a government has come into power which issues cruel decrees against us . . . we ought by rights to bind ourselves not to marry and beget children.*"

Thus, in these *midrashim* Moses is transformed from a firstborn and only child to a child born to his parents late in life, after his two older siblings. Indeed, according to the Sages' calculations, Yocheved was one hundred and thirty years old when she bore Moses.[159] Hence the wonderment expressed in the *Gemara*:[160] איפשר בת מאה ושלשים שנה וקרא לה בת, דאמר ר' חמא בר חנינא זו יוכבד שהורתה בדרך וכו' אמר רבי יהודה בר זבידא, מלמד שנולדו בה סימני נערות נתעדן הבשר נתפשטו הקמטין וחזר היופי למקומו. "*How could it be that at age one hundred and thirty she was called 'daughter'? For R. Ḥama b. Ḥanina said: It was Yocheved who was conceived on the way [when Jacob and his family came down to Egypt]. . . . R. Judah b. Zebida said: This teaches that marks of youth re-appeared on her. Her body became resilient again, her wrinkles smoothed out, and her beauty was restored.*" Thus, in addition to the miracle of the son being delivered from Pharaoh's decree the *Midrash* presents the miracle of Yocheved bearing

---

[157] Cf. our chapter on Rashi, note 19.

[158] *Torah Shelemah*, Vol. 8, p. 51. Also cf. *ibid.*, p. 51, n. 2, and *ibid.*, p. 50, n. 1; p. 53, n. 6; p. 54, n. 11; p. 58, n. 21 for many other parallel versions. Also cf. Ginzberg, *op. cit.*, Vol. 5, p. 394, n. 27.

[159] Ginzberg, *op. cit.*, p.396, n. 36; *Torah Shelemah*, Vol. 7, p. 1690, n. 148. According to the Sage's approach, which sought to account for seventy souls coming down to Egypt, Yocheved was born "between the walls." In *Baba Batra* 123a we read: בעא מיניה אבא חליפא קרויה מר' חייא בר אבא, בכללן אתה מוצא שבעים בפרטן אתה מוצא שבעים חסר אחד וכו' אמר מרגלית טובה היתה בידי ואתה מבקש לאבדה ממני, הכי אמר ר' חמא בר חנינא זו יוכבד שהורתה בדרך ולידתה בין החומות שנאמר (במד' כו, נט) אשר ילדה אותה ללוי במצרים, לידתה במצרים ואין הורתה במצרים. "*Abba Ḥalifa of Keruya inquired of R. Ḥiyya b. Abba: Why do you find a total of seventy, and in their enumeration only seventy minus one? . . . He said: I possessed a precious pearl and you seek to deprive me of it. Thus said R. Ḥama b. Ḥanina, 'It was Yocheved who was conceived on the way and born between the walls [of Egypt], for it is said,* Who was born to Levi in Egypt *(Num. 26:59), implying that her birth was in Egypt but her conception was not in Egypt.*" According to a computation of the generations, Yocheved was one hundred and thirty years old at the time she bore Moses. Cf. Rashi on Ex. 2:1: "She was then 130 years old; for she was born 'between the walls,' when they were about to enter Egypt, and they remained there 210 years, and when they left Egypt Moses was 80 years old; consequently when she became pregnant with him she was 130 years old."

[160] *Baba Batra* 120a; Ginzberg, *op. cit.*, Vol. 5, p. 396, n. 38; *Torah Shelemah*, Vol. 8, p. 53, n. 8.

a child in her old age.¹⁶¹ The way in which these motifs are drawn together resembles the combination of the motifs of old age and barrenness in the stories of Abraham and Luke 1. For example, note what is said in *Midrash Samuel* 4 (p. 28a):¹⁶² רבי שמואל בר נחמן בשם רבי יונתן בת מאה ושלשים נפקדה חנה, כשם שנפקדה יוכבד. "R. Samuel b. R. Naḥman said in the name of R. Jonathan: Hannah was one hundred and thirty years old at the time of her visitation, just as Yocheved was at her visitation."

THE THREE MONTHS OF CONCEALMENT

Amram's remarriage to Yocheved, taking her back to wife after having divorced her, is a prolific motif in the *Aggadah* and has various implications. Aside from explaining the existence of Miriam and Aaron, it is associated with the three-month period of concealment. As we read in *Sotah* 12a:¹⁶³ ותצפנהו שלשה ירחים, דלא מנו מצרים אלא משעה דאהדרה והיא הות מיעברא ביה תלתא ירחי מעיקרא. "She hid him three months. [She was able to do this] because the Egyptians only counted [the period of her pregnancy] from the time that she was restored [to Amram as his wife], but she was already three months pregnant then."¹⁶⁴ ¹⁶⁵

RESTORATION OF THE RIVER

As noted above, after Loewenstamm, the restoration of the river motif

---

¹⁶¹ Cf. *Baba Batra* 119b: "That a miracle happened to them [the daughters of Zelophehad, who were wed at an advanced age] as had happened to Yocheved." Compare the remarks of R. Judah b. Zebida with the *Gemara*, *Baba Meẓia* 87a (*Torah Shelemah*, Vol. 3b, p. 761, n. 154) on the verse, After I am waxed old shall I have pleasure (Gen. 18:12): "R. Ḥisda said: After her flesh had worn old and wrinkled, her flesh became resilient, her wrinkles smoothed out, and her beauty was restored."

¹⁶² Ginzberg, *op. cit.*, Vol. 6 (*Samuel*), p. 218, n. 15.

¹⁶³ *Torah Shelemah*, Vol. 8, p. 58, n. 21.

¹⁶⁴ The *Gemara*, however, does not make do with this answer, as we read in *Sotah* 12a: "And when she could not longer hide him—why? She should have gone on hiding him. But whenever the Egyptians were informed that a child was born, they would take another child there so that he should hear him and cry with him; as it is written, Take us the foxes, the little foxes ... (Song 2:15)." (*Torah Shelemah*, Vol. 8, p. 58, n. 24. Also see the other parallels listed in the commentary.) On the Egyptian's mistakes, see pp. 106–108 above.

¹⁶⁵ A general remark: The *Midrash* does away with the elliptical nature of the biblical narrative and goes to pains to explain why "his sister stood afar off." (According to Ginzberg, *op. cit.*, p. 398, n. 46, the *Midrash* gives the mother's command as the reason the sister stood watch, due to its inclination towards absolving Yocheved of blame for abandoning Moses.) The *Midrash* also addresses itself to the phrases, "And the daughter of Pharaoh came down," "And she had compassion on him," "This is one of the Hebrews' children," and others, according to its usual approach. These midrashic commentaries should not be viewed as particular to the Moses nativity story or to the tension that resulted from the history of the text. Therefore, these interpretations will not be discussed here.

to the story should be viewed as an indication that the force of the ark pattern is stronger than the biblical inclination to tone down the element of abandonment. So great is the force of this pattern that, from earliest to most recent times, it has appeared self-evident to readers of the biblical narrative that the ark containing Moses was placed in the river. In his article,[166] Loewenstamm cites the passage from *Sotah* 12b: "After Moses had been thrown [into the water] ...," as well as the surprising statement in *Sotah* 12a: "**and laid it in the reeds *(סוף)*—R. Eleazar said, in the Red Sea (ים סוף).**"[167] A further example of the ark's location is provided by *Dibre Yeme Moshe Rabbenu* 4:[168] ותרא בתיה את התיבה צפה על פני המים. "And Bithiah saw the ark floating on the water." The formulation in *Pirke R. Eliezer* 48[169] is instructive: ולאחר שלשה ירחים לא יכלה עוד הצפינו ושמתהו בתיבה והשליכתהו ליאור. "After three months she could no longer hide him; so she placed him in an ark and cast him into the Nile." The *midrash* replaces the edge of the Nile with the Nile itself. This in turn leads to "casting" the ark into the river (using the verb that appears in Pharaoh's edict), instead of the biblical formulation, "placing." Note the *midrashim* cited in *Torah Shelemah*, Vol. 9, p. 44, n. 80, which explain that the Nile was not struck by Moses because it had protected him when he was cast into it. Also note Rashi's commentary on Ex. 7:19. According to the *Gemara*:[170] ותקח לו תבת גמא, מ"ש גומא כר׳ רבי שמואל בר נחמני אמר דבר רך, שיכול לעמוד בפני דבר רך ובפני דבר קשה. "**She took for him an ark of bulrushes**—*why just bulrushes?* ... *R. Samuel b. Naḥmani says: because they are a soft material which can withstand both soft and hard materials.*" *Lekaḥ Tob* adds: בפני המים ובפני האבנים והסלעים, שאם יבואו גלי היאור וישליכו התיבה על הסלעים לא תשבר. "*It could withstand both the water and the rocks and stones; so that the ark would not break if waves should come in the Nile and cast the ark against the rocks.*"

From the careful attention which the text pays to the details of the

---

[166] "Die Geburtsgeschichte Moses," p. 196.

[167] This reference to the Red Sea has perplexed early and late talmudic scholars. Cf. *Torah Shelemah*, Vol. 8, p. 59, n. 29 of the commentary. Perhaps one should associate R. Eleazar's remark with what we find in the *Asatir* 9 (*Tarbiẓ*, Vol. 15, p. 74; also cf. *Torah Shelemah*, Vol. 8, p. 50, n. 1 of the commentary) about the water drying up when Moses was cast into the river; and should view the remark in the *gemara* and the words of the *Asatir* as taking the motif of the miracle at the Red Sea and applying it to the miracle involving the water of the Nile. For a juxtaposition of these notions, also cf. Biblical Antiquities 9:10; Miriam receives tidings that the son destined to be born will be cast into the water, and that the water will be dried up by him.

[168] *Torah Shelemah*, Vol. 8, p. 54, n. 11.

[169] *Ibid.*, p. 58, n. 22.

[170] *Sotah* 12a.

ark's construction, the *Midrash* draws the obvious inference that the purpose of the ark was to withstand the ravages of the river; thus the *Midrash* removes the tension found in the Bible between the lengthy and detailed account of the ark's construction and the role, or rather the lack of role, played by the ark, insofar as it was placed on the edge of the river. Indeed, in *Tībat Marqe* 6.1, p. 45, we read: נטרת אף יתך לגו נהרה דמצרים "*I also protected you in the Nile.*"[171]

As far as we can tell, restoration of the river to the story and of the ark to its original purpose do not raise any doubts in the *Midrash* as to the correctness of Yocheved's act, nor is there any tendency to argue in her defense against those who would claim that she had abandoned her child. It is clear to the *Midrash* that placing the ark in the Nile was intended to save Moses' life, and that this act stemmed from his mother's love for him.

A hint of apology may be found in *Exodus Rabbah* I.21: "Why did she cast him into the river? So that the astrologers might think that he had already been cast into the water, and would not search for him." There are no parallels to this passage, and Shinan believes it should be ascribed to the redactor. A similar point is made in the commentary of Rabbenu Ephraim[172] on the Torah: הטעם שהשליכה אותו ביאור כדי להטעות לאיצטגניני פרעה כדי שיתיאשו ממנו ולא יבקשו אחריו, שהרי כבר הושלך במים. "*The reason she cast him into the Nile was to mislead Pharaoh's astrologers, so that they would despair of [finding] him and would not seek him [any longer], since he had already been cast into the water.*" Abarbanel also mentions this approach.

The following remarks[173] however, could perhaps be viewed as implying censure of Yocheved's act: אדם אחד מאלף מצאתי (קהלת ז, כח) זה עמרם, אשה בכל אלה לא מצאתי ואפילו יוכבד. "**One man among a thousand have I found** *(Eccl. 7:28)—that is Amram,* **And a woman among all those have I not found**—*not even Yocheved.*" Perhaps Amram was not included in the story of the ark for fear lest he be tainted by censure for having abandoned his son. Indeed, the distinction between the two parents is particularly prominent in the Septuagint, which, when it comes to "**she took for him ...**," switches to the singular and explicitly mentions the mother, who does not appear explicitly in the masoretic formulation.

Perhaps greater weight should be given Loewenstamm's suggestion[174]

---

[171] Also cf. *Tībat Marqe* 296.2, p. 366.
[172] *Torah Shelemah*, Vol. 8, p. 60, n. 30.
[173] *Leviticus Rabbah* II.1; similar versions appear in *Ecclesiastes Rabbah* VII.28 and *Ecclesiastes Zuta*. Also cf. Ginzberg, Vol. 5, p. 395, n. 30 and p. 398, n. 46; *Torah Shelemah*, Vol. 8, p. 52, n. 3.
[174] "Die Geburtsgeschichte Moses," p. 196.

that originally the words "his mother" were included in the formulation of this phrase and that these words prevented changing the verb to the plural. Loewenstamm justifies his conjecture by the fact that this formulation also appears in the Samaritan version of the Bible, in which all the verbs are in the singular. On the other hand, it is not clear that Kasher is correct in his remarks on *Exodus Rabbah* I.21, "The *midrash* seeks to answer the question which has perplexed exegetes, namely how Yocheved could have done such a thing as to endanger her child with her own hands by putting him into the river, ... "[175] It seems more likely that the query of the *midrash*, "Why did she cast him into the river? ...," was directed at discovering the logic of such an act, and not at defending Yocheved's deed.

Medieval commentaries frequently grapple with Yocheved's act and sometimes proceed from the erroneous assumption that she placed the ark in the Nile. For example, note the contradictory elements found in Rabbenu Ephraim, cited above, who immediately after explaining that Moses' mother *cast him into the Nile* in order to mislead the astrologers, continues, "*She placed him on the banks of the Nile, in a discreet place, so that she could go and nurse him in hiding.*" Similarly in Rabbenu Bahya[176] we read: "**And she took for him an ark of bulrushes**—*for him, i.e., for his benefit and deliverance. Yocheved acted wisely, practicing a great deception by placing him on the banks of the Nile so that Pharaoh's astrologers would see and say that the savior had already been cast into the Nile, ...*" In contrast to all of these *midrashim*, note *Midrash ha-Ḥefeẓ*, which stresses that the ark was placed "*On the banks of the Nile, not in the Nile.*"[177]

One of the Hebrews' Children

Pharaoh's daughter's exclamation, "**This is one of the Hebrews' children**," is intended to explain Miriam's response, which follows directly: "**Shall I go and call to thee a nurse of the Hebrew women.**" The outcome is that the princess goes against her father's decree (cf. p. 23, above). Sometimes the usual nativity pattern also has the person destined to be the king's nemesis brought into the king's very own house; but this happens unbeknownst to the king or his relatives. Although this tension is not so prominent in the biblical narrative because there the king does not fear a specific individual, nevertheless in the *Midrash* it is quite evident:[178] ותרא את התבה בתוך הסוף, כיון דחזו דקא

---

[175] *Torah Shelemah*, Vol. 8, p. 60, n. 30.
[176] Exodus 2:3.
[177] See above, Chapter 2, note 43.
[178] *Sotah* 12b; *Torah Shelemah*, Vol. 8, p. 63, n. 42.

בעו לאצולי למשה, אמרו לה, גבירתנו, מנהגו של עולם מלך בשר ודם גוזר גזירה, אם כל העולם כולו אין מקיימין אותה, בניו ובני ביתו מקיימין אותה, ואת עוברת על גזירת אביך, בא גבריאל וחבטן בקרקע. "And she saw the ark among the reeds. When [her maidens] saw that she wished to rescue Moses, they said to her, 'Mistress, it is the custom of the world that when a king of flesh and blood makes a decree, even if the entire world does not obey it, at least his children and the members of his household obey it; but thou dost transgress thy father's decree!' Gabriel came and beat them to the ground."

In the version of the foundling story in which those who raise the child know the foundling's identity, their knowledge is based on first hand information from the person finding the child, who was ordered to put the child to death, or from some other hint providing at least partial disclosure of the foundling's (elevated) origins, such as his clothes, a letter, etc. Pharaoh's daughter's exclamation indicates that she knows the child's identity. The biblical narrative ostensibly provides sufficient foundation for such knowledge; nevertheless, the *Midrash*[179] still senses how basically foreign this motif is to the Moses story and tries to explain it: ותאמר מילדי העברים זה, מנא ידעה א"ר יוסי ברבי חנינא שראתה אותו מהול. "*Of the Hebrews' children is this. How did she know? R. Jose b. R. Ḥanina said: Because she saw that he was circumcised.*"

The motif of the king not knowing the true identity of the child being raised in his home is preserved in the *Midrash*, as in Philo, by means of Pharaoh's daughter not revealing the truth to her father:[180] איום ונורא הוא (חבקוק א, ז). זה פרעה שהיה קוסמוקטור שנאמר מושל עמים ויפתחהו (תהלים קה, כ), ממנו משפטו ושאתו יצא (חבקוק א, ז), זה משה שהיה מגודל בתוך ביתו והיה סבור שהוא בן בתו שנאמר ויגדל הילד ותביאהו לבת פרעה ויהי לה לבן (שמות ב, י). עמד והביא עליו עשר מכות. "*Terrible and dreadful is he (Habakkuk 1:7)—this refers to Pharaoh, who was ruler of the universe (κοσμοκράτωρ), as it is said,* **the ruler of the people, and let him go free** *(Ps. 105:20).* **His judgment and his dignity shall proceed from him** *(Habakkuk 1:7)—this refers to Moses, who was raised in his [Pharaoh's] home, and believed that he was his daughter's son, as it is said,* **and the child grew, and she brought him unto Pharaoh's daughter, and he became her son** *(Ex. 2:10). He [Moses] arose and brought down upon him ten plagues, ...*" Note that the pressure of the pattern leads the *midrash* to assume naïvely that the person who issued the decree is the one who is punished, in spite of what is written in Exodus 2:23. Perhaps this *midrash* assumed, as does Targum Yerushalmi, that "**the king of Egypt died**" (Ex. 2:23) means that he was stricken with lep-

---
[179] *Sotah* 12b; *Torah Shelemah*, Vol. 8, p. 66, n. 56.
[180] *Tanḥuma Buber* (חזריע 10); *Torah Shelemah*, Vol. 8, p. 69, n. 69.

rosy.[181] Also note what is said in *Tībat Marqe* 6.1, p. 45: ורביתך בבית דבבך בשלום. "*I saw to it that you be reared safely in your enemy's house.*"

As we have said, the exclamation of Pharaoh's daughter, "**One of the Hebrews' children is this**" is nothing but a pretext for undoing the child's severance from his mother, which fits in with the general biblical inclination towards toning down the element of abandonment. Restoring the son to his mother brings the narrative back to its starting point, reestablishing the circumstances that forced the mother to hide her son and build the ark. Indeed, note the following interpretation in *Midrash ha-Gadol*:[182] היליכי את הילד הזה והיניקהו לי, אמרה לה יראה אני מגזרה שגזר אביך, אמרה לה לי את מיניקתו. "**Take this child away, and nurse it for me.** She [Moses' mother] said to her, 'But I am afraid of the decree which your father issued.' She answered, 'For me, you are his wet-nurse.'"

Pharaoh's daughter

As Gressmann has noted, the ancient tradition of exile, bondage, and exodus is not cognizant of the nativity legend. This feature of the biblical tradition was somewhat obscured by the *midrashim* that stress the connection between the plagues on Egypt, especially the death of the firstborn, and Pharaoh's murder decrees. Nevertheless, it is notable that the *Midrash* does not enlarge upon the details of the nativity legend that concern the individual. Pharaoh's daughter, however, is the only figure that the *Midrash* could not leave in obscurity:[183] בתיה בת פרעה בכורה היתה, ובזכות מה היתה נצולת, בתפלתו של משה, דכתי׳ (משלי לא, יח) טעמה כי טוב סחרה לא יכבה בלילה נרה, ליל כתר׳, כד״א ליל שמורים הוא לי״י (שמ׳ יב, מב). "*Bithiah, the daughter of Pharaoh was a firstborn. By what merit was she spared? Through the merit of Moses' prayer for her. Of her it is written,* **She perceiveth that her merchandise** (סחרה) *[which may also be understood as her shield, i.e., Moses]* **is good: her candle** *[i.e., her soul]* **goeth not out by night** *(Prov. 31:18). Since 'night' is rendered here as* ליל, *the verse should be read in the light of another verse which also renders night in this unusual way:* **It was a night** (ליל) **of watching unto the Lord** *(Ex. 12:42) [which refers to the night when the firstborn of Egypt were smitten].*" Moreover, she even merited being counted among the Israelites:[184] ואלה בני בתיה בת פרעה, ר׳ יהושע דסיכנין בשם ר׳ לוי, אמ׳ לה הקב״ה לבתיה בת פרעה, משה לא היה בנך וקראת אותו בנך, אף את לא את בתי ואני קורא אותך בתי (שנאמר) (דהי״א ד, יח) אלה בני בתיה אשר לקח מרד זה כלב. ר׳

---

[181] Cf. the commentary in *Torah Shelemah*, Vol. 8, p. 102, n. 178.
[182] *Torah Shelemah*, Vol. 8, p. 68, n. 64.
[183] *Pesikta de R. Kahana* 7 (ויהי בחצי הלילה), p. 129; also cf. Mandelbaum's commentary there. *Torah Shelemah*, Vol. 8, p. 57, n. 18, and p. 62, nn. 37, 38.
[184] *Leviticus Rabbah* I.3; *Torah Shelemah*, Vol. 8, p. 69, n. 70.

אבא בר כהנא ור׳ יהודה בר סימון, ר׳ אבא בר כהנא אמ׳ זה מרד בעצת מרגלים וזו מרדה
בעצת אביה, יבוא מורד ויקח את המורדת, ר׳ יהודה בר׳ סימון אמ׳ זה הציל את הצאן וזו
הצילה את הרועה, יבוא מי שהציל את הצאן ויקח מי שהצילה את הרועה. "And these
are the sons of Bithiah, the daughter of Pharaoh, whom Mered
took *(I Chron. 4:18)*. *R. Joshua of Siknin said in the name of R. Levi:
The Holy One, blessed be He, said to Bithiah the daughter of Pharaoh:
'Moses was not your son, yet you called him your son; you, too, though
you are not My daughter, yet I will call My daughter,' even as it is said,*
These are the sons of Bithiah, *i.e., Bat Yah (the daughter of God).*
Whom Mered took. *Mered is Caleb. R. Abba b. Kahana and R. Judah b. Simon had a difference of opinion. R. Abba b. Kahana said: he
[Caleb] rebelled (*מרד*) against the counsel of the spies and she [Bithiah]
rebelled against the counsel of her father. Therefore let him who rebelled come and take in marriage her who rebelled. R. Judah b. Simon
said: he [Caleb] delivered the sheep and she [Bithiah] delivered the shepherd. Let him who delivered the sheep come and take in marriage her
who delivered the shepherd."* According to the account given by Artapanus in his book Ἰουδαϊκά or περὶ Ἰουδαίων (*On the Jews*), cited in
Eusebius, *Praeparatio Evangelica*, Book IX, 27.15, Pharaoh's daughter
(Maris) died before the exodus. Perhaps this happened in order that
she not be abandoned during her lifetime. In Artapanus' version of the
story her death also precedes the plagues on Egypt, perhaps for apologetic reasons, lest Moses be accused of ingratitude.[185] With respect to
the concern of the *Midrash* with the figure of Pharaoh's daughter, cf. the
opposition in Jewish tradition to abandonment, discussed in Chapter 1,
note 33 above.

Typological Motifs

In analyzing Moses nativity legends one should try, as far as possible,
to distinguish between two types: legends that are directly related to
specific literary features of the biblical story; and legends that are characteristic of the nativity of heroes in general. Thus far we have discussed
legends in terms of their being a reflection of the biblical story. In other
words, we have attempted to show how the singular features of the Moses
nativity story, its complex structure, and the tension between its components are reflected in various *midrashim*. In addition to the features
discussed thus far, we must introduce other elements that should not
be viewed as particular to the Moses nativity story, but rather as typological elements which are drawn towards nativity stories in general in
order to exalt the miracle of the birth and the deity's involvement in it.

---

[185] Cf. the section on Philo, n. 26 above; also cf. Ginzberg, *op. cit.*, p. 401, nn. 60,
61 and p. 435, n. 226.

According to *Sotah* 12a,[186] the birth of Moses was not like other births: ותהר האשה ותלד בן, מקיש לידתה להורתה מה הורתה שלא בצער אף לידתה שלא בצער, מכאן לנשים צדקניות שלא היו בפיתקה של חוה. "**And the woman conceived and bare a son.** *The bearing of the child is compared to its conception; as the conception was painless, so was the bearing painless. From this we learn that righteous women were not included in Eve's chit.*[187]"

This motif calls to mind the opposite motif of giving birth with pain, as in Genesis 25:22 and 35:16–20, as well as I Samuel 4:19–22.

The *Midrash*, unlike Josephus, does not draw a connection between Yocheved's easy labor and her managing to conceal having given birth. It stands to reason that Josephus took the motif from the *Midrash* and related it directly to the biblical story; or perhaps he had a different version of the legend. Hints of such a development can be found in later midrashic works such as *Lekaḥ Tob* and *Sekel Tob*. Following the usual pattern in the development of the motifs of our story, these *midrashim* transfer the motif from the individual to the generality:[188] בטרם תבוא אליהן המילדת וילדו, שהרי עבריות אינן בפתקה של חוה. "**Ere the midwife comes to them, they are delivered;** *for the Hebrew women are not included in Eve's chit.*" Nevertheless, *Sirāj al-'uqūl* remarks on Yocheved's birth, "*That it was not in pain, to fulfill that which is said,* **for they are lively.**" Perhaps this *midrash* wishes to intimate, like Josephus, that there was a connection between the ease of the birth and the fact that it was not discovered. The similarities between the general structure of the story in *Antiquities* and *Sirāj al-'uqūl* are discussed above, p. 95.

At the time of the birth, the house was resplendent.[189] ותרא אתו כי טוב הוא, חכמים אומרים בשעה שנולד משה נתמלא הבית כולו אור, כתיב הכא ותרא אתו כי טוב הוא וכתיב התם (ברא' א, ד) וירא אלהים את האור כי טוב. "**And she saw him that he was good.** *The sages say that when Moses was born, the whole house was filled with light; for it is written here,* **And she saw him that he was good,** *and it is written elsewhere,* **And God saw the light that it was good** *(Gen. 1:4).*"

The child was born already circumcised:[190] ואף משה יצא מהול שנאמר ותרא אותו כי טוב הוא, וכי מה ראתה אמו בו שאה ומשובח מכל אדם, אלא שיצא מהול. "*And Moses, too, was born circumcised, for it is said,* **And she saw him that**

---

[186] Ginzberg, *op. cit.*, p. 397, n. 41; *Torah Shelemah*, Vol. 8, p. 55, n. 12.
[187] Rashi interprets Eve's chit (פיתקה של חוה) to mean "her sentence and bill of decrees comprising her curse of sorrow and pregnancy."
[188] *Sekel Tob* 19; *Torah Shelemah*, Vol. 8, p. 43, n. 188.
[189] *Sotah* 12a; Ginzberg, *op. cit.*, p. 397, n. 42, and the many other appearances of this motif mentioned there; *Torah Shelemah*, Vol. 8, p. 56, n. 16.
[190] *The Fathers according to Rabbi Nathan* version A, Ch. 2; *Torah Shelemah*, Vol. 8, p. 57, n. 17.

he was good *(Ex. 2:2)*. Now, what did his mother see in him that made him more comely and magnificent than all other human beings? Only that he was born circumcised."

The *Midrash* also notes Moses' beauty:[191] ולפי שהיה יפה היו הכל מוציאין אותו מחאים לראותו. "Because he was so handsome, everyone would take him out, eager to see him." In *Pirke Rabbi Eliezer* 48 we read:[192] ר' נתנאל אומר ראו אבותיו של משה תארו של משה כמלאך אלהים. "R. Nethanel says, Moses' fathers saw Moses' aspect as an angel of God." Other references to his handsomeness have been mentioned in the sections on Philo and Josephus.[193]

Moses also grew up miraculously.[194] ויגדל הילד: כ"ד חדש היניקתהו ואת אמרת ויגדל הילד אלא שהיה גדל שלא כדרך כל הארץ. "And the child grew *(Ex. 2:10)*. She suckled him twenty-four months, yet you say: *And the child grew?* This is to teach that he grew in a manner unlike the rest of the world."

The Tale of the Crown

As we have said, these motifs should not be viewed as arising specifically from the particular literary structure or history of the biblical story, but rather as the continuation of a process whereby motifs are gathered and drawn to the figure of Moses. The most complex of the additional elements that were attracted to the figure of Moses is the story of the crown, which first appears in *Antiquities* 2.233–237 and is repeated in various versions.[195] The history of this tale is enlightening. First of all, it bears a resemblance to the Moses nativity story in the Bible. There is a threat to Moses' life which originates with the king, but divine intervention saves the newborn's life. The resemblance between this story and the pattern of the reconstructed biblical story is even more evident. A certain detail, in this case trampling on the crown, indicates to those capable of interpreting the sign that at some time in the future

---

[191] *Exodus Rabbah* I.26; *Torah Shelemah*, Vol. 8, p. 69, n. 69.

[192] *Torah Shelemah*, Vol. 8, p. 57, n. 16.

[193] Also cf. Ginzberg, *op. cit.*, p. 399, n. 50 and p. 401, n. 63.

[194] *Exodus Rabbah* I.26 and the parallels listed there; Ginzberg, *op. cit.*, p. 397, n. 43 and p. 401, n. 64; *Torah Shelemah*, Vol. 8, p. 68, n. 65; p. 69, n. 68, p. 72, n. 80.

[195] *Exodus Rabbah* I.26, *Dibre Yeme Moshe Rabbenu*, and *Sefer ha-Yashar*, pp. 289–291. For the non-Jewish sources, cf. Ginzberg, *op. cit.*, Vol. 5, p. 402, n. 65. In addition to those cited by Ginzberg, one should mention Παλαιά Ἱστορικά, published by A. Vassiliev in *Anecdota Graeco-Byzantina*, Moscow (1893), p. 227ff. This book was reviewed by D. Flusser in *Scripta Hierosolymitana* XXII, Jerusalem (1971), p. 48–79. and by S. Lieberman, "זניחין," *Tarbiẓ*, Vol. 42, pp. 42–54. What we say below about Παλαιά is all second-hand, based on the above sources. Also see the legend as it appears in pictures, as cited in Gutmann's article, *Eretz-Israel* 6, pp. 18–19.

the babe will be a threat and therefore must be put to death.¹⁹⁶ But, of course, the plot to kill him miscarries, and retrospectively it becomes clear that the omen foretelling danger had not been false. The sequence of events in this motif is clearly set forth in Josephus' version, in which, "the sacred scribe who had foretold that this child's birth would lead to the abasement of the Egyptian empire rushed forward to kill him with a fearful shout: 'This,' he cried, 'O king, this is that child whom God declared that we must kill to ally our terrors; he bears out the prediction by that act of insulting thy dominion and trampling the diadem under foot. Kill him then and at one stroke relieve the Egyptians of their fear of him and deprive the Hebrews of the courageous hopes that he inspires'" (2.234–235). Later sources add an ordeal to Josephus' version: Moses is brought gold and a red-hot coal (*Exodus Rabbah*); or a precious stone and a fiery coal (*Dibre Yeme Moshe Rabbenu*); or a date and a coal (*Midrash Rabbi David ha-Nagid*, p. 29); or a sparkling gold crown and a glinting unsheathed sword (Παλαιά, as cited in Lieberman), and the like, and Moses chooses one of the objects (with or without the intervention of an angel) and is saved.

Here, too, various features of the story indicate that it comes from a non-Jewish source. The story is indicative of recognition that the fate of man is subordinate to an independent, supreme force which man cannot change, even if he succeeds in disclosing this force. Josephus indeed adds the remark, "whom God declared ... ," although in his account of the forewarning itself (2.205) God is not mentioned. The child's deliverance, as well, is not attributed to the force of fate but rather to the king's "hesitation induced by God" (2.236). For parallel versions, see the sources cited by Lieberman.¹⁹⁷

In our study of nativity story models we saw that the motif opposing the birth, preventing or threatening the life of the newborn, can appear before, during, or after the birth. The great advantage in the story

---

¹⁹⁶ Peter Comestor puts forth an interesting explanation in his book, *Historia Scholastica* on Exodus 5: "*Erat autem in ea* [the diadem] *Ammonis imago fabrefacta*; i.e., "There was a picture of Ammon wrought in it [the diadem]." Cf. Lieberman, *op. cit.*, p. 49.

¹⁹⁷ We quote Lieberman, *op. cit.*, p. 50: "The core of the legend, about testing the intentions of a child who has committed a crime, was widespread in the ancient world. Cf. the legend in Hyperides (4th century, B.C.E.) in par. 199, about discerning between a doll and a tetradrachma (cf. Jensen ed., p. 147; H. Willers, *Numismatische Zeitschrift*, I (1899), p. 318, n. 9). Also see the formulation in Aelianus, *Varia Hist.* V,16." Emanuel Bin-Gorion (שבילי האגדה, p. 96) had already remarked on the parallel to Aelianus. It should be noted, however, that the ordeal motif does not appear in the most ancient version, i.e., the one found in Josephus. Even the Cyrus legend is familiar with the story of a child revealing his true inner nature when at play. Cf. Herodotus, Book I, 114.

of the crown is the late timing of the motif, which makes its easier to append it to the biblical story. In contrast, the story of the midwives and the story of the ark both take place at the time of the birth itself, and this proximity in their timing created the clash between them, signs of which remain evident in the Bible and are reflected in the surprising structure of the nativity story in Josephus. Indeed, the story of the crown is incorporated lucidly and smoothly in Josephus' narrative.

For all its smooth incorporation, the story pattern in Josephus still does not suffer from being associated with the figure of Moses. By *Exodus Rabbah* I.26, the *Midrash* has already added Jethro and Gabriel and an etiological explanation of Moses being "**slow of speech and of a slow tongue.**" (Compare the way in which the etiological motif, "**Because I drew him out of the water,**" is added to the basic pattern in the biblical narrative. Cf. p. 12 above.) In *Dibre Yeme Moshe Rabbenu* (Jellinek ed.) the story of the crown, whose main thrust is fear of an individual, is placed in close association with the king's fear of the masses which ends in his enslaving them. Although the story of the crown is more shielded from being connected to the masses because the child's identity is known, nevertheless the *midrash* moves increasingly closer to the biblical story.

The main significance of the story of the crown emerges from the conjunction of all the details discussed thus far. Here we have an originally foreign narrative pattern, structured according to the usual model of nativity stories. This pattern is drawn towards the figure of Moses, essentially trebles the structure of the nativity legend, and little by little is impressed with the characteristic marks of the Moses story. We are witness to a process such as presumably occurred in the biblical narrative, which, according to the theory we have advanced, gave rise to the Moses nativity story in the Bible. (Further development can be seen in Παλαιά, where the story is doubled; in the first story, Moses tramples the crown, and in the story which follows directly after it, Moses pulls Pharaoh's beard.)

Concluding Remarks

This chapter looked at *midrashim* as continuing the creative life of the biblical story and as arising out of a direct link with Scriptures. These two features of the *Midrash* were the focal point of our analysis. Many aspects of these legends seemed a continuation of the basic elements, or more precisely a continuation of the struggle between the basic elements, that gave rise to the biblical narrative. We have noted this and attempted to follow the evolution of each motif. Aside from the intrinsic interest in tracing this development, it can also assist us in understanding how the biblical narrative arose. Of course the utmost caution and reservation is called for in drawing inferences about the beginning of a motif from the subsequent evolution of that motif in a body of literature which mostly postdates the Bible.

To the extent that the *Midrash* stems directly from the scriptural text, it is akin to exegesis and certainly has a deliberate exegetical leaning. The *Midrash* surely stems in part from a desire to interpret Scripture, and hence should be viewed to a certain extent as a commentary on portions of Scripture which the Rabbis found problematic. We have noted this feature of the *Midrash* repeatedly; indeed, it was this feature that led to its incorporation in biblical exegesis, primarily in Rashi's commentary. Even though one cannot deny the exegetical inclination of the *Midrash*, only on rare occasions can one extract the full significance of the *Midrash* by viewing it as exegesis alone. Often it is preferable to say that the problematic aspect of Scripture finds expression in the *Midrash* or, especially in our case, that the complexity and tensions of the biblical narrative have been translated into midrashic legends. The fact that the *Midrash* rarely states the difficulty which gave rise to it and for the most part resolves the difficulty in passing is further indication that those who created it did not view it only as commentary. Lastly, this is also attested by the anecdotal literary nature of the *Midrash*, which deviates from a commentary on Scripture in the same instances in which it interprets the text. The literary genre of the *Midrash* is also what dictated the limits of our attempts to understand how it was created, for like every work, the wonders of its creation remain hidden from the human eye.[198]

We would like to give a concrete illustration of this point, but before presenting the *midrash* itself, one general remark is in order. The approach we have taken in this chapter may have given a distorted impression and has not truly characterized the *Midrash*. In our discussion of each motif, we looked at various *midrashim* in order to see how that motif appears in a specific legend. It is rare, however, for a *midrash* to contain only the elements we sought to present. Mostly it draws together many elements which, aside from the separate impressions of each, in their totality create a certain general impression.

Now for our illustration:[199] וימררו את חייהם, ד״א לא שלוחי (איוב ג, כו) מגזירה הראשונה שגזר פרעה עלי שאמר וימררו את חייהם, והעמיד לי הקב״ה גואל זו מרים על שם המירור, ולא שקטתי מגזירה שניה אם בן הוא והמתן אותו, והעמיד הקב״ה גואל זה אהרן על שם ההריון, ולא נחתי מגזירה שלישית שגזר ואמר כל הבן הילוד היאורה תשליכוהו, והעמיד הקב״ה גואל על שם המים זה משה שנאמר (שמות ב, י) כי מן המים משיתיהו. "And they made

---

[198] The above remarks should be qualified. They do not apply to halakhic *midrashim*, or *midrashim* whose connection with Scripture is tenuous or those which, although connected with Scripture, move far afield.

[199] *Exodus Rabbah* XXVI.1, Vilna ed.; *Torah Shelemah*, Vol. 8, p. 33, n. 145.

their lives bitter *(Ex. 1:14). Another interpretation:* **I was not at ease** *(Job 3:26) on account of the first decree that Pharaoh decreed against me, as it is said,* **and they made their lives bitter***; but the Holy One, blessed be he, produced a redeemer, namely Miriam, after 'making bitter,'* (מירור)*.* **Neither had I rest** *(Job 3:26) on account of the second decree,* **If it be a son, then ye shall kill him***; but the Holy One, blessed be He, produced a redeemer, namely Aaron, after the pregnancy* (הריון)*.*[200] **Neither was I quiet** *(Job 3:26) on account of the third decree that he issued, saying* **Every son that is born ye shall cast into the river***; but the Holy One, blessed be He, produced a redeemer, after the water, namely Moses, as it is said,* **because I drew him out of the water** *(Ex. 2:10)."*

This *midrash* is arranged according to the typological pattern of an ascending tri-part structure.[201] This pattern echoes the structure of the biblical narrative, except that in the *midrash* the structure is presented with a clarity not found in the Bible. In the Bible the structure is obscured by the great difference between the nature of the first decree, enslavement, and the two murder decrees which follow. In the *midrash*, on the other hand, the three decrees appear in a unified form, with each decree introduced by a verse from Scripture: **I was not at ease, neither had I rest, neither was I quiet**, and concluded with "the Holy One, blessed be He, produced a deliverer," and the names of Miriam, Aaron, and Moses in turn. The appearance of these names, one at the end of each unit, not only intensifies the similarity between the component parts of the progression, but also brings out its graduated structure, with the severity of each decree being mirrored by the status of the deliverer whom the Holy One, blessed be He, produced to counter the decree.[202] In the *midrash*, as well, the juxtaposition of the

---

[200] In his commentary Abarbanel says: "He was called Aaron since casting the Hebrews' children into the Nile commenced after his birth." It seems that he must have had a somewhat different version, which associated the explanation of Aaron's name with the Nile (יאור) and not the pregnancy (הריון). The explanation of Aaron's name in Abarbanel's version is associated with an event which took place after his birth. It may be, however, that Abarbanel altered the original version, for later he explains, "But, behold, none of this happened to Aaron, and he was not cast into the Nile, since when he was born the decree, '**Every son that is born** ...' had not yet been issued."

[201] Cf. Zunz, *op. cit.*, p. 366, n. d in the German edition (p. 173, n. 164 in the Hebrew edition) on the affinity of the *Midrash* for triple structures.

[202] Compare this to the similar structure in *Sotah* 12a (cited above, in Chapter 2, n. 51; *Torah Shelemah*, Vol. 8, p. 47, n. 205): "**And Pharaoh charged all his people**. R. Jose b. R. Ḥanina said: He issued three edicts: first, **if it be a son, then ye shall kill him**; *then* **every son that is born ye shall cast into the river***; and lastly he even imposed the same decree upon his own people.*" In *Sotah* the addition of Pharaoh's decree even to his own people transforms the double structure

enslavement to the two murder decrees leads even more strongly than in Exodus to a loss of the depth in time that originally characterized the bondage, as attested by scriptural sources excluding Exodus 1 and 2.[203]

The appearance of Miriam as the central figure in the enslavement motif and Aaron as the central figure in the story of the midwives is an innovation introduced by the *midrash*, without the slightest allusion to it in Scripture; but this should not lead one to think that it is therefore a 'stray' motif. The mode of expression and content may indeed be new, but they carry on a feature whose origins lie in the Bible. Clearly the last link—*the Holy One, blessed be He, produced a deliverer, after the water, namely Moses, as it is said*, **because I drew him out of the water**—should be viewed as giving rise to the first two links in parallel to it. This observation shows that the ancient trend discussed above, of the impact of the individual on the entire narrative, continues here as well. In the Bible it found expression in the murder decree being transferred from the individual to the masses; in the *midrash* it is completed by the deliverance of the individual being extended to the masses (cf. p. 108–115 above). The *midrash* which we have here goes even further, and sets forth the entire story in the context of a single individual. We may add that there is no similarity between associating Miriam with the enslavement and associating Aaron with the first murder decree. Involving Miriam in the story has no foundation in the history of the enslavement; but bringing in Aaron as having been deliv-

---

found in the Bible into a triple structure, condensed and confined within the bounds of the murder decrees.

[203] In addition to the sources cited on pp. 78–84 above, also cf. the following *midrash* from *Yalkut Shimoni*, n. 241: פתח עוזא שר של מצרים ואמר לפניו: רבש״ע אתה גזרת על אומה זו שיהו משועבדין תחת ידי אומה של׳ ת׳ שנה, שנאמר ועבדום וענו אותם ד׳ מאות שנה, ועדיין לא עבדו בהן אלא פ״ו שנה משנולדה מרים ועדיין לא הגיע זמנם לצאת, אלא תן לי רשות ואחזירם תחת ידי אומה של׳ ת׳ שנה, כשם שאתה קיים כך שבועתך קיימת וכו׳. "*Uzza, the tutelary angel of the Egyptians, spoke up and said to him: Lord of the Universe, you decreed that this people be enslaved by my people for four hundred years, as it is said*, **and they shall serve them; and they shall afflict them four hundred years** *(Gen. 15:13). But they had served them only 86 years by the time Miriam was born, and the time for their exodus had not yet come. So, permit me to return them under the service of my people four hundred years; for as You exist, so too your oath stands* ... " (*Torah Shelemah*, Vol. 3, p. 656, n. 144; *ibid.*, Vol. 14, p. 85, n. 197; citing *Midrash Abkir*). Shiloni, who edited the edition of *Yalkut Shimoni* put out by the Rab Kook Institute, believes that the origin of this legend is from *Midrash Wa-Yosha'*. According to the approach taken by the *midrash* here, Miriam was born three years before Aaron, who himself was three years older than Moses (Ex. 7:7). Perhaps this view was also in the consciousness of the authoer of the above *midrash* from *Exodus Rabbah* XXVI.1. If so, this would imply that there was an equal span of three years between each decree, thus creating a balance which further strengthens the similarity between the decrees.

ered²⁰⁴ from Pharaoh's instruction to the midwives to put every male son to death should be viewed, to a certain extent, as restoring the decree to its roots. The individual, the hero of the story from the outset, is restored; but since the original hero of the story of the midwives is captive in the story of the ark, the story of the midwives had to make do with a substitute, Moses' brother Aaron.²⁰⁵ The fact that the *midrash* associates Aaron with the first murder decree indicates that it no longer senses the connection between Moses and this decree; thus it marks another step in the story of the midwives becoming more detached from Moses, its original hero.

It is hard to say whether it was the aim of this legend to solve the problem, with which the *Midrash* grapples, of Miriam appearing on the scene and of Aaron existing before the birth of Moses, although it does so in passing. Here they appear before the birth of Moses and in relationship to him; but their appearance before Moses in no way detracts from his preferential status. Quite the contrary, the structure of the *midrash* skillfully transforms Moses' late appearance into an expression of his greater importance, as in the motif of the younger brother in Genesis and, even more strikingly, as in the anointment of David, the youngest among his brothers (I Samuel 16).

---

²⁰⁴ It seems this is how the legend should be understood. Compare *Dibre Yeme Moshe Rabbenu*: "*And she conceived again and bore a son, and she called him Aaron, for during her pregnancy* (הריונה) *Pharaoh began spilling the blood of their males on the ground and casting some of them into Egypt's river* (יאר) *(sic)*." Also compare *Sefer ha-Yashar*, p. 283.

²⁰⁵ The passage cited by Neubauer in *Chronicles*, Vol. 1, p. 196, describes Aaron's birth as follows: "*Aaron was born on the first day of the month of Tamuz, in the year two thousand three hundred and sixty-five, and on the preceding 15th of Sivan there had been a [large] eclipse [of the sun]. Moses, our Teacher of blessed memory, was born in the year two thousand three hundred and sixty-eight.*" The words in brackets are unclear. The omen, which all the sources associate with the birth of Moses, actually preceded the birth of Aaron.

CHAPTER FOUR

THE ASATIR

In the *Asatir*,[1] as well, the legend of the individual pushes aside the national tradition of the enslavement. The decree enslaving the people is not mentioned at all, and only at the end of the legend of the individual do we learn indirectly of its existence (Chapter 9, p. 75; Moses is appointed to oversee the work for Pharaoh). This change makes the time scheme of the book of Exodus fall naturally into place, so that all the events take place under a single king. Like Josephus and the Midrash, the *Asatir* explains the murder decrees in terms of the king's fear of the birth of the savior. Only a vestige remains of the fear lest the people multiply after the midwives' refusal to comply with the king's decree: "*And the people grew numerous and waxed very strong.*"

The version of the nativity story given in the *Asatir* is noteworthy

---

[1] See Appendix C for an English translation. The *Asatir* is a Samaritan legend, which Gaster dates to the third century, B.C.E., but Ben-Ḥayyim dates between the eighth and the 12th centuries, C.E. (*Tarbiẓ*, Vol. 14, pp. 105–112.) It has many close points of contact with Jewish tradition: the reason given for the edicts is the fear of a certain individual's birth; and, aside from prophesying the destined birth, the words of the seer also mention the mother's conception and Moses being thrown into the Nile (cf. above, pp. 95–104). The women are separated from their husbands (p. 88, above). The seer states that "*his death shall be by water,*" (p. 107, above). Pharaoh's daughter finds Moses on the seventh day; compare Jubilees, p. 31, above. He is given pure milk to suckle; cf. Ben-Ḥayyim's remark, *op. cit.*, Vol. 15, p. 75. Moses is appointed to oversee the Pharaoh's works; cf. *Tanḥuma* (Oxford manuscript), ואראאל 17, cited in Buber's note 151, *ibid.* (*Torah Shelemah*, p. 73, n. 84. Also cf. above, The Midrash, note 6).

According to Ben-Ḥayyim's proposed translation— ורב העם והתחזק מאד וציווה פרעה את כל העם לזרוק את היילודים אל הנהר "*and the people grew numerous and waxed very strong; and Pharaoh commanded all the people to cast the newborns into the river*" (Vol. 15, p. 73)—alongside the biblical tradition, the *Asatir* also includes the tradition appearing in Jubilees 47:2, Ezekiel the Tragedian, and Acts of the Apostles 7:19, according to which the children of Israel were ordered to cast their own sons into the Nile; except that the *Asatir* adds that the Israelite women cast themselves into the Nile along with their sons. However it is doubtful whether one can accept his rendition, because the formulation in the *Asatir*—ופקד פרעה לכל עמה (Vol. 14, p. 121)—is parallel to the formulation of the Samaritan Targum on Exodus 1:22. Therefore, it seems to us that this passage should be rendered as "And Pharaoh commanded all his people."

primarily for the way it arranges the story presented in Exodus. The double structure of the Bible (the story of the midwives and casting the sons into the Nile) is replaced in the *Asatir* by a narrative consisting of three stages, in which each stage (with the exception of the last) is arranged according to the following structure: a threat, the king's response, and the failure of his response.

The first stage is clear and simple. First comes the danger inherent in the tidings of Palti the seer: *"From the offspring of this man there shall arise a man great in faith and wisdom, and the heavens and the earth shall obey him, and the destruction of Egypt shall be wrought at his hands."* This is followed by Pharaoh's reaction: to separate the women from the men.[2] The general nature of the edict—*"The women shall be separated from the men"*—was inherited from the Midrash and the Bible; but in the *Asatir*, where the father's identity is semi-known to the seer and the king—as is common in this story pattern in other folk literature—such a general formulation is actually out of place. This difficulty becomes more pronounced in later Samaritan legends, which present the reasonable formulation that the man whom Palti saw was Amram. Indeed, these later versions attempt to reconcile this difficulty. Lastly comes the failure of the king's reaction: *"There went a man from the house of Levi."*

The second stage is a direct result of the first. It begins with the danger: a star has arisen; the mother of the child is pregnant with him. Then comes the response: Shiphrah and Puah are charged to oversee the births. Lastly, its failure: *"and the fear of God was in their hearts, and they did not do as Pharaoh had commanded."* The midwives' refusal, which is the third element in the second stage, is less clear. Firstly, we note that despite the appearance of the story of the midwives, the *Asatir* also contains a covert desire to omit the appearance of Shiphrah and Puah; for the seer's words to Pharaoh after the rise of the star, that *"his death shall be by water,"* lead towards the edict to throw the sons into the Nile and not towards the instruction given the

---

[2] In the Midrash, separation of the women from their husbands is presented as the object of the enslavement (cf. p. 88, above); but here it appears by itself, without reference to the enslavement, and is limited to a span of forty days, apparently because the savior's conception was prophesied to take place during this period. Compare the *Asatir*'s account of the birth of Abraham (Chapter 5), where the wise men say to Nimrod, "In another forty days his mother shall have conceived him." Also compare *Sanhedrin* 22a: "Forty days before the creation of the fetus a divine voice (בת קול) calls out and says 'The daughter of so and so is destined for so and so.'" The *Asatir* does not use separation of the women to account for the appearance of Moses' sister, as the Midrash does with the story of his parents' second marriage. (Of course Miriam's appearance at the end of the story in the *Asatir* is inherited from the biblical narrative.)

midwives. Omission of the midwives story, especially in sources that include the motif of foreknowledge, is discussed at greater length above (cf. p. 96).[3] Secondly, the *Asatir* moves up the verse, "*There went a man from the house of Levi,*" which in the Bible appears after the two murder decrees, and places it immediately after the edict separating the women from their husbands. Thus, Moses' mother conceives before the instruction to the midwives, whose role in the *Asatir*'s version of the story is to prevent the birth of the savior. The clear impression given by this editing of the story is that the midwives' refusal to obey the order is what leads to the birth of the savior. Indeed, the story does not note this explicitly; rather, true to the biblical story, the *Asatir* mentions the birth after the edict to throw the sons into the Nile. According to our theory, loyalty to the source proved stronger here than the conclusion that should have followed from the structure. The *Asatir*'s narrative hedges, as it were, and refrains from taking the obvious step and openly involving the midwives in the birth of Moses; but, and this is the main point, the story does lean in this direction. Likewise, it should be noted that by juxtaposing the instruction to the midwives with the edict given all the Egyptians—"*So Pharaoh commanded the Egyptians: 'Let not a single Hebrew male remain alive.' Shiphrah and Puah were charged to oversee the births of the Hebrew women, ...*"—the *Asatir* not only gives the impression that the midwives are Egyptian,[4] but also does

---

[3] *Molad Mosheh*, which is structurally parallel to the *Asatir*, emends the structure as follows: "*And the king of Egypt said to the midwives mentioned previously, 'Every son that shall be born to the Hebrews ye shall throw into the Nile and every daughter ye shall let live.' Thus said the impudent tyrant; and the midwives feared God, the righteous and just God, and did not do as the wicked Pharaoh had said,*" etc. (Cited in Miller, p. 14, ll. 3–9.) Compare this with Josephus, *op. cit.*, 2.206; also, see the section on Josephus, pp. 55–57 above. Also, compare the structure in the *Asatir*'s treatment of the birth of Abraham (Ch. 5).

[4] Perhaps one should include the Samaritan *Asatir* in the list of sources cited above, p. 92 ff., that hold that the midwives assisting the births of the Hebrew women were Egyptian. The formulation here is: "*So Pharaoh commanded the Egyptians: 'Let not a single Hebrew male remain alive.' Shiphrah and Puah were charged to oversee the births of the Hebrew women, and Pharaoh said to them: 'Let every male be killed, and every female let live.' Now Amram was a good doctor, well-received in Egypt. Shiphrah felt kindly to the Levites and Puah felt kindly to the Hebrews; and the fear of God was in their hearts, and they did not do as Pharaoh had commanded.*" Mentioning Shiphrah and Puah immediately after the Egyptians gives the impression that they, too, were Egyptians. Also, the remark that "*Puah felt kindly to the Hebrews*" is more appropriately said of an Egyptian. Against these arguments, one should note that this remark is made immediately after mentioning Amram—"*Now Amram was a good doctor.*" Perhaps one should infer from this that the Samaritan legend also identified Shiphrah and Puah with Yocheved and Miriam. It is not beyond the realm of possibility that two different approaches have been combined here.

away with the element of a covert plot that is not known to the entire population.

The transition from the second stage to the third is somewhat obscure. This is due, firstly, to the incorporation of the Biblical quotation, "*And the people grew numerous and waxed very strong*," which brings in a motif that is altogether foreign to the *Asatir*'s version. Secondly, as we have already noted, the edict to throw the sons into the Nile follows from the seer's words that "*his death shall be by water*"; whereas, according to his prophesy, the edict to throw the sons into the Nile ought to have come in place of the instruction to the midwives, which intervenes between the astrologer's prediction and the steps taken to prevent its realization. Thirdly, the relationship between the edict to throw the sons into the Nile and the instruction given the midwives is far from sufficiently well illumined; for, from the formulation of the text, it is not clear whether the midwives' refusal to follow orders is what led to the birth of the savior. If the savior was indeed born because of their refusal to comply, then one could say that the edict to throw the sons into the Nile was aimed at drowning the child who had meanwhile come into the world. In other words, in terms of the narrative's structure it is not clear whether the danger in the third stage was that Moses had already been born, or that he was destined to be born.

The conclusion of the story is most complex. To the failure of the king's response the author appends the miracle of the ark, which incidentally he elides with the miracle of the level of the river dropping.[5] He adds to this double miracle that Palti the magician was cognizant of what was happening, but that Pharaoh's daughter saved the child. This embellishment essentially creates an additional stage in the structure of the story. The element of the danger stemming from the seer's discovery is present, as is the contrasting element of the child's deliverance, but the element of the king's response, which in all the other stages appears between the danger and the deliverance, is missing.[6]

In *Molad Mosheh* (Miller edition), which largely repeats the version in the *Asatir*, the midwives of the Hebrews are described in the Arabic as "*the midwives of the magnificent people*" (p. 19). In the parallel version we read: וישלח פרעה ויקרא למילדות עם ישר דשם האחת שפרה ושם השנית פועה. "*And Pharaoh sent and called for the midwives of the righteous people, one of whom was named Shiphrah and the other named Puah*" etc. (pp. 13–14). Perhaps these later versions, as well, attest that the tradition they reflect understood למילדות העבריות as referring to women who assisted the Hebrews' births, not to midwives who themselves were Hebrews.

[5] The *Asatir* reduces the tension between the river—"*and when he was cast into the river*"—and the riverbank; for Palti noted that "*his ark was in the reeds*" after the level of the river had dropped; and the riverbank is not mentioned at all.

[6] Recall that the Jewish sources also present the magicians as being well aware that Moses was "cast" into the river; but, in contrast to the *Asatir*, this discovery

The double structure of the Moses nativity story in Exodus, which contains two originally independent nativity patterns, comes closest to a harmonious resolution in the *Asatir*. The pattern begins with the annunciation of the birth of a child who is destined to be a threat to the king. The king's response, initially, is the instruction to the midwives, the aim of which is to prevent the birth; but since the midwives refuse to comply, the infant is born; and since he has already been born, the king orders all the newborns to be thrown into the Nile. The *Asatir* even goes one better, and prefaces this structure with the king's first measure, designed to prevent the marriage of the parents. The result is a graded typological structure, consisting of three stages and paralleling the three stages in the appearance of the savior: 1) The child is destined to be conceived, 2) has been conceived, and 3) is born. Hence the structure which emerges through this overlay of motifs is: A) Forewarning (the child is destined to be conceived), then the edict to separate husband and wife, followed by the parent's marriage. B) Annunciation (the child has been conceived), then the instruction to the midwives, followed by their refusal to comply. C) The king's fear or knowledge that the child has been born (a stage which does not appear explicitly in the text), then the edict to throw the sons into the Nile, followed by the child's deliverance and adoption by the daughter of his would-be killer. Indeed, we may compare this latent structure to the pattern of the Abraham nativity story in the *Asatir* (Chapter 5). There the author did not have to adapt the structure of his story to a biblical version. The three stages of destined to be conceived, having been conceived, and being born are clearly evident, and the element of being cast into the fiery furnace appears after the element of the birth.

This development is apparently due to the literary genre of the *Asatir*, which weaves various legends together with the biblical account in order to form a single narrative, in contrast to the genre of the Midrash, with its independent units that have no pretense of forming a single, continuous story. In the next section we shall attempt to show that Rashi's commentary has a similar structure, paralleling the latter two stages of the *Asatir*. In Rashi, too, the structure can be explained as a

---

leads to Moses being rescued and the edict being repealed (see the mistakes of the magicians, p. 107, above). Perhaps this motif was originally borrowed by the Samaritan legend, but then evolved in such a way as to become severed from the motif of deliverance and associated, under the influence of the prior prophesies, with the threat to the savior's life. The miracle of the water receding is similar to the drying of the Red Sea (see above, The Midrash, note 167). Here, too, the motif might be of Jewish origin. Lastly, Pharaoh's daughter requests her handmaidens not to divulge the secret of the child's discovery. Most likely the Samaritan legend was grappling with a difficulty which the Bible seems to ignore: how Pharaoh could have consented to Moses being raised in his palace. Compare pp. 124–126, above.

result of the literary genre. His commentary necessarily adheres to the biblical text, and this brings the commentator to arrange the individual motifs in a natural order. It is important to note that the solution to the biblical structure that is offered by the *Asatir* is extremely close to the Jesus nativity story in Matthew, Chapter 2. This structural affinity leads to important conclusions regarding the relationship of the New Testament story to the Old Testament story, however we shall reserve these conclusions until the end of our chapter on Rashi.[7]

---

[7] As we have intimated in the notes, the *Asatir* represents a decisive step in the evolution of the Samaritan legends. This, however, is not the place to go into deeper analysis of these legends.

CHAPTER FIVE

NOTES ON RASHI'S COMMENTARY

Rashi's position between the homiletical approach and the plain sense approach to biblical exegesis sometimes raises the question whether his commentary should be viewed as an interpretation aimed at reconciling difficulties in the text, or whether it should be included in the same class as *aggadah* and should be viewed more as reflecting the difficulties of the text than resolving them. The difficulty in determining the literary genre is bound up with the question of whether his commentary should be viewed as a work which is separate from the Bible and analyzes the biblical text from without, or whether it should be viewed, like the Midrash, as a further evolution of motifs in the biblical narrative.

First we shall take up the elements borrowed from the Midrash, which pertain to the subject at hand and do not introduce a substantive innovation.[1] Like the earlier and later exegetes, Rashi grapples with the relationship between the motif of dealing wisely and the motif of enslavement. Rashi's remarks, "**Let us deal wisely with them**: *i.e., with the people; let us consider wisely what to do to them,*" are taken from *Sifre*, Deut. 13, and are parallel to Targum Yerushalmi (which was not known to Rashi): נחיעט עליהון בהלין דינין נזערא יתהון "*Let us take counsel regarding them, how we shall reduce their numbers.*"[2]

Rashi explains why Moses' mother ceased concealing him (Ex. 2:3): "**And she could no longer conceal him** *because the Egyptians calculated the period from when he [Amram] took her back. She, however, bore him after a term of six months and one day*—*for a woman who gives birth to a child in the seventh month may not necessarily complete the seventh month*—*and they [the Egyptians] made enquiry regarding her at the end of nine months.*" This commentary comes from *Sotah* 12a, except for the explanation about not completing the seventh month, which

---

[1] For Rashi's sources, see Zunz, *op. cit.*, Albeck's note 112 on p. 316 of the Hebrew edition; also see the Berliner edition of Rashi's commentary; Avineri, היכל רש"י; Ginzberg; and *Torah Shelemah*. Note that aside from his commentary on the Torah, one should also examine his commentary on *Sotah* 12 and *Baba Batra* 119b–120a. English translations of Rashi have mostly been taken or adapted from the Rosenbaum–Silbermann edition.

[2] Berliner does not give the source. Also cf. the Neophyti Targum.

comes from *Niddah* 38b and *Rosh ha-Shanah* 11a. Rashi's account of the Egyptians' other mistakes also follows his sources (*Sotah*). The first time Rashi cites the Midrash concerning the Egyptians' first mistake—that they thought to use their wisdom against Israel's deliverer, the Holy One blessed be He, by sentencing the children of Israel to death by water—is in Ex. 1:10, paralleling *Sotah* 11a, because at this point the subject of the narrative is still the people, and no allusion has yet been made to the single savior. Rashi incorporates the Midrash about their second mistake—that they thought to use their wisdom against Israel's deliverer, Moses, by sentencing him to death by water—again after *Sotah* 12b, in his commentary on verse 22, immediately after Moses appears in the story.

Rashi is sensitive to the problem posed by the presence of Miriam, and offers the midrashic solution (Ex. 2:1)—"*He had lived apart from her ... Now he took her back and entered into a second marriage with her*"—but does not state the difficulty of the biblical text explicitly. However, on the Gemara, *Baba Batra* 120a—"**And he took [to wife]**—*the text should have read 'and he took her [to wife] again,'*" Rashi comments, "*Much time must have elapsed since his first marriage to her, since Aaron and Miriam had already been born.*" Rashi also associates Amram's remarriage to Yocheved with the miracle of bearing child in one's old age: "*and she also became young again.*" Note how his commentary on *Sotah* 12a, that "*she returned to the days of her youth, again had a menstrual cycle (*ארח נשים*),*" points out the connection with the miracle of Sarah conceiving Isaac (Gen. 18:11). Also, Rashi comments on the *Gemara*'s remark about "*giving birth until age sixty*" (*Baba Batra* 119b, with regard to the daughters of Zelophehad) that "*they were sure a miracle would be done for them due to their righteousness, as had been done to Yocheved.*" Rashi calculates Yocheved's advanced age with great precision.[3] He also notes, again after *Sotah* 12a, that at the birth itself

---

[3] Cf. The Midrash, note 159. With respect to Yocheved having been born "between the walls" see Rashi's commentary on Genesis 46:26: "**All the souls that came (**הבאה**) with Jacob**—*every soul that left Canaan to go to Egypt. The word* הבאה *here is not a past tense, but a participle with a relative present sense, as 'In the evening she is coming (*באה*)' (Esther 2:14) and 'and, behold, Rachel his daughter is coming (*באה*) with the sheep' (Gen. 29:6). Therefore the accent is on the last syllable, on the* א*, because when they left, coming from the land of Canaan, they were only sixty-six. But the second time this is mentioned, 'all the souls of the house of Jacob, which came (*הבאה*) into Egypt, were threescore and ten,' it is a perfect tense and therefore it is accented on the penultimate syllable, on the* ב*. The reason is that when they came there they were seventy, for they found Joseph and his two sons there, and Yocheved was added to their number 'between the walls'*" (*Torah Shelemah*, Vol. 7, p. 1690, n. 148). Also cf. his commentary on Numbers 26:59. All these commentaries are after his sources; cf. The

the house became filled with light.

Now we proceed to Rashi's commentaries in which his own mark is more evident. On Exodus 1:1 Rashi writes: "*Although Scripture has already enumerated them by name whilst they were living, it again enumerates them when it tells us of their death, thus showing how dear they were to God.* (להודיע חבתם)" Rashi's explanation of the repetition follows *Tanḥuma Buber* (שמות 2); but, as Avineri has shown,[4] Rashi adds "thus showing how dear they were to God" to the explanation in the Midrash.[5] On Genesis 1:1 Avineri notes,[6] "Rashi's intention was to begin on the note of God's love for the children of Israel and the honor of the children of Israel. Indeed, we see that this is Rashi's way of beginning his commentary on each of the five books of the Pentateuch: Exodus and Numbers he begins with remarks implying love for the children of Israel, Leviticus he begins with love and respect of Moses, and Deuteronomy with an allusion to the honor of the children of Israel." Rashi's commentary on Numbers 9:1 further supports Avineri's point. Thus, we see an inclination which parallels the ancient tendency, already evident in Scriptures, not to conclude on a disparaging note.[7] Rashi, after the Midrash, frequently explains a repetition in the text as being a sign of endearment, a sort of *Bis repetita placent*. The beginning of Exodus merits redoubled emphasis, because it is set against the desire to justify the hardships of the exile on the grounds of transgression.[8] Signs of the latter approach are even evident in Rashi, as in his commentary on Exodus 2:14: "**And Moses feared**: *Explain it in its literal sense. A Midrashic explanation is that he felt distressed because he saw that there were wicked men among the Israelites—common informers. He said: Since this is so, perhaps they are not worthy to be delivered.* **Surely the thing is known**: *Explain it in its literal sense. A Midrashic explanation is that now there is known to me that matter about which I have been puzzled—how has Israel sinned more than all the seventy nations, that they should be oppressed by this crushing servitude? But now I see that they deserve this.*" It should be noted, however, that love of Israel predominates in Rashi, and disparagement of our forefathers is downplayed. Even the commentary we have cited (according to Berliner's preferred reading) places the disparaging remarks as the second interpretation, after the plain sense.

Rashi scholars have gone to great efforts to explain his grammatical

---

Midrash, note 159.

[4] היכל רש"י, Vol. 4, p. 223, n. 70.
[5] *Torah Shelemah*, Vol. 8, p. 2, n. 6; also cf. *Sekel Tob, ibid.*
[6] היכל רש"י, Vol. 4, p. 213, n. 1.
[7] Cf. Zunz, *op. cit.*, p. 91 in the German edition, p. 44 in the Hebrew edition.
[8] Cf. p. 71–76, above.

observation[9] on Exodus 1:15: "**To the midwives** (למילדת) *[the Piel participle]—This is synonymous with* מולידות *[the Hiphil participle, and both denote the women who assist the mother in bringing the child to birth]. But some verbs are used in the form of a light conjugation [לשון קל] or in forms of a heavy conjugation [לשון כבד], as e.g.,* שבר *[Kal] and* משבר *[Piel];* דובר *[Kal] and* מדבר *[Piel]; similarly we may have* מוליד *[Hiphil] or* מילד *[Piel]."*[10] It seems to us that Rashi's commentary is based on the ambiguity of the phrase למילדת העבריות, which can be understood either as "to the Hebrew midwives," or as "to the midwives assisting the Hebrew women." (Cf. p. 19, above.) Rashi finds for the latter, i.e., that העבריות is an object.

To begin with, it should be noted that in Genesis 35:17 Rashi passes over this grammatical form in silence; therefore we may proceed from the assumption that, in contrast to the Genesis occurrence of this verb, in our verse there is a problem which is resolved by comparing the forms מילדות and מולידות. Rashi wishes to use the examples of מדבר—דובר and משבר—שבר to show that the meaning of a verb need not always change when the verb form changes from one conjugation to another, and that in the present instance מילדות should be understood as equivalent to מולידות. In other words, the *Piel* form should be understood as if it were *Hiphil*.

If we look at the examples collected by Avineri,[11] we see that Rashi is very much aware of the *Hiphil* conjugation being used for transitive verbs. For example, see his commentary on Deuteronomy 30:3: "**Then the Lord thy God will turn** (ושב) **thy captivity**—*To express this idea it ought to have written 'then He will bring back (והשיב) thy captivity'*"; or Exodus 13:22: "**The pillar of the cloud did not depart** (לא ימיש עמוד הענן)— *this means He, i.e., the Holy One blessed be He, did not let the pillar of cloud depart [because a transitive verb form is used]*"; or Genesis 12:8: "**And he removed from there** (ויעתק משם)—*add the word, his tent; i.e., he removed his tent [because a transitive verb form is used]*"; or Exodus 14:10: "**And Pharaoh came near** (הקריב)—*It should have written 'and Pharaoh came near' (קרב). What is the force of* הקריב, *'He caused to come near'? He made himself come near; he*

---

[9] Our discussion of Rashi's grammatical comment is to appear in לשונו, and is published here by the gracious permission of the editor, J. Blau.

[10] By *Kal* Rashi apparently means the *Hiphil* form, מולידות, without the *dagesh*. Cf. ספר זכרון: "Rashi does not refer to the verb conjugations; rather, by *Kal*, 'light,' he means light on the tongue, and by *Kabed*, 'heavy' or 'strong,' he means heavy on the tongue; for this goes along with what Rabbi David Kimḥi wrote in his book, המכלול, שער דקדוק הפעלים, and therefore it is called *Kal*, because every letter which has a *dagesh* is produced more heavily. ... From this we conclude that Rashi would not call *Hiphil* strong, but simply augmented; i.e., an augmented *Kal* form; and this indeed is how some of the early grammarians referred to it."

[11] היכל רש"י, Vol. 3, pp. 73–77.

forced himself to go in front of them as he had arranged with them."[12] Also see the other examples cited in היכל רש"י, *loc. cit.* With respect to several *Hiphil* forms Rashi does not view this form simply as indicating a transitive verb, but adds a causative signification, despite the fact that the plain sense of these verbs hardly subsumes such a meaning. For example, see Exodus 35:1: "**And Moses assembled** (ויקהל)—*the word* ויקהל *is used in Hiphil [the verbal form that expresses the idea of causing a thing to be done] because one does not actually assemble people with one's hands, but they are assembled by his command. The Targum therefore should be* ואכניש." Also notice how Rashi stresses the causative form of the verb in his interpretation of תכריתו as to cause to be cut off, in Numbers 4:18. Further examples are cited by Avineri (*op. cit.*). Rashi's commentary on Genesis 4:18, where he distinguishes between ילד and הוליד, is crucial to our discussion. We read there: "**And Irad beget** (ילד)—*There are passages where it says of the male* הוליד, *and there are places where is says* ילד, *because this root* ילד *is used in two senses: in reference to a woman giving birth to a child, O.F. naître [Engl. to give birth to] and the act of begetting by a man, O.F. engendre [Engl. engender, beget]. When it says* הוליד *in the Hiphil form it speaks of the man in his relation to the act of giving birth by the woman—this or that man caused his wife to give birth to a son or daughter; when it says* ילד *it refers to the act of begetting by the man himself.*" Also see Rashi's commentary on Genesis 40:20: "**The day of Pharaoh's birth** (יום הלדת את פרעה). *The day of his birth* (יום לידתו). *It is called 'The birthday festival.' The causative passive form* (הלדת) *is used because the infant is born only by the assistance of others, for the midwife delivers the woman. On this account a midwife is called* מילדת *[a Piel form] 'one who brings to birth.' Similarly (Ezek. 16:4)* "**And as for thy nativity, in the day thou wast born** (הולדת אותך); *etc.*" Here too the passive form of the *Hiphil* form את הלדת stems from the action of the midwife assisting the woman at the birth of her son. Thus Rashi wishes to say that העבריות is an object, not an adjective. Rashi's commentary which we have cited from Genesis also implies that he views למילדות העבריות as meaning the women helping the Hebrew women to bring their sons and daughters to birth. Indeed, note his laconic remark on the next verse (v. 16), **When ye do the office of a midwife to the Hebrew women**, in which the object appears explicitly: "*The word* בילדכן *[the Piel form] has the same force as* בהולידכן *[the Hiphil]*." Rashi views this verse as proof that one should understand מילדות to mean מולידות, i.e., as a transitive verb which

---

[12] It is irrelevant to the point at hand that contemporary grammarians are of a different opinion and hold the examples cited here—from the verb roots מוש, עתק, and קרב—to be *Kal* forms, rathern than *Hiphil*. Cf. H. Yalon, פרקי לשון, pp. 43–55.

takes a direct object.

As we have seen (cf. p. 19, above), Rashi was neither the only nor the first commentator to rule out understanding למילדות העבריות as referring to midwives who are Hebrews; rather, he belongs to a long exegetical tradition dating back to the Septuagint. This tradition was fervently supported by Samuel David Luzzatto, cited above, who ties this interpretation to the reasonable assumption that the Septuagint meant that the midwives themselves were Egyptians.

Another commentator to address the question of the midwives was Rashi's grandson, Rashbam. His commentary, "*To the midwives, who were Hebrews* העבריות *(sic)* למילדות שהם," seems to be a polemical remark designed to exclude the possibility of thinking that the midwives were Egyptian. Rashbam, however, did not elaborate against whom his commentary was directed. Are we to infer that the tradition of the midwives' Egyptian origins was known in Rashi's circles and that Rashbam's remark was intended as a protest against this tradition? If so, we may conclude that Rashi, too, was cognizant of this tradition. Moreover, it follows naturally that Rashbam was directing his remark against his grandfather without mentioning him by name, as he has done in many other places.[13]

If so, may we take our argument one step further and may infer from Rashbam's words that, like his predecessors, Rashi too was implicitly denying that the midwives were Jewish. This possibility is supported by the logic of his commentary; for, someone who would rule out the understanding "to the midwives, who were Hebrews" and who wishes to arrive at the plain sense of Scripture, would naturally view the midwives as Egyptian. Moreover, without such an assumption it is difficult to understand why Rashi's commentary need be so lengthy. If this rather far-reaching hypothesis is true, then how are we to explain the seeming contradiction in the continuation of Rashi's commentary: "*Shiphrah was Yocheved, because she used to straighten the limbs of the babe* (משפרת); *and Puah was Miriam, because she used to call aloud* (פועה) *and speak and croon to the babe,* ..."? We suggest that this be viewed as another instance of the structure often found in Rashi, in which he first presents the plain sense and then the midrashic interpretation.

Rashbam's commentary demands interpretation; but one cannot disregard the difficulties inherent in the solution which we offer here. Primarily, it must be admitted that this solution does not follow directly from the commentary itself. For, understanding העבריות as the object

---

[13] Cf. D. Rosin, *R. Samuel b. Meir als Schrifterklärer*, Breslau, 1880, pp. 68–71; also Rosin's edition of Rashbam's commentary, pp. XXVIII–XXIX and his footnotes there.

does not necessarily entail ruling out the midwives having been Jewish.[14] Nor may one overlook the obvious fact that Rashi did not juxtapose a remark on the Egyptian origin of the midwives to his grammatical analysis.

Perhaps we ought to consider a closely related suggestion. Rashbam's remark might indeed be directed against Rashi, but only against understanding העבריות as the object. In other words, perhaps Rashbam wishes to say that the Hebrews refers to the midwives themselves and not, as Rashi maintains, to the women whose births the midwives assisted. This suggestion, as well, has its problematic aspects. It forces us to cast aside the natural understanding of Rashbam's remark. If this is indeed what he meant, then one wonders why he phrased his commentary as he did.

Rashi is consistent in the way he presents the possibility of viewing the various kings as being one and the same. His commentary includes legends which originally were not found in a single continuous source.[15] On Exodus 1:8 Rashi says: "**Now there arose up a new king**—*Rab and Samuel differed in their interpretation. One said he was really new, while the other said that his decrees were made new.* **Who knew not Joseph**—*who comported himself as though he did not know him.*" On Exodus 2:23 Rashi writes: "**The king of Egypt died**—*he became a leper [who is deemed as one dead*[16]*], and he used to slaughter Israelite children and bathe in their blood [as a cure for his disease].*" On Exodus 12:29 we read: "**From the firstborn of Pharaoh**—*Pharaoh, too, was a firstborn, but he alone was allowed to remain of the firstborn; and regarding this it states (Ex. 9:16)* **But for this cause I have maintained thee in life in order to show thee my power**—*i.e., at the Read Sea.*" Lastly, on Exodus 14:4, we have: "**Through Pharaoh and through all his host**—*He began the wrongdoing, and with him began the punishment.*"

The main point of interest for us in Rashi's commentary is the way he treats the astrologers' warning to Pharaoh. To begin with, we must note that Rashi does not make do with mentioning the words of the astrologers only before the king's edict, "**Every son that is born ye shall cast into the river**," but also mentions their words before the king's instruction to the midwives. Surely Rashi did this because he felt that otherwise the order to put to death all the male children would be incomprehensible. See his commentary on Exodus 1:16: "*He was particular only about the male children because his astrologers had told him that there was to be born a son who would become their deliverer.*"

---

[14] Ginzberg *op. cit.*, Vol. 5, p. 393, n. 17. Note that Ginzberg did not include the Septuagint in the sources which he cited on the midwives' Egyptian origin.
[15] Cf. The Midrash, note 26.
[16] See The Midrash, note 26 above.

Thus, the astrologers' warning appears twice, but its wording is not the same. The second time, Pharaoh's astrologers told him: "*Today their deliverer has been born, but we know not whether he is born of an Egyptian father or of an Israelite; but we see that he will ultimately suffer misfortune through water.*" Rashi continues: "*Pharaoh therefore made a decree that day regarding the Egyptians also, as it is said here,* **Every son that is born [ye shall cast into the river]**, *and it is not stated [every son]* **who is born to the Hebrews**. *They [the astrologers], however, were not aware that Moses was ultimately to suffer misfortune through the waters of Meribah.*" At first glance, Rashi's commentary introduces no innovation; for the astrologers' words both the first and second time are taken from the Midrash. However, closer analysis reveals that Rashi has arranged the sources according to a scheme not found in the original aggadic material that he had before him, and in this way has created a narrative structure not found either in the legends that he used or in the biblical story he was interpreting. This overall scheme is evident, provided we draw the fullest conclusions from the components of the structure.

Placing the astrologers' warning before the instruction to the midwives restores the story to its primal form in the sense that it gives this instruction back its original justification—fear of the birth of a single individual destined to be a savior. Moreover, according to Rashi's reading, the midwives' refusal to comply with the king's command is what leads to the birth of the savior; for according to his version the astrologers' warning, "*Today their deliverer has been born,*" comes after the birth of Moses. The king's first measure to prevent the birth did not succeed; therefore, on the advice of his astrologers who see that this savior will ultimately suffer misfortune through water, the king decrees: "**Every son that is born ye shall cast into the river.**" This edict is directed against the Egyptians, too: "*Pharaoh therefore made a decree that day regarding the Egyptians also.*" We noted above (p. 98), after Loewenstamm, that such an understanding of the edict completely frees the murder decree from its unnatural association with the fate of the masses, of all the Israelites. The decree is no longer associated with them at all; rather, it stems from the fear of a single individual who might even be an Egyptian. Moreover, after Gressmann, if we explain the act of casting the sons into the Nile on the grounds of the astrologers having seen that the savior would ultimately suffer misfortune through water, then we can also explain the disappearance of the edict in the continuation of the story; for, as we recall, the omen disappeared with the act of casting the sons into the Nile:[17] "*This one will fall [into the*

---

[17] *Sotah* 12b; cf. p. 99, above. Indeed, in his commentary on *Sotah* 12a Rashi

river] but no other will fall [with him]."

To make our argument clearer, let us summarize the scheme of the story as it emerges after incorporating Rashi's commentaries: Pharaoh's astrologers warn him that *"there is to be born a son who will be their deliverer."* So the king of Egypt instructs the midwives, **"if it be a son, they ye shall put him to death."** But the midwives do not carry out the king's command; and their deliverer is born. The astrologers note this development on the day of his birth and advise the king to throw every newborn into the river, i.e., those who have already been born, since they foresee that the deliverer is fated ultimately to come to misfortune through water.[18] However, Moses' mother hides her son, and after she can no longer conceal him, she places her son in an ark in the water of the Nile (on the restoration of the river motif to the story cf. pp. 122–124, above). Thus, from the outset, the decree to throw the sons into the Nile was not issued for a prolonged period. Hence it is out of place to wonder why this decree disappears in the continuation of the story. Moreover, there is a certain omen that indicates to the astrologers that *"he will suffer misfortune through water."* Placing the ark in the Nile removes this omen, and the king repeals his decree. This is how Abarbanel understands Rashi's commentary (cf. The Eighth Question, in Abarbanel's commentary on Exodus), although he views it as legend.

We prefaced our remarks with the reservation that this overall scheme is obtained only if one draws the fullest conclusions from the structure; for it is highly doubtful that Rashi consciously and deliberately meant to present such a scheme. Especially, note that Rashi's commentary on verse 22 seems not to be consonant with his commentary on Exodus 2:3: **"And she could no longer conceal him,** *because the Egyptians calculated the period from when he [Amram] took her back. She, however, bore him after a term of six months and one day ... and they [the Egyptians] made enquiry regarding her at the end of nine months."* According to verse 22, the astrologers could tell precisely when Moses was born; whereas Exodus 2:3 gives the impression that they did not know when Yocheved would give birth. (However this is not necessarily the only explanation; for they might have known exactly when their deliverer

---

noted explicitly that *"He [Pharaoh] ordained the decree unto the day he [Moses] was cast into the Nile."*

[18] Rashi takes the passive voice of the *Kal* form ילוד as a past tense. Note his comment: הילודים *means they have already come into the world"* (*Nedarim* 30b). Also, cf. ילוד in Avineri, היכל רש"י, Vol. 2.

J. Barth (*Die Nominalbildung in den semitischen Sprachen*, Leipzig, 1894, p. 41) notes that the form ילוד *yillōd* is analogous to *yullād*, substituting an *ō* for the long *ā* with dissimilation of vowels, substituting an *i* for the *u* and pointing a *Kal* form as if it were *Pual*, or alternatively, a pretonic *dagesh* with the influence of the *Pual* form.

would be born, but not have suspected Yocheved of being his mother.¹⁹) On the other hand, our understanding of Rashi as implying that Moses was born due to the midwives' refusal to put him to death, is consonant with (but not dependent on) Rashi's view that the midwives were not Hebrews, i.e., were not Yocheved and Miriam.

It is reasonable to attribute the structure of Rashi's commentary firstly to the intrinsic logic of combining midrashic material, which emerges in the work of an exegete who adheres closely to the biblical text and accompanies it with various midrashim. Compare Targum Yerushalmi, which also places the astrologers' warning before the instruction to the midwives, in contrast to most of the midrashim which, as we have seen, place the warning before the edict to throw the sons into the Nile (cf. p. 95 above). A commentary which adheres closely to the text weakens the episodic nature of the Midrash and naturally builds a

---

[19] In describing the astrologers' mistake, Rashi changes the wording from that found in *Sotah* 12a. In the passage from *Sotah* cited on p. 121 the magicians' mistake is related to Yocheved having been divorced and then taken back to wife three months later. There Rashi makes the comment: "*She managed to hide him for three months, since the Egyptians did not go checking after her until a full nine months after [Amram] had taken her back, but she had been three months pregnant with him from the start [of the second marriage].*" It is clear there that the Gemara and Rashi believe Yocheved gave birth after nine months. Rashi's commentary on Exodus, however, claims that the astrologers' mistake stemmed from the birth having taken place after six months and one day. This change is quite surprising and has puzzled many Rashi scholars. For example, R. Eliyahu Mizrahi has written in this regard: "But in the *Tosafot* on *Sotah* we find the explanation that *Sefer ha-Aggadah shel Dibre ha-Yamim* agrees with Rashi and takes issue with this *gemara*." (Chavel, in his edition of Rashi's Commentary on the Torah notes, "I have not found this *Tosafot* in our Talmud." Zunz, (*op. cit.*, p. 283, note a in the German edition; p. 416, n. 99 in the Hebrew edition) probably looked for this legend in an early edition of *Dibre Yeme Moshe Rabbenu* (Yellineck ed.) and did not find it; therefore he mistakenly conjectured that perhaps Eliyahu Mizrahi was referring to a lost homiletical book on Chronicles (*Dibre ha-Yamim*). This legend, however, does appear in the later Shinan edition, p. 8, n. 3.) Eliyahu Mizrahi continues, "But I feel misgivings about Rashi simply ignoring an explicit *gemara* and taking up an *aggadah*, unless he wished to say that the *aggadah* comes closer to the plain sense of the text." Perhaps Rashi considered it bad taste to impute that Amram had divorced his wife when she was with child; indeed, see his neutral remark on Exodus 2:1: "*He had lived apart from her.*" Possibly Rashi too realized the internal contradiction between divorcing a pregnant woman and justifying the divorce on the grounds of the fear lest she give birth (cf. p. 119 above). Be that as it may, the wording here is surprising because it draws no connection between the first reason for the magicians' error—counting the time from the day she was taken back—and their second mistake—checking after her at the end of nine months. (If their mistake had indeed been a double error, Yocheved could have concealed her son for six months.) The wording which we have seems to combine two approaches: a mistake of counting the months of pregnancy from too late a date (the day she was taken back), and a mistake stemming from a premature birth. It seems one should consider the possibility of emending the formulation here.

narrative sequence to which the isolated midrashic units are not bound. This narrative sequence appears of itself to arrange the individual legends in the most logical order. Of course, only a great exegete could be sensitive to the logic of combining motifs that appear in separate sources and could succeed in reshaping them while tying them to the biblical verses. The structure of Rashi's commentary is similar to that of the *Asatir*, discussed above, and essentially parallels the second and third stages of the story in the *Asatir*. The only difference lies in the fact that his commentary states explicitly that the astrologers discerned Moses' birth; whereas the *Asatir*, which comprises three stages, has the magician discern his conception, but whether and how his birth becomes known does not move from the realm of the theoretical to the practical (cf. The Asatir). The *Asatir*, too, can be explained in terms of the logic of combining its component motifs, as we have shown there.

The reorganization of ancient components is seen clearly when we compare Rashi's commentary with his sources. Let us review briefly the details of Rashi's commentary that are found in his sources. Rashi may have derived the idea of placing the warning to Pharaoh after the birth of Moses from *Pirke Rabbi Eliezer* 48: "After he had been born they [the magicians] said to him [Pharaoh], 'Lo, he has been born but is hidden from our sight.' He [Pharaoh] answered them, 'Since he has already been born, henceforth do not cast the sons who are born into the Nile." However, *Pirke Rabbi Eliezer* does not include the instruction to the midwives.

Rashi's principle source was apparently the *Tanḥuma*,[20] which Rashi cites explicitly in his commentary on *Sotah* 12a: "R. Tanḥuma expounded that the day Moses was born the astrologers said, 'Today the savior of Israel has been born, but we do not know whether he is an Egyptian or a Jew.' So he arose and gathered all his people and requested them to give him the children born on that very day, and imposed the same decree upon his own people." We discussed the structure of the *Tanḥuma* above, p. 94. Rashi parallels the *Tanḥuma*, not only in that his commentary includes the motif of the magicians knowing about the birth of the savior yet not being able to discover his identity (a motif apparently found in *Sotah* 12a, as well, in the words of R. Jose b. Ḥanina), but also in that he connects the prophecy both to the midwives and to the edict to cast the sons into the river. He differs from the *Tanḥuma*, however, in that he splits the words of the astrologers into two separate pronouncements (verse 16 and verse 22), whereas in the *Tanḥuma* the same pronouncement serves as the reason for the first instruction to the midwives as well as the reason for the king's decree to his entire people.

---

[20] *Tanḥuma* (ויקהל 4); *Tanḥuma Buber* (ויקהל 5).

Compare the combined structure that emerges from Rashi's commentary with the Gemara on *Sotah* 12a: "**And Pharaoh charged all his people**—R. Jose b. Ḥanina said: *He issued three edicts: first, 'if it be a son, then ye shall kill him'; then 'every son that is born ye shall cast into the river'; and lastly he even imposed the same decree upon his own people.*" With some hesitation we suggest the possibility that perhaps the Gemara should be understood as hinting at the following structure: A) Annunciation of the savior's birth, followed by the instruction to the midwives, and then their refusal to comply. B) The decree to cast the sons into the Nile, followed by the savior being born, despite the decree. C) News of the birth having taken place and the astrologers surmising that perhaps the savior had been spared because he was not a Hebrew child, and consequently "*he imposed the same decree upon his own people.*" Even if this was not R. Jose b. Ḥanina's intention, Rashi may have understood his words as such. Indeed, see Rashi's commentary there: " '*He even imposed the same decree upon his own people*'—R. Tanḥuma has explained that the day Moses was born, ..."

Eight hundred years after Rashi, without mentioning him at all, Hugo Gressmann, who laid the foundation for modern scholarship on Moses nativity stories, compared the Moses nativity story in Exodus to the Jesus nativity story in Matthew 2. He wrote: "From here [i.e., Matthew 2] we can reconstruct the original exposition of the birth of Moses. Pharaoh did not fear the people's proliferation, but only the birth of Moses, as one can still see in the present story. From some source or other, such as a dream or prophetic pronouncement, he found out that in the near future a Hebrew woman was destined to give birth to a son who would be a dangerous foe of Pharaoh and would steal both his life and his throne. The king's edict is restricted solely to the male children, because the female ones were of no account. Since Moses had not yet been born (which was not the case in the Jesus nativity legend), Pharaoh turned to the midwives. The midwives refused to cooperate, the predestined time passed, and Moses was born without there having been a threat to his life. The king's plan having failed, he had no alternative but to cast the Hebrews' sons into the Nile, and thus be sure that he would also do in the young Moses who had just been born. Thus the edict to cast the sons into the Nile was not intended for an extended period of time, but only for this purpose and would be carried out only once. This easily explains why we hear no more of it later."[21]

The interpretation which we advocate, for all its debt to Gressmann, is not identical to Gressmann's above remarks. Gressmann views the structure he has outlined as that of the original story from which the

---

[21] *Mose und seine Zeit*, p. 5.

biblical version of the Moses nativity story evolved. In our opinion, it is more likely that the story of Moses was comprised of two independent nativity story archetypes which through their reciprocal influence over many generations merged into a single continuous story. The structure that Gressmann describes should be viewed as the point on the horizon towards which the various motifs and patterns are likely to aspire; in other words, as the end of the process, not its beginning. Gressmann used the Jesus nativity story, which has a parallel structure, to help him reconstruct the Moses story; but precisely the converse stands to reason. The Jesus nativity story is more harmoniously structured, not because of being closer to the primal structure; but, on the contrary, because it is further away in time and is not encumbered by a legend about an individual being combined with an ancient national tradition. Gressmann, we believe, was again misled by his assumption that the logical and harmonious structure is the ancient and original one. It is inconceivable that Rashi was influenced in any way by the story in Matthew. The emergence of a parallel structure in Rashi's commentary indicates that the smooth structure in Matthew is not necessarily due to being close to the original source. Quite the contrary; it is more reasonable to assume that it reflects prolonged development and represents a later stage in the development of the tradition. Evidence in support of this conclusion is provided by the version of the story found in the Samaritan *Asatir*. Even there one can see how the flow of the narrative aspires towards a harmonious structure that eliminates the tension between the original elements of the story.

CHAPTER SIX

CHRISTIAN SOURCES

In this chapter we discuss Christian sources in which the hero is Jesus. Stephen's Oration, although Christian, is included in Chapter 2 because it deals with the birth of Moses.

THE GOSPEL ACCORDING TO MATTHEW

It is easy to see that the nativity story in Matthew and the account of the birth of Moses in Exodus are closely related. To begin with, the general structure of the stories is parallel: an edict against the male children, divine intervention, the rescue of a single son. There is also considerable similarity in the details of the story. In both stories the public edict of annihilation is preceded by an attempt to achieve the same objective secretly, by a devious design—in the Moses story, by means of the midwives (Ex. 1:15), and in Matthew, by means of the wise men (Mt. 2:8–12). And in both stories, the second murder attempt arises from the failure of the first.

Nevertheless, we cannot ignore the decisive difference between the Christian work and the works we have discussed thus far. The Jewish works relied overtly on the nativity story in Exodus, whereas here the stories are covertly related. This difference entails another point of divergence. Although one cannot deny the similarity to the midrashic work as revealed mainly by the use of the formulation "**that it might be fulfilled**" which we shall discuss below, nevertheless the differences remain decisive. Despite its marked dependence, the story here preserves considerable independence with respect to the Old Testament story. Unlike the Midrash, it aspires to stand side by side with the Exodus story. Therefore, one must reject the frequently made definition of the story in Matthew as belonging to the genre of midrash.[1] This difference between the aspirations of the creators of the Christian nativity stories and the creators of the *Midrash* explains why the work which is closer to the Old Testament in terms of literary genre is precisely the Christian work. The Christian authors aspired to recound a story as in the Bible, whereas

---

[1] See Y. Kaufmann's perceptive distinction in *Apokryphen*, in the German *Encyclopedia Judaica*, Vol. 2, p. 1161.

"pure" *Midrash* is always set alongside the biblical story as a comment on the text proper. This gives rise to the episodic nature of the *Midrash*, shedding light only on a specific detail in the story.

The processes described in Chapter 1 stand out even more clearly in the nativity stories of the New Testament. Firstly, the nativity stories are created after the literary account of the hero as a grown man has taken shape. In the New Testament this is taken to the farthest extreme; the story of the crucifixion and resurrection of Jesus provides the core from which the history of his life emerged retrospectively, as is evident from ancient passages in the New Testament (cf. Acts of the Apostles 2:23–24, 32; 3:14–15; 4:10; 10:39–40; I Corinthians 15:3–4)[2] and from the fact that this core appears as a continuous unit in all the Gospels, whereas the nativity story itself appears only in Matthew and Luke. Neither Mark, the most ancient of the Gospels (according to the prevailing, although sometimes contested, scholarly opinion), nor John makes any reference to the nativity. Nor is there any sign of the nativity story in the rest of the New Testament, even in those sections that predate the Gospels.[3] Moreover, while these stories appear in the beginning of Matthew and Luke, there are many indications that the Gospels themselves were altogether uncognizant of the story found in their introductions.

Secondly, one sees clearly that the New Testament nativity traditions were cast into preset patterns, thus leading to a wealth of forms which, by the very nature of the process by which they were created, are self-contradictory.

Thirdly, the New Testament also clearly reveals the superior force of the pattern, insofar as its hero is the Son of God. There is no need to reconstruct this motif in the pattern's past, since the forms that in other stories range over an historical continuum may be found side by side here.

In Matthew determining the boundaries of the unit comprising the nativity story is simple.[4] It is included in Chapters 1 and 2. Even the

---

[2] See R. E. Brown, *The Birth of the Messiah*, pp. 26–32. Brown presents an extensive review of nativity story literature, along with his own commentary.

[3] Cf. especially Usener, *Das Weihnachtsfest*, p. 71 ff.; E. Petersen, *Die Wunderbare Geburt des Heilandes*; Gressmann, *Das Weihnachtsevangelium*; Hennecke and Schneemelcher, *New Testament Apocrypha*, Vol. 1, pp. 363–369. Also see Bultmann, *The History of the Synoptic Tradition*, pp. 291–301, who deals specifically with the independence of the individual units. His views on the relationship between the entire narrative and the Gospel is unclear. Cf. also Fitzmyer's commentary in *The Anchor Bible*, Vol. 28, p. 304 ff. Additional sources are cited in Brown, Fitzmyer, and the (rather conservative) overview by Kümmel in his introduction to Luke, pp. 105–107.

[4] Matthew is referred to here in the sense generally accepted in scholarly research as the anonymous author of the Gospel. See Kümmel's survey in his introduction,

boundaries within this larger unit are clear: 1:1–17 outlines the genealogy of Jesus, presenting him as a descendant of the House of David; 1:18–25 tells of the birth of Jesus to the Virgin Mary, who conceived by the Holy Ghost; 2:1–23 recounts how he was saved from the king's murderous designs. The independence of the unit from 1:18 to 2:23 vis-à-vis the rest of the Gospel can be seen from all the unique elements constituting the two nativity stories found here. We shall list these elements, so immediately apparent. In all of Matthew there is not the slightest reference, either from Jesus himself, or from his supporters or his opposition, to the miracle of the virgin birth or to the preferential status due Mary in the wake of this story. Quite the contrary (cf. Matthew 12:46–50).[5] The father, the dominant figure in Chapters 1 and 2, does not appear at all in the Gospels proper, aside from one reference whose explicit purpose is to point out his lowly status (Mt. 13:55). Moreover, the events described in 2:1–23 are not reflected at all in the subsequent text. According to the narrative, the first contact which the priests and scribes of the people had with Jesus was at his birth; yet we can search in vain for any reference to this in all of Jesus' appearances before them or contact with them. This silence is complemented by the absence of any allusion to the wise men and the star in the east, or to the slaughter of all the children in Bethlehem and its surrounding areas.[6]

That the nativity story is external to the Gospels proper is further supported by the correlation that exists between Matthew, Mark, Acts, and Luke regarding the starting point for the history of Jesus, provided the nativity story is separated from the Gospels. All of these works view Jesus' baptism in the River Jordan and his contact with John as the beginning of his history.[7] The Acts of the Apostles, attributed to Luke, deserves special attention, since it shows clearly that Luke is not cognizant of the beginning of the Gospel that bears his name. Both in Matthew and in Luke the verse immediately following the nativity story looks like an introductory formulation (Matthew 3:1; Luke 3:1).

It is also clear that each of the units, 1:18–25 and 2:1–23, is independent with respect to the other. Moreover, what we have said about the relationship of the two traditions to the rest of the Gospels holds also for their relationship to each other. Neither narrative mentions

---

pp. 91–92.
[5] Cf. the parallel texts in Mark 3:31–35, Luke 8:19–21. The Ebionites actually concluded from this episode that Mary was not the mother of Jesus at all. Epiphanius *Panarion*, haer. 30, 14; also cited in K. Aland, *Synopsis Quattuor Evangeliorum*, p. 173.
[6] Cf. Matthew 13:53–58; and the parallel text in Mark 6:1–6; also cf. Luke 4:22.
[7] Cf. Matthew 3:1; Mark 1:4; Luke 3:1–2; Acts 1:22, 10:37; and elsewhere.

the miraculous events included in the other.[8] Furthermore, the absence in Chapter 2 of any mention of the main thrust of the tradition—the miracle of the virgin birth—is especially noticeable.

Matthew 2:1-23

As we have said, the nativity story in Matthew 2:1-23 parallels the story of the birth of Moses in many respects. Comparing the two, we see that Matthew has only the murder pattern and lacks the ark pattern, which actually holds pride of place in the Moses narrative. In contrast to Exodus, in Matthew the murder pattern appears in its entirety in that it preserves the motif of foreknowledge. This pattern, as we have mentioned, belongs to the genre of migratory legends, and its primal form was certainly neither biblical nor even Jewish.

The mark of the pattern can still be discerned in Matthew; indeed, it can be fully reconstructed. There is a prophecy—the star in the east (2:1-2); the king panics (2:3); he takes steps to prevent the prophecy's fulfillment (2:7-11); and those steps fail (2:12). In this part of the story, as in most of the parallel versions (cf. above, Chapter 1, p. 8 ff.), the mother is the central figure. Aside from the name of the king, Herod, the place names Bethlehem and Jerusalem, and the names of the infant and his mother, Jesus and Mary, there are no specifically Jewish or Christian motifs here. We concur with the view held by many scholars that this segment of the narrative is the core of the unit.

The pattern assumes that "he that is born King of the Jews" is destined to depose the current king and inherit his crown; this provides further evidence of the original independence of the pattern. Indeed, Celsus' taunting remarks are quite revealing: "If Herod did this in order that when you were grown up you might not reign instead of him, why then when you had grown up did you not become king?"[9] It is not clear why Jesus' star did not lead the wise men directly to Bethlehem. This mix-up probably stems from adapting the pattern to the specific circumstances of the Christian legend. The king is in Jerusalem, and the savior is in another city.[10]

Thus all the parallel elements clearly show that the Jesus nativity pattern which appears in Matthew 2 belongs to the genre of the migratory legend.[11] Indeed, it is doubtful if these legends had any direct impact

---

[8] Excluding 1:1-17. The relationship of this passage to the Gospel and to the nativity tradition which follows immediately after it is far more complex.

[9] Celsus I,61; cited in Stern, *op. cit.*, Vol. 2, p. 267.

[10] Cf. p. 173 below, the *Protevangelium of James*, which omits Jerusalem. In that version the wise men come to Bethlehem without any intermediate stops along the way. Typically, he does not take geographical or historical facts into consideration.

[11] The belief in a star accompanying a man's birth and disappearing upon his

on the Christian community. It is more reasonable to attribute the more decisive impact to the parallel versions in the Jewish sources, which we discussed at length above.[12] Recall (cf. p. 25, above) that this was not originally a religious-monotheistic pattern, and that rescuing the child stems from man's inability to change that which is foreordained.

In the narrative's introduction we find two motifs—the star (the cos-

---

death was prevalent in the ancient world, as we may infer indirectly from the rejection of this notion by Pliny in *Hist. Nat.*, Book II, 6.28. The birth of Alexander Severus was accompanied by the appearance of a star (*Script. Hist. Aug., Alex. Sev.* 13,5). An omen (the burning of the shrine of Diana at Ephesus) preceded the birth of Alexander. It was this omen that foretold the Persian wise men about the birth of the man who would lay waste to Asia (Cicero, *De Divinatione,* I XXIII 47). The Roman senate issued a decree forbidding the raising of male sons in order to prevent the birth of Augustus (Suetonius, *Augustus,* 94,5). A star led Aeneis to the place where Rome was to be founded (Virgil, *The Aeneid,* II 694). Usener, p. 78 ff. presents many more examples, but his conclusion that the legend emerged on Hellenistic soil contradicts the striking parallel to the Moses nativity story in the Old Testament and Jewish legends, and apparently stems from his insufficient knowledge of the Jewish sources. Billerbeck's work was not yet available to Usener at the time. Also see Lohmeyer, p. 20; Brown, p. 170; Gnilka, *Das Matthäusevangelium*, pp. 42–43; and Strack and Billerbeck, Vol. 1, p. 76. Also see the Testament of Levi 18:2: *And his star [of the new priest] shall rise in the heavens*; As well as the *Damascus Covenant* 7:18–19. One should not exaggerate the importance of the parallel between Jesus' star and Numbers 24:17, because the appearance of a star as an omen of the birth of a hero is widespread. See also the convincing arguments advanced by Weiss, *Die Schriften des Neuen Testaments,* p. 235.

[12] On the wise men coming from the east, compare *Kohelet Rabbah* VII.23, and the parallel texts: כתיב ותרב חכמת שלמה מחכמת כל בני קדם ומכל חכמת מצרים (מלכ״א ה, י) ומה היתה חכמתן של בני קדם שהיו יודעין במזל וקוסמין בעופות ובקיאין בטייר. "*It is written:* And Solomon's wisdom excelled the wisdom of all the children of the east, and all the wisdom in Egypt *(I Kings 5:10). What, then, was the wisdom of the children of the east? They were skilled in astrology and divination with birds and expert in augury.*" Ginzberg, Vol. 5 (*Abraham*), p. 265, n. 311, wonders whether there is a connection between the wise men coming from the east to bow down before the Messiah and the legend presented in *Midrash ha-Gadol* (Gen. 25:6), according to which Abraham sent the sons of his concubines to the eastern ends of the world to await the coming of the Messiah. And in the time of Solomon, the inhabitants of the land of Sheba (the descendants of Sheba son of Keturah; cf. Gen. 25:3) imagined that Solomon was the King Messiah and came to bow down before him. כיון שראו שאינו המלך המשיח מיד ותהפך לארצה (דהי״ב ט, יב) שחזרו למקומם ועתידין לבוא בימי המלך המשיח כשיגלה במהרה בימינו שאמר שפעת גמלים תכסך בכרי מדין ועיפה כולם משבא יבאו זהב ולבונה ישאו ותהלות ה׳ יבשרו (יש׳ ס, ו). "*When they saw that he was not the King Messiah, they immediately turned and went away to her own land (II Chronicles 9:12). They returned to their lands and will come in the time of the Messiah, may he appear speedily in our day, as it is said:* The multitude of camels shall cover thee, the dromedaries of Midian and Ephah; all they from Sheba shall come: they shall bring gold and incense; and they shall shew forth the praises of the Lord *(Isaiah 60:6).*"

mic sign bearing tidings of the savior's birth) and alongside it the response of the priests and scribes, a prophecy which, citing Micah 5:1, adds where the savior was born. These motifs have a certain tension between them; not only does the star have no need for the verse from Micah in order to bear tidings of the savior's birth, moreover it does not need the verse either in theory or in practice in order to find the birthplace. Indeed, the wise men actually find Jesus solely by following the star (2:9).

Combining the Jewish element with the universal element was unsuccessful also insofar as the king's interest in the Messiah destined to be born is far greater than the interest shown by the priests, who disappear from the story as soon as they have said their lines. In the universal pattern the role of the priests is played by the king's astrologers and advisors, who naturally are less involved than the king in the anticipated birth.[13] Therefore we must agree with the prevalent opinion, which views verses 4–6 as a Christian or Jewish addition to the universal pattern.[14]

As for the description of the king (and his people) being troubled by the tidings and gathering all the chief priests and scribes, compare this to the account in *Dibre Yeme Moshe Rabbenu* (Jellinek ed.): *"And Pharaoh awakened, and lo, it was a dream. And he gathered all the people of Egypt and all his magicians, and Pharaoh told them his dream; and all the people were frightened by the dream, until one of the ministers came before the king and said to him: This dream signifies a great evil to Egypt, and trouble. And the king said to him: And what is the nature of this evil? And he said: A son shall be born to the Children of Israel who shall lay waste all of Egypt. And therefore, my lord king,*

---

[13] Lohmeyer (*Das Evangelium des Matthäus*, p. 26) clearly discerns a difference between the king and the priests, but draws far-fetched inferences from it.

[14] Cf. Gunkel, *Das Märchen im Alten Testament*, p. 119. We may reasonably assume that what the scribes and priests say to the king is an addition. However, there is also the possibility, albeit less probable, that the Jewish core—the Messiah destined to be born in Bethlehem—attracted the universal pattern. The history of the text goes back further than we can trace, so we cannot say anything definitive. The important thing is to discern that what we have here is a general pattern and a Judeo-Christian stratum, with tension between the two. Ancient commentators have wondered why Herod did not follow the wise men to Bethlehem; and even some modern exegetes have found this point troublesome. Cf. Lohmeyer, *loc. cit.*, p. 24, who seriously cites Calvin's explanation: *Pollebat certe non vulgari astutia Herodes; erat in eo rara animo magnitudo.* Also see Petersen, *Die Wunderbare Geburt des Heilandes*, p. 11. E. Schweizer (*The Good News according to Matthew*, p. 37) sees Herod as being absurdly trusting. It is the modern scholars, however, and not the king, who should be accused of naïveté, since they ask inappropriate questions of the legend, a genre that follows different criteria. Cf. also Klostermann's note on Matthew 2:7 (*Das Matthäusevangelium*, p. 15).

let me give you some good advice, that you order every son born to the Children of Israel to be killed. Etc." Aside from the parallelism to this version of the legend in terms of detail, we note in general that the role played by Pharaoh's magicians is split between the wise men, who first notice the omen and interpret it correctly, and the chief priests and scribes of the people, who add to what the wise men have said. This comparison shed light on the great difference between the account in Matthew and the legends of Moses and Abraham. In the latter case the king's sundry astrologers and advisors are mostly evil; whereas here the wise men are completely righteous, and the people's leaders and scribes, as well, are not portrayed in a negative light, even though that would seem to be the natural way to present them. Perhaps we may deduce from this that the pattern of the basic unit in Matthew (2:1–12) does not depend on the legends of Moses and Abraham, but actually on another archetype. Be that as it may, refraining from portraying the people and their leaders in a negative light suits the overall line of the nativity stories in Matthew and Luke, stories which have not the slightest sign of any tension between the Messiah and his people. We may draw certain conclusions from this about the origins of the stories.[15]

Determining how verses 13–18 relate to the core of the unit is more complicated. The parallel patterns in other folk literature do not include the motif of wholesale slaughter as in Matthew 2:16; hence we may assume that this motif does not belong to the core of the story. The major figure in this part of the story is Joseph, a character who does not appear at all in the first part. In addition to these considerations, we must add the literary factor that the core of the unit ends naturally with verse 12. The wise men going to their own country and not returning to Herod balances their having come from their country to Herod.[16]

The supplementary passage of verses 13–18 is strongly connected with the Judeo-Christian addition in the unit extending from verse 1

---

[15] Matthew has an affinity in the Gospel for the term συνάγω (to assemble) to describe gatherings of Jesus' enemies, particularly the priests, scribes, and elders. Cf. 26:3,57; 27:17,27,62. The contrast in content—the sole evil figure here being the king—is further underscored by using the same term. This divergence between use of language and content is instructive. The simple solution would be to view the linguistic formulation as the last stage in the evolution of the text, (perhaps) the only stage that should be attributed to Matthew. Cf. Cohen, *Masorot*, p.232–233. The plural form, ἀρχιερεῖς (chief priests), used here is also found in Josephus. Cf. Strack and Billerbeck, *op. cit.*, Vol. 1, p. 79.

[16] One cannot, however, rule out the possibility that the original pattern also included a second attempt on the part of the king to kill the infant, after the departure of the wise men; but the pattern's parallels do not support this theory. The expression κατ' ὄναρ (in a dream) in verse 12 also raises doubts, because it is characteristic of the angel's revelation (cf. 1:20; 2:13,19); thus perhaps the original conclusion of the story has not come down to us in its entirety. Cf. also note 20, below.

to verse 12. The evil king is Herod, and the Messiah's place, Bethlehem. Perhaps therefore one should connect the supplementary passages and view them as part of a single literary stratum. In any event, we may infer from Bethlehem being mentioned in verse 16 with no explanation that, as far as we can tell, the external supplement (verses 13–18) cannot have predated the addition within the core unit.

The appearance of the angel in verse 13 parallels his appearance in 1:20 and is repeated in 2:19. Since the two units (1:18–25 and 2:1–23) were not connected at the outset, it is reasonable to view the appearance of the angel as a later literary element joining an ancient tradition; and it is hard to say whether it comes from Matthew himself, or from an earlier writing. In view of the fact that this pattern of the angel's appearance does not recur later in the Gospel, and considering the tension between this pattern and 2:22–23, it seems that this element in the story predates the narrative's final redaction (by Matthew?). The tension between the appearance of the angel in verses 19–21 and verses 22–23 is due to the fact that the angel's second appearance looks like a natural conclusion for the supplement to the core of the narrative. The beginning of the secondary unit (13–14) parallels its conclusion (19–21). The angel's words in the introduction even include a promise presaging his second appearance: **until I bring thee word.** Verses 22–23 disrupt the structure of the narrative, and even are disconsonant with what the angel says in verses 13 and 19. The dream seems to be an emendation to the angel's words, and from the narrative it is far from clear why Joseph was not instructed to go to Nazareth by the angel directly. Therefore verses 22–23 should be viewed as a later addendum to the story. The motivation for this addendum is not hard to discover. The next chapter will tell of Jesus coming from the Galilee (3:13), whereas Chapter 2 states his home as being in Bethlehem. Verses 22-23 were thus designed as a transition to the Gospel proper. Therefore it seems that this unit belongs to the last stratum in the formation of the text.

One other argument can be added to the above. The transitional addendum concludes with the stock phrase **"that it might be fulfilled"** ($\H{o}\pi\omega\varsigma\ \pi\lambda\eta\rho\omega\theta\bar{\eta}$). This expression appeared previously in 2:15, 2:17–18, and in the previous chapter, 1:22–23. From its appearance in 1:22-23 we may infer, as we did from the appearance of the angel in this passage, that it does not belong to the core of the narrative; but unlike the appearance of the angel, this phrase is one of the hallmarks of Matthew and appears even in the Gospel (cf. 4:14–16, 8:17, 12:17–21, 13:35, 21:4–5, and 27:9–10).[17] One can reasonably view it as Matthew's own mark

---

[17] Cf. the similar formulations in 13:14–15 and 26:56; also cf. Brown, *op. cit.*, p. 98.

and attribute it to the last stage in the development of the text.[18]

The tenuous connection of this stock phrase with the story is also brought out by the fact that it can be omitted without affecting the flow of the narrative, except for its last occurrence.[19] Unlike the case in 1:22-23 and 2:15, 17-18, deleting this phrase from 2:23 would remove the underpinning for the direct divine instruction to Joseph to dwell in Nazareth. Therefore one can reasonably attribute the phrase, **"that it might be fulfilled"** to the same source as the entire transitional addendum of 21-23, i.e., to Matthew himself.[20] Furthermore, in Matthew we find quotes appended to complete literary units in other places besides the nativity story. In particular compare Mark 1:14 and Luke 4:14 with Matthew 4:12-16; or Matthew 21:1-8 with Mark 11:1-7 and Luke 19:28-35. The fact that Matthew 4:12-16 has no parallel in the synoptic Gospels and should thus be seen as a pure Matthean unit is further evidence of that 2:22-23 should be attributed to Matthew; since 4:12-16 and 2:22-23 form an impressive parallel.[21] It is a widely accepted assumption among scholars that the quotes represent the latest stage in development of the narrative.

There is a measure of similarity between the way the stock phrase, "that it might be fulfilled," is used and the way the prophecy from Micah is incorporated in the text. However, since the formulation introducing the reference to Micah uses the words οὕτως γὰρ γέγραπται διὰ τοῦ προφήτου ("so it is written by the prophet") instead of the usual formulation ἵνα (τότε, ὅπως) πληρωθῇ τὸ ῥηθὲν ("to fulfill what had been spoken"), and since the quote from Micah is more closely connected with the narrative, it seems that this should not be associated with the other quotes. Furthermore, the Matthean formulation of the verse from Micah is quite different from the formulation of this verse in the masoretic text and the Septuagint. In contrast, the other verses cited from the Old Tes-

---

[18] The actual formulation is not Matthew's; rather, it reflects the Jewish phrases typically found in the Midrash: לקיים מה שאמר "to fulfill that which was said"; זהו שאמר ברוח הקודש על ידי פלוני "as was said through holy inspiration by so-and-so"; זה הוא שאמרה רוח הקודש על ידי "which the holy spirit said through ..."; etc. Cf. Strack and Billerbeck, Vol. 1, p. 74. It should be noted, however, that the regular incorporation of these formulations in Scriptural literary genres such as Matthew makes the biblical literary form closer to the midrashic patterns.

[19] Too much weight should not be placed on this argument, because this phrase of its very nature accompanies the plot, but is not strictly part of it. Nevertheless, there is a striking difference between the connection of this phrase to the story in its earlier occurrences as opposed to its last occurrence in verse 23.

[20] Also the phrase κατ' ὄναρ (in a dream) most likely was determined by its earlier appearances (1:20; 2:12,13,19).

[21] See Brown, p. 107, whose approach to the text does not enable him to carry through to the farthest conclusion. Also see the variety of views presented by him, pp. 99-101.

tatment are rendered much closer to their masoretic formulation. This is further evidence that the quote from Micah may have come from another source than the other quotes.[22] Ascertaining the source of the quotes and determining whether they should be attributed to Matthew himself or were taken from some other source are a separate issue.[23]

In analyzing Matthew, Chapter 2, we have not simply tried to identify the literary units but also to reconstruct the order in which these units were assembled into the finished text. In our opinion the narrative crystallized according to the following stages:

(1) first came the core of the narrative: 2:1–3 (or 2:1–2) and 2:7–12;
(2) then the prophecy from Micah (2:4–6) was incorporated into this core;
(3) the angel's revelations to Joseph (2:13–21) were added to the story;
(4) lastly the stock phrase, "that it might be fulfilled," of vv. 15 and 17–18 and the transitional passage of vv. 22–23 were added.

Having thus discerned the basic units and the order in which they were incorporated, we can proceed to discuss the result of blending the various units.

Incorporation of the Supplementary Unit

As in the Moses nativity story, the core of the narrative in Matthew (2:1–12) makes no explicit mention of divine intervention. This feature of the core was toned down by adding the verse from Micah and by the cautious formulation of verse 12: **And being warned in a dream**[24]; and it disappears completely with the addition of the unit consisting of verses 13–21.

If we combine our remarks on the way the narrative in Matthew was formed with our general analytic method, we can offer an explanation for the father's absence from verse 11, which has been a quandary to many scholars. The father's absence is not surprising, but rather quite to be expected; for one should note that the father figure is altogether absent from the core of the narrative, just as it is essentially absent in the Moses nativity story and either absent or purely marginal in the murder

---

[22] On Matthew 2:23, see note 32, below.
[23] Cf. Kümmel, *Einleitung*, p. 81 ff., and Brown's conclusion, pp.101–104, for further bibliographical references.
[24] καὶ χρηματισθέντες κατ' ὄναρ: the identical formulation is found in verse 22, which belongs to Matthew's own addition. The passive use of this verb, meaning to be divinely commanded or admonished, is rare. Cf. the entry for this word in Bauer, Arndt, Gingrich, *Greek-English Lexicon*. Therefore the parallel to verse 22 casts doubt on the originality of the formulation in verse 12. Cf. also note 16, above.

pattern in general. The figure of the father intrudes into the story only in the supplementary unit (13–21). This development is paralleled in the evolution of the Moses nativity story in the Bible, the Targumim and post-biblical literature, and is likewise found in the development of nativity stories of other heroes in Jewish traditions. Therefore, one should view the rise in prominence of the father figure as a unifying line of the biblical traditions. We attempted to account for this development in our analysis of the Moses nativity story (cf. p. 48, above) and believe that similar factors account for it in Matthew, as well; namely, an antimythological inclination. Here we can only allude briefly to the fact that the dominance of the father in the supplement to the core of the narrative in Matthew (2:13–23) parallels his dominance in the story of the virgin birth (1:18–25).[25]

It should be noted that the newborn child took refuge[26] in Egypt, along with his mother and father. This is particularly noteworthy since in the vast majority of murder patterns[27] in folk literature and in the parallel Moses nativity story, which is the principle source of inspiration for the supplement, at this stage of the story the child is separated from his family and taken in by strangers. In addition to stemming from the pressure of other Christian traditions, this part of the story line may also have been inherited from the Jewish biblical tradition, insofar as we have seen opposition to the foundling motif and to the child's abandonment in the stories of the birth of Moses and of Samuel and in the legends of the birth of Abraham.

Incorporation of "that it might be fulfilled"

The immediate effect of this formulation on the narrative is to increase the deity's involvement, and in this respect it should be seen as rounding out the unit of verses 13–21. Yet, this phrase, "that it might be fulfilled," also serves a further purpose: it connects the events recounted in Matthew to the Old Testament by stressing the continuity of what has just happened with the hallowed prophecies of the past, which appear to the author of the narrative to have been realized by what he has just recounted.[28,29] As we have said, this formulation is quite tenuously connected to the narrative, except for its last occurrence in verse 23, where

---

[25] A detailed and extensive discussion of this subject may be found in Cohen, *Masorot*, passim.

[26] The angel instructs Joseph φεῦγε (flee); but when this instruction is carried out, the wording is toned down, and Joseph ἀνεχώρησεν (departs, retreats) into Egypt. Cf. Targum Onkelos, Genesis 27:43; Philo, note 26 in the section on Philo, above.

[27] Cf. the examples cited by Redford, *op. cit.*

[28] Cf. L. Baeck, *Das Evangelium als Urkunde der jüdischen Glaubensgeschichte.*

[29] The verses from Jeremiah (31:14–16), which Matthew cites as proof that the

it supports Jesus living in Nazareth; we note that dwelling in Nazareth stems only indirectly from the instruction given in the dream and is not supported by an explicit divine instruction. It should be added that the reason given for Joseph going to the Galilee is also far from simple. The divine instruction, "**being warned in a dream**," which, like verse 12, carefully refrains from using an active verb,[30] is juxtaposed to a human reason: "**he was afraid to go thither**" (2:22). This complex structure apparently reflects the theological notion that the Galilee, and within it Nazareth, are in no way special. Nazareth, of itself, is but one of the cities of the Galilee. The Greek refers to Joseph going εἰς πόλιν (to a town), without the definite article τήν.[31] Thus, it seems purely by chance that Jesus dwells there without any divine instruction to do

---

slaughter of the children in Bethlehem was the fulfillment of an ancient prophecy, are interesting in terms of exegetical history, since the original verses are in no way connected with Bethlehem (*Encyclopedia Biblica*, Vol. 7, pp. 360–363). Jeremiah preserves the ancient tradition according to which Rachel's tomb is in the land of Benjamin, near the city of Ramah, as we read in I Samuel 10:2: "**When thou art departed from me to day, then thou shalt find two men by Rachel's sepulchre in the border of Benjamin at Zelzah.**" Compare Jeremiah 40:1: "**The word that came to Jeremiah from the Lord, after that Nebuzaradan the captain of the guard had let him go from Ramah, when he had taken him being bound in chains among all that were carried away captive of Jerusalem and Judah, which were carried away captive unto Babylon.**" From this verse we learn that Jeremiah was bound in chains in Ramah; and there, while watching his people being driven into exile, he composed his famous verse, "**A voice was heard in Ramah, lamentation, and bitter weeping; Rachel weeping for her children ...**" (Jeremiah 31:14). The antiquity of the Benjamin tradition is actually evident from Genesis 35, as well; for, the story of Benjamin's birth is most likely a tradition belonging to the tribe that bears his name, and we would expect such a tradition to set the scene of the action in the territory of the tribe of Benjamin. The fact that Bethlehem is mentioned in Genesis should be viewed as a Judaic redaction, transferring the site of Rachel's burial to the inheritance of Judah, similarly to what was done with the burial of Jacob. Cf. Bruston, "La Mort et Sépulture de Jacob," and Loewenstamm, "פרשת האומה בבראשית"; "מותם של אבות"; also see *Sifre* (וזאת הברכה 352); *Torah Shelemah*, Vol. 7, p. 1750, nn. 57, 58; הוספתא כפשוטה *Sotah* 11, p. 725. Again we have confirmation of the well-known rule that, given competing sources, generally one should give preference to the unknown place, Zelzah (near Ramah, Samuel's city), over the more famous place, Bethlehem, David's birthplace. Klostermann, (*op. cit.*, p. 18) and Brown (*op. cit.*, p. 205) note that Matthew 2:17 begins with the phrase "then was fulfilled," in contrast to "that it might be fulfilled," found in the parallel formulations. A probable explanation is that this formulation was used to do away with the problematic idea that the slaughter of the children was God's will. Compare Matthew 27:9.

[30] Cf. Strack and Billerbeck, Vol. 1, p. 443.

[31] Cf. "**Can there any good thing come out of Nazareth?**" (John 1:46); "**Shall Christ come out of Galilee**" (John 7:41); and "**Search, and look: for out of Galilee ariseth no prophet**" (John 7:52).

so. But in hindsight it turns out that even this chance occurrence was divinely guided and was presaged by his prophets.[32] The anonymity of the Messiah's dwelling place had been removed by the addition of the verse from Micah which set his dwelling as Bethlehem. Historical reality (Jesus actually came from the Galilee) and the pressure of the Gospels restore this anonymity and make it the point of departure for developing a theological idea.

Combining the Various Elements of the Narrative

As one might expect, the dependence of the story in Matthew on its Old Testament origins is evident primarily from the supplementary passage (2:13–21). We say as one might expect, because this passage should be viewed as the first stage in putting a Jewish mark on the universal pattern found in the core of the narrative. Indeed, this supplement is responsible for the incorporation of the mass murder motif in 2:16, a motif unparalleled in any but Jewish sources (in Exodus and in the legends about the birth of Abraham). In Chapter 1 we set forth several conjectures accounting for the motif's creation. The supplement is also responsible for the double structure which resulted from incorporating the mass murder motif: the first murder attempt (2:8), its failure (2:12), the second murder attempt (2:16), and its failure (2:13).[33] The relationship of the supplementary unit in Matthew to the core of the narrative is not the same as that of the murder pattern in Exodus to the ark pattern, because the supplementary unit has no independent existence. It is from the outset a supplement to a literary source, whose very existence was the reason for its creation.

The narrative in Matthew is more continuous because, unlike the Exodus narrative, both murder attempts focus on the individual, and the failure of the attempts result in the rescue of the individual; whereas in Exodus (p. 12 ff.) the unification of the two patterns and the disappearance of the annunciation of the birth of the individual resulted in the story of the midwives being severed from the story of the lone

---

[32] The origin and meaning of this verse are a question in their own right. This verse is not found in the Old Testament, and many conjectures have been advanced to explain it. In the Dead Sea Scrolls one finds similar occurrences of a text quoting verses with which we are unfamiliar. See the examples in Fitzmyer, "The Use of Explicit Old Testament Quotation in Qumran Literature and in the New Testament," and compare the example in Rabbinic literature, *Berakot* 61a, "And Elkanah went after his wife."

[33] Perhaps making Egypt his place of refuge is another expression of the impact of the Exodus story; but cf. I Kings 11:17–23,40 and Jeremiah 26:21, 43:5–7. F. W. Beare's commentary on the verse adds Onias III, from the third century B.C.E., to the biblical list. On the other hand, we may assume Exodus 4:19 had an influence on Matthew 2:20, as is attested by the use of the plural in Matthew.

savior. It should be noted that the Moses nativity story could have had a structure like that found in Matthew. One could have told the story in such a way that the midwives save Moses and do not prevent his birth, and therefore, since the child had already been born, the Pharaoh orders all his people to cast all the infants, one of whom is the lone savior, into the Nile. Indeed, the Moses nativity story, in its biblical stages, developed differently due to the story of the individual being combined with the history of the nation; nevertheless, as we have seen, later works channeled the Moses nativity story more towards this direction.[34]

Incorporating the motif of the mass murder in the supplement to the core was also accomplished successfully, and in certain respects even better than in the original Exodus narrative. In Matthew the entire story focuses on the individual from the outset, and therefore the tension between the course of the narrative and the point it seeks to make, which we discussed after Gressmann, does not exist. Nor does the absence of a description of the people's reaction to the terrible slaughter detract from the story in Matthew, because the people essentially do not figure in the story, rather, only the individual.

In contrast, the story in Matthew does not have the colorful complexity of the Old Testament story. In Exodus the double structure of the murder attempt and its failure mirrors the double pattern underlying the story—the murder pattern and the ark pattern—even though the way in which these two patterns are combined, transforming the first deliverance to a merely momentary deliverance, is not smooth. In Matthew the relationship of the structure, doubling the murder attempt and the deliverance from it, to the contents of the narrative is rather pale and lacks the richness produced in the Exodus story by uniting the two patterns. This impression is reinforced by the rigidity of the formula for the angel's intervention, which forces the narrative to open the supplementary passage with the angel's appearance, and thus have the deliverance precede the mass slaughter. This order of narrative does violence to the structure of the story and to its underlying tension, because, unlike the Moses nativity story, the mass slaughter does not endanger the newborn, even though the story revolves entirely around the fate of the individual. This lays bare the shortcoming of the final structure, which does not rule over its component elements.

The supplementary passage heightens the importance of the slaughter in Bethlehem. This is so, firstly, because of the horrifying nature of wholesale slaughter; secondly, because the story calls in the angel to deliver the hero from the slaughter; and thirdly, because the very fact of this section being a supplementary passage puts the slaughter in Beth-

---

[34] Cf. our discussion of the *Tanḥuma* (p. 94 ff.), the *Asatir*, and Rashi, above.

lehem in a climactic position relative to the first attempt. However, the supplement itself undermines these elements and weakens them due to its typological character, having the angel introduce the unit.

The Protevangelium of James

General Remarks

Our citations from the *Protevangelium of James* (henceforth *PEJ*) are taken from the version in the Bodmer Papyrus, ed. M. Testuz. Occasionally this version will be compared with that presented by Tischendorf, *Evangelia Apocrypha*, pp. 1–50 (henceforth EA).[35]

---

[35] Prevalent scholarly opinion (cf. Hennecke-Schneemelcher, *New Testament Apocrypha*, Vol. 1, p. 372 for a review of the literature) attributes the *PEJ* to a Christian, not a Jewish, author (but see *Oxford Dictionary of the Christian Church*, under *James*). We concur with this opinion. The author of the *PEJ* is not conversant with Jewish customs, nor does he know the geography of the land of Israel. For example, according to his approach, Mary grew up in the Temple and even danced before the Lord there (7; 8; and 15:3); it seems, moreover, that the author viewed this as a common practice, requiring no explanation. The geographical relationship of Mary's house, Joseph, the Temple, and Elizabeth's house is obscure. Anna sits beneath a laurel tree (2:4), etc. The nationalist content of the tidings of predestination is also toned down; Jesus will be spoken of in the whole world (4:1), and the nationalist part of the Gospel according to Luke is omitted (11). Of course, as one might expect, the tidings were adapted to what actually happened, and the discrepancy between the tidings and their realization, which is evident in the Gospels was reduced. Even though the author ostensibly adheres to the biblical pattern of a barren woman giving birth, the literary genre of his work departs from the general world of biblical forms. As often happens, this departure is evident even in those places where the author is ostensibly imitating the source. The author does not give an etymological explanation of the name Mary (מרים). It seems that the absence of commentary on the name stems from the absence of the name Mary in the examples which the author was imitating. It stands to reason that the author did not know Hebrew and was incapable himself of composing a commentary on the name. Also, see Anna's lamentation (3) and her hymn of thanksgiving (6:3), and compare these to Hannah's prayer in I Samuel 2:1–10 and to the hymns in Luke. Also the formulation, "that it might be fulfilled," routinely attached to a biblical verse, has disappeared.

Nevertheless, despite all this evidence, one may not simply conclude that all the sources of the *PEJ* are non-Jewish. Aside from the nationalist heritage, whose origins lie in the canonical version, "The Lord ... will manifest his redemption to the children of Israel" (7:2), and from Jesus being destined to become King of Israel (20:4) (not found in the Bodmer version), there are points of contact with Jewish traditions. Compare the complaint of Anna, mother of Mary, about her barrenness (3) to the complaint of Hannah, mother of Samuel: "*Of all the people before You, You do not remember me as one of them ... how many houses of abominable, disgusting creatures are there before You, and yet You do not remember me as one of them*" (Midrash Samuel, Ch. 2, p. 48). In the *PEJ* the priest's plate ($\pi\acute{\varepsilon}\tau\alpha\lambda ov$=ציץ; cf. the Septuagint on Ex. 28:32 (28:36) [on the mitre]) shows that no sin lies with Mary's father (5:1); compare this with Ginzberg, Vol. 6 (*Moses*), p. 145, note 861. The *PEJ*

The separate versions of the Jesus nativity story could not remain isolated for long. Attempts to reconcile their differences and give the story continuity were not long in coming. This process of drawing a story together is not restricted to nativity stories, and is also evident primarily in the various version of the Gospels being brought closer one to another. A prime expression of such unification is Tatian's *Diatessaron*.[36] We are interested in the *PEJ* not only because of the unification of the various traditions, but also because this unification is accompanied by a further development of individual elements.

Aside from the fact that the *PEJ* unifies two fundamentally separate traditions, one can readily discern certain other traditions and blocs of text in it.[37] The author(s) of the *PEJ* collected and appended various sources, but did not exert himself overly much to obscure their original character and to imbue them all with a unified literary form. See the striking example of the transition to the first person in the words of Joseph (18:2 in EA; not found in the Bodmer papyrus). In this respect the *PEJ* resembles Biblical Antiquities (see our section on the same). Comparing the various versions of the *PEJ* reveals marked differences.[38]

The relationship of the *PEJ* to its sources displays characteristics typical of the development of legends in general as ornamental enlargements on the text. Sometimes the story is extended with no seeming reason; for example, in the *PEJ* Joseph's son leads his ass (17:2). We

---

stresses the fact that Jesus was delivered by a Hebrew midwife (18:1); compare to the Gemara, Abodah Zarah 26a. Compare the world standing still at the moment of Jesus' birth (18:2; not found in the Bodmer version) with Exodus Rabbah XXIX.9. Also see Ginzberg, Vol. 6, p. 39, note 213. Compare the virgins making a veil for the Temple (10) with *Pesikta Rabbati* 26 (p. 131) and the Syriac Apocalypse of Baruch 10:18–19; also see Ginzberg, Vol. 6 (*Exile*), p. 396, note 30 (although Ginzberg does not cite the *PEJ* there). Also see Lieberman's remarks in *Hellenism in Jewish Palestine*, pp. 167–168. On the snake who defiled Eve (13:1) see Ginzberg, Vol. 5 (*The Ten Generations*), p. 133, n. 3. Mary (5:2) (and perhaps also Jesus, 13:1) was born in the seventh month; compare our remarks in the section on Jubilees, note 2, and the section on Midrash, p. 108 ff. The later versions, failing to understand the significance of the seventh month, are uncertain about this figure and change it to nine or eight months. Cf. EA and the alternate versions given there. Also see Lieberman, *Hellenism*, p. 76, note 240; and Testuz (*op. cit.*, p. 51), who feels constrained to remark that, "One must assume that the angel brought the annunciation of the birth in the second month of the pregnancy." Zacharias dies in the Temple (23); cf. Ginzberg, Vol. 6 (*Exile*), p. 396, note 30. There is an anti-Jewish (or perhaps anti-Pharisaic) note in the fact that Annas, who betrays Mary, is a scribe.

[36] Early signs of this development can be found even in the Gospels. Many manuscripts render Matthew 1:25 as "the firstborn son," apparently under the influence of Luke 2:7; the Syriac translation sy^c reads וקרא, i.e., "and she called," under the influence of Luke 1:31; etc.

[37] Cf. the various ideas advanced in Testuz' introduction.

[38] Hennecke-Schneemelcher, *op. cit.*, p. 372 ff.

also have transferal and evolution of motifs: in the *PEJ* Mary, not Elizabeth, hides herself (12:3); Zacharias lingers at the temple, but for a different reason (24); his body disappears (24:3); a dove descends on Joseph's head (9:1); etc.

The main theme of the *PEJ* is the birth of the virgin Mary, mother of Jesus. The Christian tradition that completed the story of the Messiah by creating the nativity story thus continues its course, insofar as it strives to give an account of the mother of the Messiah that goes back to the very beginning. The nativity story is created according to the usual pattern of barren woman stories; in other words, here, too, the existing literary genre becomes a receptacle that accommodates the new heroine: Mary's mother, a barren woman. The influence of the story of the birth of Samuel is particularly noticeable. The mother, named Anna, bewails her bitter fate (2:3); she dedicates the son promised her to God (4:1); and after his birth she thanks God for his grace (6). It should be noted that, in contrast to the Old Testament and Luke, the hymns are well-suited to the story (the hymns found in Luke were not cited in the *PEJ*). The story is set in the temple during a festival, and it is there that the reproach to Joachim is made; etc. On Mary's miraculous growth and development (6) see p. 129 above. As in Genesis 21:8, a feast is made to celebrate the miraculous birth (6:2). As with Samuel (I Samuel 1:22), the mother tries to delay handing over her son (7). Like Abraham, Mary receives food from the hand of an angel (8:1).[39] Mary is from the House of David; and the *PEJ* notes this fact in passing (10:1). Perhaps this represents an attempt to associate Jesus the Son of God with the House of David by way of his mother.[40] The *PEJ* does not attempt to reconcile her coming from the House of David with her being a relative of Elizabeth (12:1).[41]

The King and the Infant

The story of the star over Bethlehem appears in the *PEJ* (21:1-4) as follows: (1) *"And there took place a great tumult in Bethlehem of Judea. For there came wise men saying: 'Where is the king of the Jews? For we have seen his star in the east and have come to worship him.'* (2) *When Herod heard this he was troubled and sent officers and sent for them*

---

[39] Cf. Ginzberg, Vol. 5 (*Abraham*), p. 212, note 29.

[40] This tradition appears as early as Justin, Dialogue 45; also cf. the obscure statement by Ignatius, Ephesians 18.2: "For our God, Jesus Christ, was instructed by Mary in the plan (οἰχονομίαν) of God from the seed of David as from the Holy Spirit." Also cf. the many manuscripts cited in *The New Testament in Greek* on Luke 2:4, which read αὐτοὺς; and sy^s, which reads "both of them": מטל דתריהון מן ביתה הוו דדויד "because the two of them were from the house of David."

[41] The *PEJ* is discussed in detail in Cohen, *Masorot*; here we shall limit ourselves to a comparison with Matthew 2.

and they told him about the star. (3) *And behold, they saw stars in the east, and they went before them, until they came to the cave. And it stood over the head of the child. And when the wise men saw the [young child] standing with Mary his mother, they took out of their bag gifts, gold, and frankincense and myrrh. (4) And being warned by the angel that they should go by another way, they went to their own country."*
Comparing this text with the source in Matthew is very instructive. We see that the Bodmer papyrus version completely omits the story of the king calling the priests and scribes of the people—a unit which, as we have seen, is secondary to the original pattern. The elements of tension that went along with this implanted unit have obviously disappeared from the story. But there is yet another change that follows from this omission. In Matthew the wise men following the Messiah's star first come to Jerusalem, and only from there does the king send them to Bethlehem. In the Bodmer version we see a strong desire to simplify the story here, too, and to omit this waystation. The wise men following the Messiah's star come, as one would expect, directly to Bethlehem, where the Messiah is. The question of where exactly the Messiah is to be found is preserved to some extent, insofar as the Messiah in the Bodmer version is hidden in a cave. The Bodmer version simplifies the plot, but in so doing complicates the incorporation of the king into the story. It should be noted, however, that Jerusalem is not mentioned at all, because the Bodmer version has left out everything having to do with this intermediate station on the wise men's way from their home to Bethlehem.

The EA version: In this version, between verse 1 and verse 3 we have: *"When Herod heard this he was troubled and sent officers to the wise men, and sent for the high priests and questioned them: 'How is it written concerning the Messiah? Where is he born?' They said to him: 'In Bethlehem of Judea; for so it is written.' And he let them go. And he questioned the wise men and said to them: 'What sign did you see concerning the newborn king?' And the wise men said: 'We saw how a very great star shone among these stars and dimmed them so that they no longer shone; and so we knew that a king was born for Israel. And we have come to worship him.' And Herod said: 'Go and seek, and when you have found him, tell me, that I also may come to worship him.' And the wise men went forth. And behold, the star which they had seen in the east went before them, until they came to the cave."*

This version retains the motif of the priests (without the scribes) appearing before the king. But, since the wise men had already reached Bethlehem, their answer does not reveal to Herod the whereabouts of the Messiah; rather, it proves to him that the words of the wise men were true. In Matthew the star motif becomes superfluous because the prophecy from Micah is appended to it; here, in contrast, this superfluity does not exist. Thus Herod can send the wise men forth with the instruction to "go and seek." Here, too, the story is built around the fact that Jesus is in a cave, which explains why the wise men do not come to him directly.

The EA version describes the sight the wise men beheld (after the birth, in which "a king was born for Israel"): a star that outshone all the other stars. This passage is very similar to the legend about Abraham:[42] "A star from the east came and swallowed four stars from the four corners of the heavens."[43] Also traditions on the birth of Moses, as far as these can be traced, at first do not go into great detail (as in Josephus, *Antiquities* 2.205), and later give a fuller description in a variety of forms. (We are assuming here that the Bodmer version is the more ancient one).[44]

As in Matthew, the wise men return home, but under the influence of the other units in Matthew they are warned by an angel, whereas in the original they are **warned in a dream**. One should note the stability of the literary form, which finds expression in the fact that also in the *PEJ* the virgin birth remains beyond the limits of the story of the star in Bethlehem (21; 22). As in Matthew, the virgin birth is neither mentioned nor even alluded to. It seems that the necessity of maintaining the anonymity of the newborn helped preserve the ancient form.

The way the various traditions are drawn together and motifs developed finds expression particularly in the handling of the motif of deliverance. We have already discussed the surprising structural feature of putting the deliverance before the murder attempt (see p. 170). This shortcoming is set right in the *PEJ*, which inverts the order (22). In its description of the deliverance, the *PEJ* departs radically from the story line in Matthew. The angel's revelation and the flight to Egypt are altogether absent. In other words, the supplement to the core of the story (Matthew 2:13–23) is neglected. The flight to Egypt is replaced by the manger in which Mary hides her son after having swaddled him. Unfortunately, the story is broken off at this point, and we do not know whether the mother remains with her son or whether, as in the parallels in other folk literature, like Yocheved, she abandons her son, leaving him in the manger, where the shepherds will find him later. Perhaps the story is broken off here deliberately, because, due to the pressure of the canonized tradition, the author could not bring the story to the conclusion that necessarily followed from the structure of its pattern.

---

[42] *Ma'aseh Abraham* Version B, in Jellinek, *Bet ha-Midrash*, Vol. 2, pp. 118–119.
[43] Also cf. the Arabic version, *ibid.*, p. XXXIII.
[44] Also compare Ignatius, *Ephesians* 19.2.

It seems that here, too, one need not assume that the *PEJ* is based on an ancient tradition; nor may we view this version as proving the conjecture, to be taken up later in the appendix, that the story of the manger in Luke is an adaptation of a foundling story. (While this text does not provide us with proof, it does give some slight support to the conjecture.) That the manger is turned into a secret refuge for the swaddled infant apparently should be explained in terms of the text's desire to unify the canonical versions, the pressure of the pattern which strives to justify the manger motif, and also perhaps the influence of the story of the ark in the Old Testament.[45]

The affinity of the *PEJ* story to the Old Testament story is not limited to the manger and the ark playing similar roles; rather it also extends to the fact that, as in the Old Testament, only the mother plays an active part in the child's deliverance, and the father has disappeared from the story. It seems that the mother's restoration to the story should be attributed to the triple combination of the literary pattern, the Old Testament influence, and primarily the fact that the mother is the dominant figure in the *PEJ*.

In any event, whatever the reasons for dropping out the supplement to the core of the narrative as it appears in Matthew, in terms of the history of the tradition one should view the restoration of the figure of the mother and the replacement of the flight motif by the manger motif as a regression to an earlier stage of the story. As a result the *PEJ* version is closer to the Moses nativity story than is the Matthew version, even though the latter version is earlier and served as the principal source for the *PEJ*.

The reader may have observed that the stages of evolution conjectured here resemble the history of the ark described above, especially in the section on Philo, pp. 45–46. There, too, we saw more ancient elements returning to younger versions of the story. Yet there is a crucial difference here, which may not be ignored. One cannot suspect that Josephus, the authors of the Midrash, or Gregory of Nyssa knew the Akkadian story; thus their versions, which restore the ark to the river, can only be explained in terms of the pressure of the literary pattern. In contrast, the author of the *PEJ* certainly was cognizant of the story of the ark, and this story may well have influenced him either directly or indirectly.

---

[45] The inexplicable element of the manger (cf. appendix, below) becomes a creative element in later legends, attracting animals to it. See Seeligmann's note, *The Septuagint Version of Isaiah*, p. 28, which refers the reader to the Septuagint, Habakkuk 3:2.

APPENDIX A

THE TIDINGS TO THE SHEPHERDS (LUKE 2:6-20)

Thus far we have discussed nativity traditions whose direct or indirect connection with the Moses nativity story was immediately apparent and which did not require any attempt to reconstruct their original form. We now proceed to the version of the Jesus nativity story found in Luke 2:1-20.[46] In its present form this tradition does not come within the scope of our study; but, as Gressmann has noted,[47] the original form of this story was different, and another pattern can be detected through the present formulation. Gressmann prefaces his specific arguments with the general remark that, in a cycle of legends, each component legend taken individually is generally more ancient than the composite cycle in which it appears; and therefore one can assume *a priori* that the story of the tidings to the shepherds was originally independent. Close analysis of the story's details confirms this hypothesis. Verses 18-19 read: "**And all they that heard it wondered at those things which were told them by the shepherds. But Mary kept all these things, and pondered them in her heart.**" It is clear that for "all they that heard," and especially for Mary, the tidings brought them were altogether new to them. In line with this, the story indeed makes no mention of the virgin birth described in the previous chapter, even in those places where one might expect a reference to it, as in the words of the angel to the shepherds (vv. 11-12), or as an explanation for the wonderment of those hearing the tidings in verse 18 (for it would seem that the miracle of virgin birth is far greater, and certainly no lesser, than the miracle of finding a child in a manger). The general argument concerning the unit's independence also leads one to exclude Luke 2:1-5 from the story of the tidings to the shepherds, because the primary role of this passage is to connect the previous story, set in Nazareth, with the current story, which takes place in Bethlehem. Moreover, the motif

---

[46] Or through verse 21, which now serves as a transitional verse connecting the story of the tidings to the shepherds with Jesus' being presented in the Temple, but which certainly was not the original concluding verse of the story of the shepherds.

[47] *Das Weihnachtsevangelium auf Ursprung and Geschichte untersucht*. Unless explicitly stated otherwise, the discussion that follows has been taken from Gressmann.

of the tax disappears from the story altogether, having performed its role of explaining why Joseph left the city where he had been living. It should be added that the reason given in verse 7 for placing the child in the manger, is not further developed in the story.

The focal point of the story is the swaddled child in the manger (originally φάτνη, whose exact meaning is not crucial to our analysis). There is a natural connection between the manger and the shepherds; however this connection is not felt in the story, because there is no causal relationship between these two elements in the story as we have it today. It is not because of their being shepherds that they find the child. Moreover, it is far from clear why the manger should be the focal point of the story. Why choose precisely this object? Why should it serve as a sign, in the angel's words? Or as a mark of recognition for the shepherds? And how did they know where in Bethlehem to seek it? Even the reason for choosing the shepherds as the ones to receive the tidings is not explained by the story. Why them, and not the child's parents? or the entire people? The shepherds' response upon discovering the child is surprisingly brief. One would expect them to bow down before him, bear gifts, or show some other sign of adoration as they stand facing the Messiah. In this regard, comparing the text with Matthew 2:11 is instructive. Perhaps some explanation can be found for each question in turn, but taken together they pose a weighty problem.

All these difficulties, coupled with the story's central motif of finding the child in a manger, led Gressmann to the conclusion that the original core of the story was built around the foundling pattern, which tells of a child being discovered without his parents. This daring conjecture resolves all the problems mentioned above. The child is placed in the manger at night, unbeknownst to anyone, and is in great danger. The angel of God appears to the shepherds, in whose manger the child has been placed,[48] and brings them tidings of the birth of the Savior that night, and the sign proving his words is that they will find the Savior as a babe wrapped in swaddling clothes and lying in their manger. The passage of the angel's tidings (verses 10–12) is preserved in a form relatively faithful to the original pattern; for the tidings do not yet mention the child's parents, and the only part of the passage which perhaps may be viewed as a modification of the original is the reference to the city of David (v. 11). The shepherds find the child and, as is typical of the pattern, take him into their home and raise him. This pattern was adapted and bent to fit other traditions. The child's parents were brought into the picture, the role of the shepherds as adoptive parents was eliminated,

---

[48] Contrary to Gressmann; for the location of the manger cannot be severed from the location of the shepherds. It seems the manger was close by, where the shepherds spent the night.

and a new reason was given for finding the child in a manger. These changes did violence to the structure, creating an element of tension between the pattern around which the story is built and the details that were added to the story.

Gressmann's conjecture is very far-reaching. It does not simply fill in a single detail; rather, it reconstructs an entire structure. The question as to our ability to piece together fragments in such a way cannot be disregarded; but his conjecture does appear well-founded. In our opinion, as well, the structure that Gressmann extracted practically glares at us through the lines of the narrative's current form; and without assuming the existence of this structure, we would have no answer to the difficulties raised above, and all alternative explanations do not stand to reason. Gunkel's appraisal is well-put: "Of course it is only a conjecture, but perhaps quite attractive."[49] Nevertheless, we do not view this conjecture as sufficiently well-proven, and therefore decided not to include it in the body of our book, but rather present it here as an appendix.

This cautious approach also leads us to take issue with the detailed stages in the evolution of the pattern as proposed by Gressmann. Precise reconstruction of the pattern is impossible. It would be preferable to assume a minimal, three-stage, process of change. We begin with the foundling pattern, which belongs to the group of migratory legends and thus is clearly not originally Jewish. In the second stage this pattern became the setting in which the Jesus nativity story was shaped. In the third stage the pattern was subjugated to other traditions in the New Testament. One may ask whether the foundling pattern was taken up directly by the Christian tradition, or whether the Christian reworking of the pattern was preceded by the Jewish adaptation, mediating the development, and the Christian tradition simply completed the work of adaptation? Was there a stage at which the story was a completely independent tradition, not at all dependent on other traditions? These are all important questions, but the text does not give us sufficient information to answer them reasonably.

The extent of the role played by Luke himself in reworking and adapting the unit is a question in its own right. This problem is discussed at length in *Masorot*, and here is not the place to repeat ourselves, since to answer this question one must evaluate all the nativity traditions appearing in Luke. Be that as it may, one immediately sees a resemblance between the story as reconstructed and the story of the ark in Exodus 2. In terms of the evolution of the traditions, it is interesting that Matthew (ch. 2) has a parallel to the annihilation pattern without the ark, whereas Luke (if we accept Gressmann's conjecture) has a parallel

---

[49] *Das Märchen*, p. 118.

to the ark motif, but without the annihilation, and the *Protevangelium of James* actually combines both of these approaches. It should, however, be stressed that the tradition in Luke differs from the traditions that we have discussed thus far in two important respects: firstly, it is a tradition which, at the end of the evolutionary process, reaches complete obliteration of the foundling motif; secondly, we have, in any case, an independent foundling story which should not be directly connected with the Moses nativity story.

In conclusion, we cannot know whether the *PEJ* retained vestiges of the ancient foundling tradition, or whether the *PEJ* itself came up with this motif and restored it to a tradition that had obliterated the motif. Nor may we ignore the possibility that the given elements of the text led the *PEJ* to implant elements of the foundling pattern into a tradition that had never known such a pattern. Either way, the very fact of our wavering between these three possibilities is intrinsic to the evolutionary process that this study has sought to describe.[50]

---

[50] Compare our remarks at the end of the previous chapter, on the return of the ark motif, and our frequent references throughout the book to the latent aspiration of the literary pattern to restore motifs that have been rejected. There is an interesting parallel between the literary tendency reviewed here and a similar tendency noted by Ben-Ḥayyim in the realm of grammar. In his article, "בדבר מקוריותה של הטעמה מלעיל בעברית," he investigated whether the penultimate accentuation in Samaritan preserves the penultimate accentuation that was practiced in Hebrew at a stage prior to the Tiberian tradition, a stage many scholars assume existed. The article's conclusion is that accentuation as practiced today in Samaritan was preceded by another stage, equivalent to the tradition from Tiberias. In other words, the usual penultimate accentuation of Samaritan is not a continuation of the direction set by the conjectured penultimate accentuation of its Hebrew predecessor. Nevertheless, Ben-Ḥayyim concludes his article thus: "If we have not succeeded in deriving an answer from the Samaritan tradition regarding the complex question of the emergence of the Tiberian accentuation of Hebrew, nevertheless the Samaritan tradition indirectly supports the views of those scholars who assume, each in his own way, a consistent penultimate accentuation at a stage preceding the Tiberian one. For, the basic trends of a language, having been disturbed by phonetic processes (such as the elimination of short vowels in Hebrew at the ends of words), tend to work their way back to their original form. It seems to me likely that the penultimate accentuation, which spread throughout the Hebrew language towards the end of the Second Temple period, is one of these basic trends which re-emerges in Hebrew, as a child takes after his parents."

APPENDIX B

NOTES ON IBN EZRA'S SHORT AND LONG COMMENTARIES

The reason for the exile: Ibn Ezra, like his predecessors in the *Midrash*, casts the story in the usual form. In his long commentary on Exodus 2:23 we read: "*Israel repented. Ezekiel reminds us that Israel used to worship Egyptian idols, therefore the Lord oppressed them and, for not having worshipped Him, made them serve cruel masters.*" Thus Ibn Ezra restores the four basic components of sin, retribution, repentance, and redemption to the story. Compare this to R. David Kimḥi's commentary on Genesis 15:14, and to Sforno on Genesis 15:13, and Exodus 1:7.

With respect to the midwives (Ex. 1:15), in his short commentary he writes: "**To the midwives.** *They [i.e., these two] were in charge of all the midwives.*" (Ibn Ezra is addressing the question of how two women could have assisted the births of an entire nation. He gives a similar interpretation in his long commentary as well.) Was Ibn Ezra the first exegete to find this verse problematic? In his long commentary he adds, "*According to received tradition (*בדרך קבלה*), they were the mother and daughter [i.e., Moses' mother and sister]; and this is so.*" Ibn Ezra's proclamation, faithfully accepting this tradition, should put the reader on alert, as we shall show below.

With respect to **the daughter of Levi** (Ex. 2:1), he specifies, "*That is, Levi, the son of Jacob,*" (in the short commentary; likewise in the long) in order to explain the presence of the definite particle את. But compare his commentary on Genesis 46:27.

Ibn Ezra, like his predecessors, the Sages of the *Midrash*, also found the existence of Miriam (and Aaron) problematic. However, he took a completely different approach than his predecessors to this grave contradiction. Early exegetes were shielded from having to draw the necessary conclusions by their practice of interpreting Scripture within the context of *Aggadah* or in conjunction with it (e.g., Rashi). In the world of *Midrash* everything, or at least very much, is permissible.[1] Ibn Ezra did not enjoy the aegis of the *Aggadah*. Moreover, by his natural inclination, he was extremely sensitive to contradictions. His handling of the problem here is typical of his treatment of such difficulties. Four of his

---

[1] Cf. Heinemann, דרכי האגדה.

frequently employed techniques are called upon here: A) proclaiming his faith in the tradition; b) expressing his own opinion under the guise of an attack upon it; C) expressing his own opinion and spontaneously also contradicting himself, as well as presenting other contradictory views, although not as alternate possibilities among which the reader is free to choose; D) providing an answer which implies an even greater problem. All these are naturally accompanied by deliberate obfuscation, designed to camouflage the exegetes true intention.

In his long commentary (Ex. 6:26) Ibn Ezra wrote: "**It is Aaron and Moses.** *Aaron is mentioned before Moses because he was the senior in years.*" As proof, in his commentary on verse 27 he cited Numbers 26:59: "**and she bare unto Amram Aaron and Moses, and Miriam their sister,**" with respect to which he wrote, "*In the order in which they were born, so are they mentioned, and the proof is* ... **and she bare.**" Thus, in Ibn Ezra's opinion Miriam was younger than Moses. This interpretation in his long commentary matches the one in his short commentary: אחותו, יתכן להיות אחותו ממשפחתו "**His sister—** *perhaps meaning that she was from his family*" (i.e., not actually his sister Miriam, since she had not yet been born, but one of his relations; as in Genesis 13:8: **for we be brethren**, Genesis 29:15, and elsewhere).[2]

In his long commentary (Ex. 2:2), Ibn Ezra also cites Ben Zuta, a 10th century Karaite exegete, who supports the view that Miriam was younger than Moses: "*Ben Zuta said that no one telling of a deed would show favoritism to the more honored person by mentioning him first. It is written,* **and she bare unto Amram Aaron and Moses, and Miriam their sister** *(Num. 26:59), which shows that she was the youngest. But this blind man forgot about Shem, Ham and Japheth (Gen. 5:32), as it is written,* **and Noah begat Shem, Ham and Japheth,** *and Japheth was the eldest. Moreover, we read,* **There they buried Abraham and Sarah his wife** *(Gen 49:31), although she was*

---

[2] The fact that this explanation appears both in his long and his short commentaries exempts us from having to take a stand on the complex question of the relationship of these commentaries one to the other. This relationship is discussed in Fleischer's introduction, pp. xxxii–xxxix. The extent of Ibn Ezra's authorship of the long commentary has been a matter of controversy since the latter half of the fourth century (!), when Joseph ben Eliezer Tob Elem (Bonfils) wrote צפנת פענח, where we read (in the introduction to Exodus, p. 181, Herzog edition): "On this I have to say that by all reason the long commentary is not his work; rather, it was composed by one of his disciples who collected commentaries from Ibn Ezra's books, embellishing Ibn Ezra's writings in certain places and abridging them in others, altering Ibn Ezra's opinion in certain places and contradicting it in others." Also see Friedlaender, *Abraham Ibn Ezra*, p. 153. We shall not elaborate further on this controversy, but merely wish to point out that one can hardly deny a given commentary belongs to Ibn Ezra simply on the grounds that it contradicts something he has said elsewhere. Such a criterion must be applied with the utmost care.

buried in the cave thirty-eight years before Abraham." In view of the method used by Ibn Ezra in his short and long commentaries, we may presume that here, as elsewhere, he was presenting his own opinion under the guise of an attack on his adversaries. Fleischer[3] expressed surprise at Ibn Ezra's attack on Ben Zuta and naïvely remarked, "He ends up contradicting himself."[4]

Ibn Ezra contradicts the midrashic tradition which typically makes the obscure definite and says that the unknown women, Shiphrah and Puah, were none other than the mother Yocheved and her daughter Miriam, and thus necessarily implies that Miriam was older than Moses. Therefore Ibn Ezra goes to pains to preface his (long) commentary with an affirmation of loyalty to the tradition: "**to the Hebrew midwives (Ex. 1:15)**—*According to received tradition, they were the mother and daughter; and this is so.*" Later, in his commentary on Exodus 2:2, he says: "**And the woman conceived.** *There can be no doubt, as we have mentioned, that Aaron was older than Moses; and indeed, it is the accepted tradition of our forefathers, that Puah was Miriam, as it is written,* **and his sister stood afar off.**" (The fact that she stood watch over the child proves that she was older than he.) The very way Ibn Ezra puts his words raises doubts; for it is hard to believe of Ibn Ezra that he truly held that "there can be no doubt ... that Puah was Miriam," especially when, in his short commentary he infers from the "sister" standing watch that she was actually older than Moses and hence not his sister.[5]

---

[3] *Op. cit.*, p. 6, n. 2.

[4] It is worth noting that to prove his remarks here Ibn Ezra cited Genesis 5:32. Indeed, most of the Sages believe that Japeth was the oldest (cf. *Genesis Rabbah* XXVI.3 (p. 245), and XXXVII.7 (p. 349); and *Sanhedrin* 69b). There are, however, some who dispute this view. (Cf. Ginzberg, Vol. 5, p. 179, n. 30; *Torah Shelemah*, Vol. 2, p. 364, n. 84; Rappaport, p. 97, n. 64.) Ibn Ezra seems to be among those who cast doubt on Japeth's being the elder; since, on Gen. 10:21, he remarks: "Some hold that Shem was Japhet's older brother, and that therefore Scripture mentioned him first." Hence Ibn Ezra clearly believes that this verse cannot be used as incontrovertible proof; indeed, compare R. David Kimḥi on Genesis 5:32. On prefering the last-mentioned, see Chapter 1, note 40.

[5] Ibn Ezra's commentary is further obscured by the fact that he inserts a discussion of the order of the generations between his remarks on the received tradition of our forefathers that "Puah was Miriam" and his citation from Ben Zuta. Perhaps Ibn Ezra's addition to the ancient sources (especially *Seder Olam Rabbah* 3) of something which one finds only in his commentary—"*When did this new king rule, and how many years did they build treasure cities? For close to the birth of Moses the decree was passed against the males*"—may be taken as an indication that he sensed that viewing the enslavement as a preface to the birth of Moses shortens the length of the enslavement, thus contradicting the four hundred years mentioned in Genesis 15:13. Thus, here he intended to hint that whether or not Miriam's birth came first, it is difficult to connect the nativity story with the history of the enslavement. In Fried-

Scripture (Numbers 26:59) lists Miriam last, and she was the youngest; whereas Aaron is mentioned first. According the Ibn Ezra's approach, this order proves that Aaron was older than Moses. Ibn Ezra provides an interesting response to the question why, if this was indeed so, was Aaron not mentioned between the verse, **and took to wife a daughter of Levi,** and the verse, **and the woman conceived, and bare a son.** In his short commentary on Exodus 2:2 he writes:[6] *"Scripture did not mention him because nothing of note happened to him as had happened to Moses in his youth. Likewise, regarding Bathsheba, Scripture says* **and called his name Jedidiah** *(II Sam. 12:25)*[7]—*this was Solomon, although Shimea, Shobab, and Nathan had already been born to her before Solomon [cf. I Chron. 3:5:* **And these were born unto him in Jerusalem; Shimea, and Shobab, and Nathan, and Solomon, four, of Bathshua the daughter of Ammiel]."*[8] If we are to uphold Ibn Ezra's interpretation of the verse from Chronicles, then we would have to assume that the birth of Solomon to Bathsheba, the wife of Uriah the Hittite, which is described in II Samuel 11–12, was preceded by three other births. But this is impossible. Quite the contrary, if we were to follow Ibn Ezra's approach, that Bathsheba is the same as Bathshua and that the sons mentioned in I Chronicles and in II Samuel were her children, then we would be compelled to admit that the order in which the sons are mentioned in the verse does not necessarily reflect the order in which they were born, or that Bathsheba cannot be identified with Bathshua and that the Solomon mentioned in I Chronicles is not the same as the Solomon mentioned in II Samuel. Clearly Ibn Ezra perceived this complex array of contradictory implica-

---

laender's opinion (*Ibn Ezra*, p. 153) part of the difficulty in his text stems from the fact that not all of it was written at the same time and that mistakes were made in copying it. His remarks, which apply to the entire long commentary on Exodus, must be studied. Be that as it may, whether or not we accept his proposed reconstruction of Ibn Ezra's text, our remarks still stand.

[6] Note that in his short commentary Ibn Ezra did not bother to explain the existence of Miriam, since in that commentary he took the approach that she was younger than Moses and did not even mention the interpretation which held that she was older than Moses. In his long commentary, however, where Ibn Ezra ostensibly agrees with the Sages' view that Miriam was Puah, he also mentioned Miriam: "Scripture did not mention the births of Miriam and Aaron because nothing changed with their births."

[7] Ibn Ezra misquotes the verse, omitting the particle את. Cf. Fleischer, p. 5, n. 6.

[8] The Rab Kook edition of Ibn Ezra's commentary reads, "had already been born to him." The version in this edition was generally copied from Fleischer's version; we do not know on what the variant reading, "him," is based. Examination of seventeen manuscripts did not reveal a single instance of "him." We surmise that the publisher "emended" the version which he had before him in order to make it match the formulation in Scripture, as is known to happen in the evolution of a text.

tions. Thus, his position on our problematic passage in Exodus could be put approximately as follows: the story of the birth of Moses in Exodus 2 contradicts other passages in the Torah, just as the description of the birth of Solomon in II Samuel contradicts the account of his birth in I Chronicles.

It is clear from the above not only that Ibn Ezra, like his predecessors, sensed these contradictions, but that unlike the Sages, he was aware of their implications. How far he went in drawing his conclusions, however, we cannot know. Contemporary research is inclined to "make Ibn Ezra a better Jew" and gloss over his oblique insinuations. Therefore it is only just and fitting to recall the words of Spinoza, who laid the foundations of modern Bible criticism and provided a good characterization of this exegete who worked through obscurities: *Et hac de causa Aben Hezra, liberioris ingenii Vir, et non mediocris eruditionis ... non ausus est mentem suam aperte explicare, sed rem obscurioribus verbis tantum indicare.*[9]

---

[9] *Tractatus*, beginning of Ch. 8. Parallels can be found elsewhere for each of Ibn Ezra's methods listed above, although this is not the place to go into further detail. Cf. Bernfeld's article on Ibn Ezra in the German *Encyclopedia Judaica*, Vol. 8, pp. 326–340, which remains an excellent article to this day. Also cf. Soloweitschik-Rubascheff, תולדות בקרת המקרא, pp. 42–47.

APPENDIX C

THE ASATIR

CHAPTER 8

And there arose a (new) Pharaoh who gathered a great multitude of Copts and ruled after him for sixty years. Now, in Egypt there was a magician, P(a)LT(i)Y by name. And (P(a)LT(i)Y) saw the greatness of Israel, having seen Levi go in to Pharaoh in a most magnificent chariot and leave in great honor; and he said, "Who is this man?" And he was told, "A Hebrew." Then he said, "Great is the honor of this man, and of what lies hidden in his loins and of what he shall have." His words were relayed to Pharaoh, who then called for the magician. (P(a)LT(i)Y) said to him, "It is so, that from the offspring of this man there shall arise a man great in faith and wisdom, and the heavens and the earth shall obey him, and the destruction of Egypt shall be wrought at his hands." Pharaoh [immediately] commanded that the women shall be separated from the men for forty days. When they had already been separated one from another for nineteen days, "And there went a man from the house of Levi." Great is the tree from which Moses comes. The magician saw through his magic that Israel's star had risen and that the child's mother was pregnant with him, and he said to the king: "Your intention [was] in vain." Pharaoh said to him, "What shall be done?" And the magician answered: "His death shall be by water." So Pharaoh commanded the Egyptians: "Let not a single Hebrew male remain alive." Shiphrah and Puah were charged to oversee the births of the Hebrew women, and Pharaoh said to them: "Let every male be killed, and every female let live." Now Amram was a good doctor, well-received in Egypt. Shiphrah felt kindly to the Levites and Puah felt kindly to the Hebrews; and the fear of God was in their hearts, and they did not do as Pharaoh had commanded. And the people grew numerous and waxed very strong. And Pharaoh commanded all his people to throw the newborns into the river. And the fathers and mothers trembled. And the Hebrew women acted with faith, and cast themselves together with their children.

CHAPTER 9

And the exalted prophet Moses, of eternally blessed memory, was born in the month of Nisan, on the [fifteenth] of the month, on the Sabbath day.

And on the fifteenth of Sivan he was cast into the river. And when he was cast into the river, the river fell. And all the women came out to see it [rise]. And as all the ⟨men⟩ [women] came down, Pharaoh's daughter (also) came down. And the river fell each day that it [should have been] rising. And the magicians and seers assembled in great distress. And P(a)LT(i)Y [the magician] comprehended the secret of the book of omens and [said] that the child had come down (i.e., been born), and that his ark was in the reeds. And Pharaoh's daughter saw it in the fifth hour of the seventh day, and she sent her handmaid to fetch it, and she opened it, "and she saw the child: and, behold, it was a boy weeping. And Pharaoh's daughter had compassion on him."—Great is compassion!— And she commanded her maidens that the incident not be revealed. All the while Miriam was standing across from her. And when she (Miriam) saw her so moved by him, she ran over and said to her, "Shall I go and call . . . ?" And (Pharaoh's daughter) answered, "Go"! And so she went and called Yocheved, her mother. And she (Pharaoh's daughter) said to her: Nurse this child and I shall pay (you) for your milk." And she nursed him [pure milk]. And he grew, and she brought him to Pharaoh's daughter; and the (latter) called him Moses.

APPENDIX D

LIST OF ABBREVIATIONS

ANET	Ancient Near Eastern Texts Relating to the Old Testament
BASOR	Bulletin of the American Schools of Oriental Research
EA	Evangelia apocrypha, ed. Tischendorf, 1876.
EJ	Encyclopedia Judaica
GCS	Griechische Christliche Schriftsteller
HThR	Harvard Theological Review
JANES	Journal of the Ancient Near Eastern Society of Columbia University
LCL	The Loeb Classical Library
MG	Migne, Patrologiae Cursus Completus, Series Graeca
NTS	New Testament Studies
OTL	Old Testament Library
PEJ	Protevangelium of James
SCS	Septuagint and Cognate Studies
ThZ	Theologische Zeitschrift
VT	Vetus Testamentum
ZAW	Zeitschrift für die Alttestamentliche Wissenschaft
ZRGG	Zeitschrift für Religions und Geistegeschichte

Note: Throughout the book, references to Ginzberg are to his *Legends of the Jews* and references to Kasher are to his *Torah Shelemah*, unless otherwise stated. Since references to these two works occur so frequently, these authors have not been included in the index. References to primary sources have been given throughout according to the editions listed in the bibliography.

BIBLIOGRAPHY

Abarbanel, Don Isaac, פירוש התורה, (*Commentary on the Torah*), Jerusalem, 1964.
Abraham, son of Maimonides, פירוש על בראשית שמות, (*Commentary on Genesis and Exodus*), Weisenberg-Sasson ed., Jerusalem, 1984.
Aland, K., *Synopsis Quattuor Evangeliorum*, 9th ed., Stuttgart, 1976.
"The Asatir (ספר אסטיר)," edited by Z. Ben Ḥayyim, with translation and commentary, *Tarbiẓ* 14 (1943), 104–125, 174–190; *Tarbiẓ* 15 (1944), 71–87.
Avineri, I., היכל רש"י, an encyclopedia of Rashi's work in the field of language and exegesis, Tel Aviv, 1940–1960.
Baeck, L., *Das Evangelium als Urkunde der jüdischen Glaubensgeschichte*, Berlin, 1938.
R. Baḥya, ביאור על התורה, (*Commentary on the Torah*), Chavel ed., Jersualem, 1982.
Bauer, W., Arndt, W. F., and Gingrich, F. W., *Greek-English Lexicon of the New Testament*, 2nd ed., Chicago, 1979.
Beare, F. W., *The Gospel according to Matthew*, San Francisco, 1981.
Ben-Ḥayyim, Z., "בדבר מקוריותה של הטעמת מלעיל בעברית", ("On penultimate accentuation in Hebrew"), in ספר חנוך ילון, (*Henoch Yalon Jubilee Volume*), Jerusalem, 1963, pp. 150–160.
Biblia Hebraica (Stuttgartensia), Stuttgart, 1984.
Bickerman, E., *Studies in Jewish and Christian History*, Leiden, 1976–1986.
Binder, G., *Die Aussetzung der Königskinder Kyros and Romulus*, Meisenheim, 1964.
Bin-Gorion, E., שבילי האגדה, (*Pathways of the Aggadah*), Jerusalem, 1950.
Blau, J., "החל בהוראת התחיל בדבר והמשיך בו", ("*Heḥel* Denoting 'To Begin and Continue'"), *Leshonenu* 32 (1968), 53–58.
Brown, R. E., *The Birth of the Messiah*, New York, 1977.
Brunner-Traut, E., "Die Geburtsgeschichte der Evangelien im Lichte ägyptologischer Forschungen," *ZRGG* 12 (1960), 97–111.
Bruston, C., "La Mort et Sépulture de Jacob," *ZAW* 7 (1887), 203–210.
Bultmann, R., *The History of the Synoptic Tradition*, Oxford, 1963.
Campbell, Y., *The Hero with the Thousand Faces*, New York, 1968.
Cassuto, U., *A Commentary on the Book of Exodus*, Jerusalem, 1967. Originally published in Hebrew as פירוש על ספר שמות, Jerusalem, 1952.
Charlesworth, J. H. (ed.), *The Old Testament Pseudepigrapha*, New York, 1983.
Chavel, Ḥ. D., פירושי רש"י על התורה, (*Rashi's Commentaries on the Torah*), 3rd ed., Jerusalem, 1983.
Childs, B. S., *The Book of Exodus*, OTL, London, 1974.
Cicero, *De Divinatione*, ..., Stuttgart, 1965.
Clement of Alexandria, *Stromata*, GCS II(15), Berlin, 1960.
Cohen, C., "The Legend of Sargon and the Birth of Moses," *JANES* 4 (1972), 46–51.
Cohen, J., מסורות הלידה של ישו על רקע סיפורי הלידה במקרא ובמסורת היהודית, (*Traditions of Jesus' Birth against the Background of the Birth Stories in the Bible and Jewish Tradition*); doctoral dissertation, Jerusalem, 1989.
Daube, D., *The New Testament and Rabbinic Judaism*, London, 1957.
R. David ha-Nagid, מדרש ר' דוד הנגיד, ספר שמות, Jerusalem, 1968.
Deissmann, A., *Licht vom Osten*, 4th ed., Tübingen, 1923.
Deuteronomy Rabbah, דברים רבה, Vilna, new edition, Jerusalem, 1961.
Deuteronomy Rabbah, דברים רבה, Lieberman ed., Jerusalem, 1940.

Diels, H. and Kranz, W., *Die Fragmente der Vorsokratiker*, 12th ed., Dublin and Zürich, 1966.

"Dibre ha-Yamim shel Mosheh," ("דברי הימים של משה"), Shinan ed., *Ha-Sifrut* 24 (1977), 100–116. We have generally used this edition unless otherwise noted.

Ecclesiastes Rabbah, קוהלת רבה, Vilna, new edition, Jerusalem, 1961.

Ecclesiastes Zuta, קוהלת זוטא, in מדרש זוטא, ed. Buber, Vilna, 1925.

Ehrlich, A., מקרא כפשוטו, (*The Bible according to its Literal Meaning*), Berlin, 1899–1901.

——, *Die Psalmen*, Berlin, 1905.

R. Ephraim, פרוש רבינו אפרים על התורה, (*Commentary of Rabbenu Ephraim on the Torah*), Halevi ed., Johannesburg, 1950.

Epiphanius, *Panarion: Haeres*, GCS I(25), Berlin, 1915–1922.

Epstein, B. L., תוספת ברכה, Notes on the Pentateuch and Megillot, Tel Aviv, 1981. First printed in Pinsk, 1937.

Eusebius, *Praeparatio Evangelica*, GCS VIII(43), Berlin, 1954.

Exodus Rabbah, שמות רבה, Shinan ed., Jerusalem, 1984. When a given *midrash* did not appear in this edition, we used the Vilna edition.

The Fathers According to Rabbi Nathan, אבות דר' נתן, Schechter ed., Vienna, 1887.

Finkelstein, L., "The Oldest Midrash," *HThR* 31 (1938), 291–317.

Fitzmyer, J., *The Gospel according to Luke*, The Anchor Bible, Vol. 28, New York, 1983.

——, "The Use of Explicit Old Testament Quotations in Qumran Literature and in the New Testament," *NTS* 7 (1960–1961); in *Essays on the Semitic Background of the New Testament*, London, 1971, pp. 3–58.

Flusser, D., "Palaea Historica, An Unknown Source of Biblical Legends," *Scripta Hierosolymitana* 22, 48–79.

Freud, S., *Der Mann Moses und die monotheistische Religion*, Frankfurt a. M., 1965.

Friedlaender, M., *Essays on the Writing of Abraham Ibn Ezra*, photocopy edition, Jerusalem, 1964.

Gaster, M., *The Asatir. The Samaritan Book of the Secrets of Moses*, London, 1927. The actual book was not available to the author.

——, *The Chronicles of Jeraḥmeel*, New York, 1971. Orig. 1899

Gaster, Th., *Myth, Legend, and Custom*, London, 1969.

Geiger, A., *Urschrift und Übersetzungen der Bibel in ihrer Abhängigkeit von der innern Entwicklung des Judentums*, Frankfurt a. M., 1928.

Genesis Rabbah, בראשית רבא, Theodor–Albeck ed., Berlin, 1903–1929. Second printing, with emendations by H. Albeck, Jerusalem, 1965. Page numbers have been given according to this edition.

Gesenius-Kautzsch-Cowley, *Hebrew Grammar*, 2nd ed., Oxford, 1910.

Ginsberg, H. L., "The Legend of King Keret," *BASOR (Supplementary Studies)* 2–3 (1946).

Ginzberg, L. (ed.), *Ginze Schechter = Geniza Studies*, Vol. 1, New York, 1928.

——, *The Legends of the Jews*, Philadelphia, 1909–1938.

——, על הלכה ואגדה, (*On Halakhah and Aggadah*), Tel Aviv, 1960.

Gnilka, J., *Das Matthäusevangelium*, Freiburg, 1986.

Goodenough, E. R., *Jewish Symbols in the Greco-Roman Period*, Vol. 9, pp. 197–226.

Gregorius, *De Vita Moysis*, Gregorii Nysseni Opera, Vol. 7, part 2, Leiden, 1964.

Gressmann, H., *Mose und seine Zeit*, Göttingen, 1913.

——, *Das Weihnachtsevangelium auf Ursprung und Geschichte untersucht*, Göttingen, 1914.
Grünbaum, M., *Neue Beiträge zur Semitischen Sagenkunde*, Leiden, 1893.
Günter, H., *Die Christliche Legende des Abendlandes*, Heidelberg, 1910.
Gunkel, H., *Das Märchen im alten Testament*, Tübingen, 1921.
Gutmann, J., "The Haggadic Motif in Jewish Iconography," *Eretz-Israel* 6 (1960), 16–22.
Heinemann, I., דרכי האגדה, (*Methods of the Aggadah*), 2nd ed., Jerusalem, 1974.
Hennecke, E. and Schneemelcher, W., *New Testament Apocrypha*, Philadelphia, 1963–1965.
Herodotos, *Herodoti Historiarum Libri IX*, G. Dindorfius ed., Paris, 1877.
Ibn Ezra, הפירוש הקצר לשמות, (*Short Commentary on Exodus*), Fleischer ed., Vienna, 1926.
Ibn Ezra, הפירוש הארוך לשמות, (*Long Commentary on Exodus*), Weiser ed., Jerusalem, 1976.
Ibn Janaḥ, Jonah, ספר הרקמה, (*Kitāb al-Lumaʻ*), ed. Wilensky-Tene, 2nd ed., Jerusalem, 1964.
Ignatius, *Epistolai*, in The Apostolic Fathers, LCL, London and New York, 1959.
Jellinek, A., בית המדרש, A collection of little-known midrashim, Jerusalem, 1938.
Josephus, *Jewish Antiquities*, LCL, 1930; קדמוניות היהודים, Hebrew translation with notes by A. Schalit, Jerusalem and Tel Aviv, 1978.
Justin, *Pros Tryphōna Ioudaion Dialogus*, MG, Vol. 6, Paris, 1857–1866.
Kahana, A., ed., הספרים החיצוניים א--ב, (*The Apocrypha, I–II*), Tel Aviv, 1937.
Kasher, M. M., תורה שלמה, *Torah Shelemah*, a Talmudic-Midrashic encyclopedia of the Pentateuch, containing a complete collection of commentaries and notes from the earliest Hebrew works, up to the gaonic period, Vol. 1–39, Jerusalem and New York, 1949–1985.
Kaufmann, Y., ספר יהושע, (*The Book of Joshua*), Jerusalem, 1976.
——, תולדות האמונה הישראלית, (*History of the Religion of Israel*), Tel Aviv, 1937–1956.
Klostermann, E., *Das Matthäusevangelium*, 3rd ed., Tübingen, 1938.
Kraeling, C. H., *The Synagogue (The Excavations at Dura-Europos)*, New Haven, 1956.
Krauss, S., *Griechische und lateinische Lehnwörter*, Berlin, 1899.
Kümmel, W. G., *Einleitung in das Neue Testament*, 21st ed., Heidelberg, 1983.
Kutscher, E. Y., *The Language and Linguistic Background of the Isaiah Scroll*, (I Q Isa^a), Leiden, 1974. Originally published in Hebrew as הלשון והרקע של מגילת ישעיהו השלמה ממגילות ים המלח, Jerusalem, 1959.
Lambert, W. G. and Millard, A. R., *Atraḥasis*, Oxford, 1962.
Lekaḥ Tob, מדרש לקח טוב לר' טוביה בן אליעזר, Buber ed., Lwow, 1878.
Leviticus Rabbah, ויקרא רבה, Margulies ed., Jerusalem, 1953–1958.
Lewis, C. T. and Short, C., *A Latin Dictionary*, Oxford, 1969.
Liddell, H. G. and Scott, R., *A Greek-English Lexicon*, new ed. rev. by H. S. Jones, Oxford, 1940.
Lieberman, S., *Greek in Jewish Palestine*, New York, 1942.
——, *Hellenism in Jewish Palestine*, New York, 1950.
——, מדרשי תימן, (*Yemenite Midrashim*), Jerusalem, 1970.
——, שקיעין, a few words on some Jewish legends, customs and literary sources found in Karaite and Christian works, Jerusalem, 1970.
——, "זניחין," ("Neglected Sources"), *Tarbiẓ* 42 (1973), 42–54.

Loewenstamm, S. E., "Beloved is Man that he was created in the Image," in *Comparative Studies in Biblical and Ancient Oriental Literatures*, Neukirchen-Vluyn, 1980, pp. 48–50. Originally published in Hebrew as חביב אדם שנברא בצלם, *Tarbiẓ* 27 (1958), 1–2.

——, "The Death of Moses, Studies on the Testament of Abraham," ed. George W. E. Nickelsburg, Jr.,, *SCS* 6 (1976), 185–217. Originally published in Hebrew as מות משה, *Tarbiẓ* 27 (1958), 142–157.

——, *The Evolution of the Exodus Tradition*, Jerusalem, 1992. Originally published in Hebrew as מסורת יציאת מצרים בהשתלשלותה, Jerusalem, 1968.

——, "Die Geburtsgeschichte Moses," in *Studies in Jewish Religious and Intellectual History in Honour of Alexander Altmann*, Alabama, 1979, pp. 195–213.

——, "The Making and Destruction of the Golden Calf," *Biblica* 48 (1967), 481–490; *Comparative Studies ...*, Neukirchen-Vluyn, 1980, pp. 236–245.

——, "פרשת מותם של אבות האומה בספר בראשית," ("The Death of the Patriarchs in the Narrative of the Book of Genesis"), in המקרא ותולדות ישראל, מחקרים לזכרו של יעקב ליור, (*Studies in the Bible and Jewish History, Dedicated to the Memory of Jacob Liver*), Tel Aviv, 1972, pp. 104–123.

Lohmeyer, E. and Schmauch, W., *Das Evangelium des Matthäus*, Göttingen, 1958.

Luzzatto, Samuel David, פירוש על חמישה חומשי תורה, (*Commentary on the Pentateuch*), Padua, 1871.

Mann, J., *The Bible as Read and Preached in the Old Synagogue*, Vol. 2, Cincinnati, 1966.

Mekilta of R. Simeon b. Yoḥai, מכילתא דרבי שמעון בן יוחאי, Epstein-Melammed ed., Jerusalem, 1955. Generally we have used this edition, unless otherwise noted. Page numbers have been given according to this edition.

Mekilta of R. Simeon b. Yoḥai, מכילתא דרבי שמעון בן יוחאי, Hoffmann ed., Frankfurt a. M., 1905.

Mekilta of R. Ishmael, מכילתא דרבי ישמעאל, ed. Horovitz-Rabin, 2nd ed., Jerusalem, 1970. Page numbers have been given according to this edition.

Meyer, E., *Die Israeliten und ihre Nachbarstämme*, Halle, 1906.

Midrash ha-Gadol on Exodus, מדרש הגדול, שמות, ed. Margulies, Jerusalem, 1956.

Midrash Samuel, מדרש שמואל, Buber ed., Cracow, 1893.

Midrash Tanḥuma, מדרש תנחומא, Buber ed., Vilna, 1891.

Midrash Tannaim on Deuteronomy, מדרש תנאים על ספר דברים, Hoffmann ed., Berlin, 1908.

Midrash Tehillim, מדרש תהלים, =*Midrash Shoḥer Tob*; Buber ed., Vilna, 1891.

Miller, S. J. (ed.), *The Samaritan Molad Mosheh*, New York, 1949.

Nachmanides, פירוש הרמב"ן על התורה, (*Nachmanides' Commentary on the Torah*), Chavel ed., Jerusalem, 1959.

The Neophyti Targum of the Pentateuch, ed. A. Diez-Macho, Madrid and Barcelona, 1968–1978.

Nestle, K. and Aland, B., *Greek-English New Testament*, Stuttgart, 1985.

Neubauer, A., *Mediaeval Jewish Chronicles and Chronological Notes*, Amsterdam, 1970. Orig. 1887

The New Testament in Greek, The Gospel According to St. Luke, Oxford, 1984.

Numbers Rabbah, במדבר רבה, Vilna version, new edition, Jerusalem, 1961.

Origen, *In Exodum Homilia*, GCS VI(29), Leipzig, 1920.

The Oxford Dictionary of the Christian Church, 2nd ed., Oxford, 1985.

Pesikta de R. Kahana, פסיקתא דרב כהנא, Mandelbaum ed., New York, 1987. Page numbers have been given according to this edition.

Pesikta Rabbati, פסיקתא רבתי, Ish-Shalom ed., Vienna, 1880.

Petersen, E., *Die Wunderbare Geburt des Heilandes*, Tübingen, 1909.
Philo, *Life of Moses*, LCL, 1932.
Pirke de R. Eliezer, פרקי דרבי אליעזר, C. M. Horowitz ed., Jerusalem, 1972.
Pliny, *Natural History*, LCL, 1949.
Pritchard, Y. B. (ed.), *Ancient Near Eastern Texts Relating to the Old Testament*, 3rd ed., Princeton, 1969.
Pseudo-Jonathan, תרגום יונתן על התורה (= תרגום ירושלמי), Ginsburger ed., Berlin, 1903.
Pseudo-Philo, *Liber Antiquitatum Biblicarum*, ed. G. Kisch, Notre-Dame, Indiana, 1949.
Rabin, C., *The Zadokite Documents*, (=*Damascus Covenant*), 2nd ed., Oxford, 1958.
von Rad, G., "Das formgeschichtliche Problem des Hexateuch," in *Gesammelte Studien zum Alten Testament*, Munich, 1958, pp. 9–87.
Raglan, L., *The Hero*, New York, 1956.
Rank, O., *The Myth of the Birth of the Hero*, New York, 1964. Originally published as *Der Mythus und die Geburt des Helden*, Schriften zur angewandten Seelenkunde, hrg. von S. Freud, 5, Leipzig, 1908.
Rappaport, S., *Agada und Exegese bei Flavius Josephus*, Vienna, 1930.
Rashi, רש"י על התורה, (*Rashi on the Torah*), Berliner ed., Frankfurt a. M., 1905.
——, *Pentateuch with Rashi's Commentary*, ed. M. Silbermann, Jerusalem, 1973.
Redford, D. B., "The Literary Motif of the Exposed Child," *Numen* 14 (1967), 221–224.
Roscher, W. H., *Ausführliches Lexikon der griechischen und römischen Mythologie*, Hildesheim, 1965.
The Samaritan Version of the Pentateuch, חמשה חומשי תורה נוסח יהודי-שומרוני, ed. Sadaqa, Tel Aviv, 1961–1966.
Samaritan Targum of the Pentateuch, התרגום השומרוני לתורה, ed. A. Tal, Jerusalem, 1983.
Schmerler, B., אהבת יונתן, a commentary on Targum Jonathan (= Targum Yerushalmi) on Genesis–Leviticus, Bilgoraj, 1933-1935.
Schweizer, E., *The Good News according to Matthew*, Atlanta, 1975.
Seder Eliyyahu Rabbah סדר אליהו רבה and *Seder Eliyyahu Zuta* סדר אליהו זוטא, Ish Shalom ed., Vienna, 1902.
Seder Olam, סדר עולם, Ratner ed., New York, 1966.
Seeligmann, I. L., "Menschliches Heldentum und göttliche Hilfe," *ThZ* 19 (1963), 385–411.
——, *The Septuagint Version of Isaiah*, Leiden, 1948.
——, "Voraussetzungen der Midraschexegese," *VT (Sup.)* 1 (1953), 150–181.
——, "מסורת פולחנית ויצירה היסטוריוגראפית במקרא," "Cultic Tradition and Historiographical Creativity in the Bible", in דת וחברה בתולדות ישראל ובתולדות העמים, (*Religion and Society in Israelite and General History*), Jerusalem, 1965.
——, "מחקרים בתולדות נוסחת המקרא," "Research into the Criticism of the Masoretic Text of the Bible", *Tarbiẓ* 25 (1956), 118–139.
Sefer ha-Yashar, ספר הישר, Dan ed., Jerusalem, 1986.
Sifre on Numbers, ספרי על ספר במדבר, Horovitz ed., 2nd edition, Jerusalem, 1966.
Sifre on Deuteronomy, ספרי דברים, Finkelstein ed., New York, 1969.
Soloweitschik, M. and Rubascheff, S., תולדות בקרת המקרא, (*A History of Bible Criticism*), Berlin, 1925.
Spinoza, Benedictus, *Tractatus Theologico-Politicus (Opera, tomus primus)*, Hagae comitum, 1914.

Stern, M., *Greek and Latin Authors on Jews and Judaism*, Jerusalem, 1976–1984.
Strack, H. and Billerbeck, P., *Kommentar zum Neuen Testament aus Talmud und Midrasch*, Munich, 1926–1961.
Suetonius, *De Vita Caesarum*, LCL, Munich, 1960.
Targum Onkelos, תרגום אונקלוס, in *Torat Ḥayyim*, R. Kook Institute, Jerusalem, 1986.
Testuz, M., *Papyrus Bodmer 5, Nativité de Marie*, 1958.
Thompson, S., *Motif Index of Folk-Literature*, Vol. 5, Bloomington, 1935.
Tibat Marqe, תיבת מרקה, A collection of Samaritan *midrashim*, Ben-Ḥayyim ed., Jerusalem, 1988.
Tosefta ke-Peshutah, תוספתא כפשוטה, Lieberman ed., New York, 1945 to 1988.
Usener, H., *Religionsgeschichtliche Untersuchungen Weihnachtsfest*, Vol. 1, Bonn, 1899.
Virgil, *The Aeneid*, LCL, 1960.
Weiss, J., *Die Schriften des Neuen Testaments*, Göttingen, 1917.
Wellhausen, J., *Der Text der Bücher Samuelis*, Göttingen, 1871.
Yalkut Shimoni, ילקוט שמעוני, Shiloni ed., R. Kook Institute, Jerusalem, 1977.
Yannai, מחזור פיוטי רבי יניי, (*The Liturgical Poems of Rabbi Yannai*), Z. M. Rabinovitz ed., Jerusalem 1985.
Zeron, A., שיטתו של בעל קדמוניות המקרא, (*The System of Pseudo-Philo*); doctoral dissertation, Jerusalem, 1973.
Zunz, L., *Die Gottesdienstlichen Vorträge der Juden*, 2nd ed., Frankfurt a. M., 1892. Hebrew translation: הדרשות בישראל והשתלשלותן ההיסטורית, Albeck (ed.), Jerusalem, 1974. Page numbers have been given both for the German original and for Albeck's Hebrew edition, which contains extensive notes.

INDEX

OLD TESTAMENT

Genesis 1:1	145
Genesis 1:4	128
Genesis 4:18	147
Genesis 5:32	182, 183
Genesis 10:21	183
Genesis 11:32	20
Genesis 12:8	146
Genesis 12:20	72
Genesis 13:8	182
Genesis 15:7	106
Genesis 15:8	73, 75
Genesis 15:13	17, 26, 61, 72, 73, 81, 134, 181, 183
Genesis 15:13–14	16
Genesis 15:13–16	59, 78
Genesis 15:14	69, 181
Genesis 15:16	26, 75
Genesis 16:7	24
Genesis 18:1–15	111
Genesis 18:11	144
Genesis 18:12	121
Genesis 18:20–21	77
Genesis 19:13	77
Genesis 20:11	19
Genesis 21:8	173
Genesis 22:12	22
Genesis 22:17	88
Genesis 25:3	161
Genesis 25:22	128
Genesis 25:24	108
Genesis 27:41	86
Genesis 28:11	24
Genesis 29:6	144
Genesis 29:15	182
Genesis 35	168
Genesis 35:16–20	128
Genesis 35:17	146
Genesis 38:27	108
Genesis 40:20	147
Genesis 41:57	73
Genesis 42:18	19
Genesis 46:26	144
Genesis 46:27	181
Genesis 49:31	182
Exodus 3:7	90, 109
Exodus 3:7–9	77
Exodus 3:8	77
Exodus 3:9	83
Exodus 3:22	110
Exodus 5	11
Exodus 5:13	88
Exodus 5:21	5
Exodus 6:18	84
Exodus 6:20	84
Exodus 6:26	182
Exodus 6:27	182
Exodus 7:7	82
Exodus 7:19	122
Exodus 7:20	71
Exodus 7:29	78, 134
Exodus 9:16	149
Exodus 11, 12	112
Exodus 12:2	81
Exodus 12:29	149
Exodus 12:36	80
Exodus 12:42	126
Exodus 13:22	146
Exodus 14:4	149
Exodus 14:10	146
Exodus 14:27	87
Exodus 15:2	111
Exodus 15:20	103, 119
Exodus 18:11	70
Exodus 35:1	147
Leviticus 1:1	145
Numbers 1:1	145
Numbers 4:18	147
Numbers 9:1	145
Numbers 11:21	113
Numbers 12:12	79
Numbers 20:13	107
Numbers 20:15	17
Numbers 20:15–16	77
Numbers 22:20	21

Numbers 22:22	21	I Kings 5:10	161
Numbers 24:17	161	I Kings 11:2	93
Numbers 26:59	120, 144, 182, 184	I Kings 16:19	17
		I Kings 18:37	22, 74
Deuteronomy 1:1	145		
Deuteronomy 23:5	68	II Kings 15:5	79
Deuteronomy 23:8	68		
Deuteronomy 25:18	19	Isaiah 6:1	79
Deuteronomy 26:5–8	14	Isaiah 19:6	52
Deuteronomy 26:5–9	16	Isaiah 19:20	77
Deuteronomy 26:7	68, 77	Isaiah 29:22	105
Deuteronomy 30:3	146	Isaiah 54:9	87
Deuteronomy 32:13	111	Isaiah 60:6	161
Deuteronomy 34:6	111	Isaiah 66:15	87
		Isaiah 66:16	87
Joshua 24:14	72	Jeremiah 31:14	168
		Jeremiah 31:14–16	167
Judges 1:11–24	111	Jeremiah 31:29	19
Judges 2–3	71	Jeremiah 40:1	168
Judges 6:15	49		
Judges 8:30	22	Ezekiel 16	114, 115
Judges 9:5	22	Ezekiel 16:4	111, 115, 147
Judges 11:1	49	Ezekiel 16:7	111, 115
Judges 13	50	Ezekiel 16:8	115
Judges 13:2	116	Ezekiel 16:9	111, 114
Judges 13:24–25	14	Ezekiel 16:9–10	110
Judges 16:22	22	Ezekiel 20:5	26
Judges 16:28	22	Ezekiel 20:5–9	71
		Ezekiel 20:14–17	72
		Ezekiel 20:23	115
I Samuel 1:1	116		
I Samuel 1:22	35, 173	Hosea 5:7	74
I Samuel 2:1–10	171		
I Samuel 2:19	20	Micah 5:1	162, 165, 166, 175
I Samuel 4:12–17	93		
I Samuel 4:19–22	128	Habakkuk 1:7	125
I Samuel 9:3	24		
I Samuel 9:16	77	Psalms 22:6	77
I Samuel 10:2	168	Psalms 63:2	110
I Samuel 12:8	33, 77	Psalms 90:4	82
I Samuel 15:27–28	20	Psalms 105:20	125
I Samuel 15:29	21, 22	Psalms 105:24	14, 74, 75
I Samuel 15:35	21, 22	Psalms 105:25	74, 76
I Samuel 16	135	Psalms 113:9	118, 119
I Samuel 17:12	117	Psalms 129:3	111
I Samuel 28:14	20	Psalms 136:15	70
		Psalms 137:8	77
II Samuel 11–12	184	Proverbs 13:24	76
II Samuel 12:25	184	Proverbs 14:23	73
II Samuel 19:42–44	17	Proverbs 31:18	126

Job 1:1	19
Job 3:26	94, 133
Job 22:28	119
Song of Songs 2:8	81
Song of Songs 2:15	121
Song of Songs 8:5	110
Ecclesiastes 7:28	123
Esther 2:14	144
Esther 7:5	95
I Chronicles 3:5	184
I Chronicles 4:18	127
I Chronicles 8:1,29	22
II Chronicles 9:12	161

Qumran Scrolls

Isaiah 19:20	77

Samaritan Version

Exodus 2:3	124

Septuagint and Vulgate

Septuagint	67
Exodus 1–2	18, 19, 39, 40, 44, 45, 47, 49, 54, 59, 71, 79, 92, 93, 100, 117, 123, 148
Exodus 7:20	71
Exodus 28:32	171
Judges 3:17	40
I Samuel 9:16	77
Ezekiel 16:5	60
Micah 5:1	165
Habakkuk 3:2	176
Vulgate	
Exodus 1–2	19, 39, 40, 92

Targumim

Neophyti Targum	
Genesis 40:12	69
Genesis 40:18	69
Exodus 1–2	38, 48, 87, 100, 143
Samaritan Targum	
Exodus 1–2	48, 100, 137

Targum Onkelos	
Genesis 27:43	44, 167
Exodus 1–2	47, 64, 100
Exodus 18:11	70
Targum Yerushalmi	
Genesis 40:12	69
Genesis 40:18	69
Exodus 1–2	38, 47, 78, 87, 96, 100, 101, 104, 108, 112, 125, 143, 152
Exodus 18:11	70

APOCRYPHA AND PSEUDEPIGRAPHA

Baruch (Syriac) 10:18–19	172
Biblical Antiquities 9	37–40, 48, 56, 79, 81, 87, 92, 100, 104, 117, 122, 172
Jubilees 46–47	29–32, 33, 34, 35, 40, 45, 56, 60, 100, 105, 137, 172
Jubilees 48:14	70
Judith 11:23	40
I Maccabees 1:11	72
III Maccabees 6:3	42
Susanna 1:7	40
Testament of Levi 17.3	82
Testament of Levi 18:2	161
Wisdom of Solomon 18:5	60, 70, 109

NEW TESTAMENT

Matthew 1:1–17	159, 160
Matthew 1:18–25	159, 164, 167
Matthew 1:20	163, 164, 165
Matthew 1:22–23	164, 165
Matthew 1:25	172
Matthew 2	11, 20, 27, 47, 106, 142, 157–171, 178, 179
Matthew 3:1	159
Matthew 3:13	164
Matthew 4:12–16	165
Matthew 4:14–16	164
Matthew 8:17	164
Matthew 12:17–21	164
Matthew 12:46–50	159
Matthew 13:14–15	164
Matthew 13:35	164

Matthew 13:53–58	159
Matthew 13:55	159
Matthew 21:1–8	165
Matthew 21:4–5	164
Matthew 26:3	163
Matthew 26:56	164
Matthew 26:57	163
Matthew 27:9	168
Matthew 27:9–10	164
Matthew 27:17	163
Matthew 27:27	163
Matthew 27:62	163
Mark	158
Mark 1:4	159
Mark 1:14	165
Mark 3:31–35	159
Mark 6:1–6	159
Mark 6:3	10
Mark 11:1–7	165
Luke	158
Luke 1	121
Luke 1–2	163, 171, 173
Luke 1:31	172
Luke 2:1–20	177–180
Luke 2:6–20	176
Luke 2:7	172
Luke 2:41–52	32
Luke 2:52	32
Luke 3:1	159
Luke 3:1–2	159
Luke 4:14	165
Luke 4:22	159
Luke 8:19–21	159
Luke 19:28–35	165
John	158
John 1:46	168
John 7:41	168
John 7:52	168
Acts 1:22	159
Acts 2:23–24	158
Acts 2:32	158
Acts 3:14–15	158
Acts 4:10	158
Acts 7	56, 59–62
Acts 7:16	115
Acts 7:18	79
Acts 7:19	31, 34, 43, 115, 137
Acts 7:20	32, 40, 49
Acts 7:22	45
Acts 7:23	36
Acts 7:38	115
Acts 7:42	115
Acts 10:37	159
Acts 10:39–40	158
I Corinthians 15:3–4	158
Hebrews 11:23	40, 44, 49, 117
Hebrews 11:24	36
Revelation of John	102

Codices

Codices Graeci
Mark 6:3	10
Luke 2:4	173
Acts 7:19	61
Acts 7:21	61

Codices Latini
Acts 7:19	61

Syriac Versions
Matthew 1:25	172
Luke 2:4	173

RABBINICS

Abarbanel
Exodus 1–2	8, 19, 35, 50, 90, 100, 123, 133, 151
Judges 13	50
(Midrash) Abba Gorion	72
(Midrash) Abkir	74, 88, 114, 134
Abraham, son of Maimonides	77

Baḥya
Genesis 15:7	105, 106
Exodus 2:3	124
(Midrash) ha-Be'ur	119

R. David ha-Nagid	91, 97, 130

Deut. Rabbah (Lieberman ed.)
p. 14	110, 111
p. 15	90
p. 16	115

Deuteronomy Rabbah
II.23	78
Dibre Yeme Moshe Rabbenu	82, 83, 94, 97, 99, 101, 103, 104, 114, 116, 122, 129, 130, 131, 135, 152, 162

Ecclesiastes Rabbah
 VII.23 161
 VII.28 123
Ecclesiastes Zuta
 VII.28 123
(Rabbenu) Ephraim 20, 123, 124
Exodus Rabbah
 I.8 74
 I.12 88, 89
 I.13 116
 I.18 92, 100, 101, 103
 I.21 52, 99, 123, 124
 I.24 41
 I.25 93
 I.26 129, 130, 131
 I.27 71
 I.28 71, 91
 I.30 75
 I.34 79, 112
 XXVI.1 94, 132, 134
 XXIX.9 172

Fathers accord. Rabbi Nathan A
 Ch. 2 128

Genesis Rabbah
 XXVI (p. 245) 183
 XXXVII (p. 349) 183
 XXXIX (p. 369) 20
 XLIII (p. 421) 74
 LXI (p. 666) 80
 LXIII (p. 686) 108
 LXXXV (p. 1043) 108
 XC (p. 1100) 79
 XCVI (p. 1192) 33, 80
 XCVII (p. 1247) 113

Hadar Zekenim 16
(Midrash) ha-Ḥefeẓ 52, 124
Ḥem'at ha-Ḥemdah 104
Ḥemdat Yamim 109

Ibn Ezra 24
 Genesis 5:31 183
 Genesis 10:21 183
 Genesis 46:27 181
 Exodus 1–2 5, 16, 34, 75, 84, 181–185
 Exodus 6:26 182
 Exodus 6:27 182
Ibn Janaḥ, R. Jonah 24
Imrei No'am 92

Kimḥi 146
 Genesis 5:32 183
 Genesis 15:14 181
Kurdistan manuscript 85, 89

Lekaḥ Tob
 Genesis 15:16 75
 Exodus 1–2 79, 96, 97, 104, 122, 128
Leviticus Rabbah
 I.3 126
 II.1 123
Luria, R. David, see Radal

Ma'aseh Abraham 105, 106, 175
Ma'oz Ẓur 69
Mekilta
 Tractate *Shirata* 10 (p. 151) 119
Mekilta of R. Simeon b. Yoḥai
 Shemot (p. 1) 90, 109
 Shemot (p. 7) 80
 Be-Shallaḥ (p. 100) 103
Mekilta of R. Simeon b. Yoḥai (Hoffmann ed.)
 Shemot (p. 3) 118
Midrash ha-Gadol
 Genesis 11:28 106
 Genesis 25:6 161
 Exodus 1–2 90, 93, 97, 99, 101, 102, 103, 104, 113, 116, 126
 Exodus 4:13 80
 Deuteronomy 23:8 68
Mishnat Rabbi Eliezer
 19 70
Mizraḥi, Eliyahu 152

Nachmanides
 Genesis 15:14 69
 Exodus 1–2 5, 21, 23, 24
 Exodus 18:11 70
Numbers Rabbah
 XV.20 55

Passover Haggadah	37, 52, 69, 83	Sotah 12b	99, 107
Pesikta de R. Kahana		Baba Batra 17a	116
5 (p. 88)	81	Baba Batra 119b	144
7 (p. 129)	126	Baba Batra 119b–120a	143
23 (p. 344)	40	Baba Batra 120a	144

Pesikta Rabbati
26   172
47   110, 114
Pirke Rabbi Eliezer
42   112
48   30, 42, 59, 82, 89, 96, 100, 101,
    103, 104, 109, 122, 129, 153

Radal   82, 83
Rashbam
  Exodus 1–2   148, 149
Rashi   1, 22, 97, 181
  Genesis 1:1   145
  Genesis 4:18   147
  Genesis 11:32   20
  Genesis 12:8   146
  Genesis 25:24   108
  Genesis 35:17   146
  Genesis 40:20   147
  Genesis 46:26   144
  Exodus 1–2   14, 38, 44, 87, 104, 120,
    141, 143–155, 170
  Exodus 7:19   122
  Exodus 7:20   71
  Exodus 12:29   149
  Exodus 13:22   146
  Exodus 14:4   149
  Exodus 14:10   146
  Exodus 18:11   70
  Exodus 35:1   147
  Leviticus 1:1   145
  Numbers 1:1   145
  Numbers 4:18   147
  Numbers 9:1   145
  Numbers 26:59   144
  Deuteronomy 1:1   145
  Deuteronomy 30:3   146
  Esther 7:5   95
  I Chronicles 8:1,29   22
  Shabbat 55b   116
  Megillah 14a   103
  Nedarim 30b   151
  Sotah 11b   85
  Sotah 12   143
  Sotah 12a   57, 104, 128, 144, 151,
    153

(Midrash) Samuel
2   171
4   121
11   93
Seder Eliyyahu Rabbah
  (7)8   89, 91
Seder Olam Rabbah
  3   83, 84, 183
Sekel Tob
  Exodus 1–2 16, 87, 96, 97, 100, 104,
    117, 120, 128, 145
Sforno
  Genesis 15:13   181
  Exodus 1–2   75, 181
Sifre (Deut.)
  13   143
  78   63, 93
  301   68, 83
  352   168
Sirāj al-'uqūl   30, 64, 95, 101, 104, 128
(Midrash) Tadshe   92
Talmud, Babylonian
  Shabbat 55b   116
  Erubin 53a   79
  Rosh ha-Shanah 11a   108, 144
  Megillah 14a   101, 103, 104, 117
  Nedarim 30b   151
  Sotah   38
  Sotah 11a   78, 79, 87, 107, 144
  Sotah 11a–13a   144
  Sotah 11b   85, 89, 110, 114
  Sotah 12   143
  Sotah 12a   48, 57, 99, 104, 108, 114,
    116, 118, 119, 121, 122, 128, 133,
    143, 144, 151, 152, 153, 154
  Sotah 12b   5, 30, 96, 99, 107, 112,
    113, 122, 124, 125, 144, 151
  Sotah 13a   104
  Sotah 46b   72
  Baba Meẓia 87a   121
  Baba Batra 17a   116
  Baba Batra 60b   120
  Baba Batra 119b   121, 144
  Baba Batra 119b–120a   143

Talmud, Babylonian (continued)
   Baba Batra 120a   120, 144
   Baba Batra 123a   120
   Sanhedrin 22a   138
   Sanhedrin 69b   183
   Sanhedrin 101b   103
   Abodah Zarah 26a   93, 172
   Niddah 38b   144

Talmud, Jerusalem
   Pesaḥim X.1 (37a)   112
Tanḥuma
   (Ginze Schechter) Vol. 1, p. 63   75
   Wa-Yesheb 3   81
   Wa-Yakhel 4   104
   Wa-Yakhel 5   153
Tanḥuma Buber
   Shemot 2   145
   Shemot 6   75
   Wa-Era (p. 32)   37, 71
   Wa-Era 17   137
   Bo 5   70
   Wa-Yakhel 5   56, 64, 94, 95, 99, 104,
      153, 170
   Tazria' 10   12, 125
   Be-Ha'alotka 23   55, 85
(Midrash) Tannaim
   Deuteronomy 23:8   68
(Midrash) Tehillim
   2.4   86, 91
   22.20   77
Tosefta
   Sotah 11 (p. 725)   168

(Midrash) Wa-Yosha'   114, 134

Yalkut Shimoni
   Exodus, n. 162   74
   Exodus, n. 163   88
   Exodus, n. 164   96
   Exodus, n. 241   114, 134
Yannai (Rabinovitz ed.)
   Vol. 2, p. 252   90, 109
(Sefer) ha-Yashar   83, 103, 129, 135
Yefeh To'ar   76
Yelammedenu
   (Ginze Schechter) Vol. 1, p. 45   74,
     75
(Sefer) Yeraḥmiel   37, 92

Ẓafenat Pa'aneaḥ   182
(Sefer) Zikkaron   146
Zohar
   Vol. 2, 19   116, 117

ANCIENT AND MEDIEVAL NON-RABBINIC SOURCES

Aelianus   130
Aeneis, see Virgil
Alexander Polyhistor   36
Aristobulus   59
Artapanus   36, 41, 127
Asatir   14, 20, 31, 34, 47, 56, 60, 101,
    102, 104, 109, 122, 137–142, 153,
    155, 170

Ben Zuta   182, 183

Celsus   160
Chaeremon   6
Cicero   161
Clement of Alexandria
   Stromateis I, 23.151–153   45, 46
   Stromateis I, 23.155 f.   32
Comestor   130

Damascus Covenant   161
Dura-Europos   51, 59, 62–65

Epiphanius   159
Eusebius
   Praep. Evan. IX, 27.3   36, 41
   Praep. Evan. IX, 27.15   127
   Praep. Evan. IX, 28.1–3   32, 36
   Praep. Evan. XIII, 12.5   59
Ezekiel the Tragedian   31, 32–37, 40,
    42, 44, 56, 60, 63, 65, 81, 137

Gregory of Nyssa   45, 46, 176

Hammurabi
   code of   9
Hecataeus of Abdera   20
Herodotus
   I, 107–122   106
   I, 111   35
   I, 112   40, 41, 60
   I, 114   130
   I, 120   106
   V, 41   36
Hilarion   20
Homer
   The Odyssey   51
Hyperides   130

Ignatius   173, 175

Josephus   67, 84
  Antiquities 1.185   55, 69
  Antiquities 2.201–238   11,
    19, 30, 33, 36, 38, 39, 40, 41, 43,
    44, 45, 46, 46–59, 63, 64, 65, 79,
    92, 94, 95, 100, 101, 102, 103, 105,
    117, 128, 129, 130, 131, 139, 175,
    176
  Antiquities 2.277   47
  Antiquities 2.281–282   5
  Antiquities 2.319   54
  Antiquities 5.213   49
  Antiquities 5.257–260   49
  Antiquities 5.276   49
  Antiquities 6.45   49
  Antiquities 8.159   47
  Contra Apionem 1.286   41
  Contra Apionem 1.292   6
  Contra Apionem 1.299–300   55
  Contra Apionem 2.202   20
Justin   173

Keret
  legend of   22

Mahabharata   41
Molad Mosheh   57, 139, 140

Odyssey, see Homer
Origen   45
Orpheus   12

Palaia Historika   129, 130, 131
Pausanias   45
Philo   37
  Life of Moses   23, 33, 36, 37, 38,
    40–46, 49, 53, 56, 59, 60, 61, 63,
    71, 93, 117, 125, 127, 129, 167, 176
Pliny   161
Pompeius Trogus   40
Praeparatio Evangelica, see Eusebius
Protevangelium of James   9, 106, 108,
    160, 171–176, 180

Sargon
  legend of   6
Script. Hist. Aug.   161
Stromateis, see Clement of Alexandria
Suetonius   161

Tībat Marqe
  14.1 (p. 59)   69
  224.2 (p. 281)   112
  296.2 (p. 366)   123
  6.1 (p. 45)   74, 123, 126
Tacitus   20, 39
Tatian   172

Virgil   39, 161

Westcar Papyrus   12

AUTHORS

Abramson   24
Aland   159
Albright   22
Allgeier   61
ANET   6, 9
Aptowitzer   94
Avineri   24, 143, 145, 146, 147, 151

Bacher   2
Baeck   167
Barth   151
Bauer   166
Beare   169
Ben-Ḥayyim   89, 137, 180
Berliner   143
Bernfeld   185
Bickerman   65
Binder   7, 9
Bin-Gorion   130
Blau   24, 146
Brown   10, 158, 161, 164, 165, 168
Brunner-Traut   12
Bruston   168
Bultmann   158

Calvin   162
Campbell   7
Cassuto   24
Charlesworth   29, 32, 34, 36, 37
Chavel   152
Childs   5
Cohen, C.   9
Cohen, J.   10, 50, 112, 114, 163, 167,
    173, 179

Daube   119
Deissmann   20
Delitzsch   60
Diels   12

Ehrlich	19, 24, 60, 77	Mann	106
Epstein	26	Meyer	6, 15
		Miller	57, 139
Finkelstein	69, 112		
Fitzmyer	158, 169	Nestle-Aland	10, 61
Fleischer	182, 183, 184	Neubauer	135
Flusser	129		
Freud	7	Petersen	158, 162
Friedlaender	182, 184		
		Rabbinovicz (Dikduke Soferim)	117
Gaster, M.	137	Rad, von	77
Gaster, Th.	7, 41	Raglan	2
Geiger	72	Rank	7
Gesenius	24	Rappaport	46, 47–59, 183
Ginsberg, H. L.	22	Redford	7, 8, 10, 12, 41, 167
Ginzberg	1, 2	Robertson	32, 34, 36, 37
Gnilka	161	Roscher	9
Goodenough	59, 65	Rosenmüler	19
Gressmann	1, 2, 3, 5–18, 47, 48, 52, 113, 126, 150, 155, 158, 170, 177, 178, 179	Rosin	148
		Scaliger	59
Grünbaum	46	Schalit	47, 52, 55, 58
Gunkel	2, 75, 162, 179	Schmerler (Ahabat Jonathan)	112
Günter	7	Schweizer	162
Gutmann	65, 129	Seeligmann	3, 22, 33, 69, 74, 75, 77, 105, 176
Harrington	37	Shadal, see Luzzatto	
Heinemann, I.	2, 93, 181	Shinan	71, 83, 123, 152
Heinemann, J.	94	Soloweitschik-Rubascheff	185
Hennecke-Schneemelcher	158, 171, 172	Speiser	6, 9
		Spinoza	22, 75, 185
Kahana	72	Stern	20, 40
Kaufmann	2, 9, 26, 52, 76, 157	Strack-Billerbeck	10, 55, 115, 161, 163, 165, 168
Kisch	37		
Klostermann	162, 168		
Kraeling	62, 63, 64, 65	Testuz	172
Krauss	71	Thackeray	47, 49, 55
Kümmel	158, 166	Thompson	7
Kutscher	77		
		Usener	158, 161
Lambert	9		
Lewis-Short	39	Vassiliev	129
Le Clerc	19		
Liddell-Scott	36	Weiss	161
Lieberman	2, 30, 62, 71, 108, 129, 130, 172	Wellhausen	92
		Willers	130
Loewenstamm	3, 6, 7, 8, 9, 17, 18, 20, 21, 24, 25, 26, 34, 44, 48, 50, 51, 52, 70, 71, 98, 100, 112, 119, 121, 122, 123, 150, 168	Wintermute	29
		Yalon	147
Lohmeyer	161, 162	Zeron	39
Luzzatto	19, 20, 22, 92, 148	Zunz	3, 47, 133, 143, 145, 152

STUDIES IN THE HISTORY OF RELIGIONS
NUMEN BOOKSERIES

4 *The Sacral Kingship/La Regalità Sacra.* Contributions to the Central Theme of the VIIIth International Congress for the History of Religions, Rome 1955. 1959. ISBN 90 04 01609 0
8 K. W. Bolle. *The Persistence of Religion.* An Essay on Tantrism and Sri Aurobindo's Philosophy. Repr. 1971. ISBN 90 04 03307 6
11 E. O. James. *The Tree of Life.* An Archaeological Study. 1966. ISBN 90 04 01612 0
12 U. Bianchi (ed.). *The Origins of Gnosticism.* Colloquium Messina 13-18 April 1966. Texts and Discussions. Reprint of the first (1967) ed. 1970. ISBN 90 04 01613 9
14 J. Neusner (ed.). *Religions in Antiquity.* Essays in Memory of Erwin Ramsdell Goodenough. Reprint of the first (1968) ed. 1970. ISBN 90 04 01615 5
16 E. O. James. *Creation and Cosmology.* A Historical and Comparative Inquiry. 1969. ISBN 90 04 01617 1
17 *Liber Amicorum.* Studies in honour of Professor Dr. C. J. Bleeker. Published on the occasion of his retirement from the Chair of the History of Religions and the Phenomenology of Religion at the University of Amsterdam. 1969. ISBN 90 04 03092 1
18 R. J. Z. Werblowsky & C. J. Bleeker (eds.). *Types of Redemption.* Contributions to the Theme of the Study-Conference held at Jerusalem, 14th to 19th July 1968. 1970. ISBN 90 04 01619 8
19 U. Bianchi, C. J. Bleeker & A. Bausani (eds.). *Problems and Methods of the History of Religions.* Proceedings of the Study Conference organized by the Italian Society for the History of Religions on the Occasion of the Tenth Anniversary of the Death of Raffaele Pettazzoni, Rome 6th to 8th December 1969. Papers and discussions. 1972. ISBN 90 04 02640 1
20 K. Kerényi. *Zeus und Hera.* Urbild des Vaters, des Gatten und der Frau. 1972. ISBN 90 04 03428 5
21 *Ex Orbe Religionum.* Studia G. Widengren. Pars prior. 1972. ISBN 90 04 03498 6
22 *Ex Orbe Religionum.* Studia G. Widengren. Pars altera. 1972. ISBN 90 04 03499 4
23 J. A. Ramsaran. *English and Hindi Religious Poetry.* An Analogical Study. 1973. ISBN 90 04 03648 2
25 L. Sabourin. *Priesthood.* A Comparative Study. 1973. ISBN 90 04 03656 3

26 C. J. Bleeker. *Hathor and Thoth*. Two Key Figures of the Ancient Egyptian Religion. 1973. ISBN 90 04 03734 9
27 J. W. Boyd. *Satan and Māra*. Christian and Buddhist Symbols of Evil. 1975. ISBN 90 04 04173 7
28 R. A. Johnson. *The Origins of Demythologizing*. Philosophy and Historiography in the Theology of R. Bultmann. 1974. ISBN 90 04 03903 1
29 E. Berggren. *The Psychology of Confession*. 1975. ISBN 90 04 04212 1
30 C. J. Bleeker. *The Rainbow*. A Collection of Studies in the Science of Religion. 1975. ISBN 90 04 04222 9
31 C. J. Bleeker, G. Widengren & E. J. Sharpe (eds.). *Proceedings of the 12th International Congress, Stockholm 1970*. 1975. ISBN 90 04 04318 7
32 A.-Th. Khoury (ed.), M. Wiegels. *Weg in die Zukunft*. Festschrift für Prof. Dr. Anton Antweiler zu seinem 75. Geburtstag. 1975. ISBN 90 04 05069 8
33 B. L. Smith (ed.). *Hinduism*. New Essays in the History of Religions. Repr. 1982. ISBN 90 04 06788 4
34 V. L. Oliver, *Caodai Spiritism*. A Study of Religion in Vietnamese Society. With a preface by P. Rondot. 1976. ISBN 90 04 04547 3
35 G. R. Thursby. *Hindu-Muslim Relations in British India*. A Study of Controversy, Conflict and Communal Movements in Northern India, 1923-1928. 1975. ISBN 90 04 04380 2
36 A. Schimmel. *Pain and Grace*. A Study of Two Mystical Writers of Eighteenth-century Muslim India. 1976. ISBN 90 04 04771 9
37 J. T. Ergardt. *Faith and Knowledge in Early Buddhism*. An Analysis of the Contextual Structures of an Arahant-formula in the Majjhima-Nikāya. 1977. ISBN 90 04 04841 3
38 U. Bianchi. *Selected Essays on Gnosticism, Dualism, and Mysteriosophy*. 1978. ISBN 90 04 05432 4
39 F. E. Reynolds & Th. M. Ludwig (eds.). *Transitions and Transformations in the History of Religions*. Essays in Honor of Joseph M. Kitagawa. 1980. ISBN 90 04 06112 6
40 J. G. Griffiths. *The Origins of Osiris and his Cult*. 1980. ISBN 90 04 06096 0
41 B. Layton (ed.). *The Rediscovery of Gnosticism*. Proceedings of the International Conference on Gnosticism at Yale, New Haven, Conn., March 28-31, 1978. Two vols.
   1. *The School of Valentinus*. 1980. ISBN 90 04 06177 0
   2. *Sethian Gnosticism*. 1981. ISBN 90 04 06178 9
42 H. Lazarus-Yafeh. *Some Religious Aspects of Islam*. A Collection of Articles. 1980. ISBN 90 04 06329 3
43 M. Heerma van Voss, D. J. Hoens, G. Mussies, D. van der Plas & H. te Velde (eds.). *Studies in Egyptian Religion, dedicated to Professor Jan Zandee*. 1982. ISBN 90 04 06728 0
44 P. J. Awn. *Satan's Tragedy and Redemption*. Iblīs in Sufi Psychology. With a foreword by A. Schimmel. 1983. ISBN 90 04 06906 2

45 R. Kloppenborg (ed.). *Selected Studies on Ritual in the Indian Religions.* Essays to D.J. Hoens. 1983. ISBN 9004071296
46 D.J. Davies. *Meaning and Salvation in Religious Studies.* 1984. ISBN 9004070532
47 J.H. Grayson. *Early Buddhism and Christianity in Korea.* A Study in the Implantation of Religion. 1985. ISBN 9004074821
48 J.M.S. Baljon. *Religion and Thought of Shāh Walī Allāh Dihlawī, 1703-1762.* 1986. ISBN 9004076840
50 S. Shaked, D. Shulman & G.G. Stroumsa (eds.). *Gilgul.* Essays on Transformation, Revolution and Permanence in the History of Religions, dedicated to R.J. Zwi Werblowsky. 1987. ISBN 9004085092
51 D. van der Plas (ed.). *Effigies Dei.* Essays on the History of Religions. 1987. ISBN 9004086552
52 J.G. Griffiths. *The Divine Verdict.* A Study of Divine Judgement in the Ancient Religions. 1991. ISBN 9004092315
53 K. Rudolph. *Geschichte und Probleme der Religionswissenschaft.* 1991. ISBN 9004095039
54 A.N. Balslev & J.N. Mohanty (eds.). *Religion and Time.* 1993. ISBN 9004095837
55 E. Jacobson. *The Deer Goddess of Ancient Siberia.* A Study in the Ecology of Belief. 1993. ISBN 9004096280
56 B. Saler. *Conceptualizing Religion.* Immanent Anthropologists, Transcendent Natives, and Unbounded Categories. 1993. ISBN 9004095853
57 C. Knox. *Changing Christian Paradigms.* And their Implications for Modern Thought. 1993. ISBN 9004096701
58 J. Cohen. *The Origins and Evolution of the Moses Nativity Story.* 1993. ISBN 9004096523
59 S. Benko. *The Virgin Goddess.* Studies in the Pagan and Christian Roots of Mariology. 1993. ISBN 9004097473
60 Z.P. Thundy. *Buddha and Christ.* Nativity Stories and Indian Traditions. 1993. ISBN 9004097414

ISSN 0169-8834

DATE DUE

NOV 15 1993			

HIGHSMITH 45-220